Asia and the Middle-Income Trap

T0361239

The term 'middle-income trap' refers to countries that stagnate economically after reaching a certain level of per capita income on the basis of labour- and capital-intensive growth, and are struggling to transition towards more skill-intensive and technology-driven development. It has resonance for the increasing number of countries in Asia that have either languished in middle-income status for extended periods of time, or are worried about growth slowdowns.

This book sets outs the conceptual underpinnings of the middle-income trap and explores the various ways it can be defined. It also focuses on the debate surrounding the trap that questions the appropriate institutional and policy settings for countries to enable them to continue past the easy phase of economic growth. The book engages with this debate by investigating the role of institutions, human capital and trade policy in helping countries increase their income levels and by highlighting factors that enable the shift to higher and qualitatively better growth. It analyses how the large emerging economies in Asia such as China, Indonesia and India are currently grappling with the challenges of transitioning from labour-intensive to technology- and knowledge-intensive production, and discusses what can be learned from the countries that have been able to escape the trap to attain high-income status.

Providing a conceptual framework for the middle-income trap, this book will be of interest to students and scholars of Asian Economics, Comparative Economics and Asian Studies.

Francis E. Hutchinson is a Senior Fellow and Coordinator of the Regional Economic Studies Programme at ISEAS-Yusof Ishak Institute, Singapore and Managing Editor of the Journal of Southeast Asian Economies.

Sanchita Basu Das is a Fellow and Lead Researcher in Economics at the ASEAN Studies Centre and the Coordinator of the Singapore APEC Study Centre, both based in the ISEAS-Yusof Ishak Institute, Singapore. She is also a co-editor of the Journal of Southeast Asian Economies.

Pacific Trade and Development Conference Series
Edited by Peter Drysdale
Australia-Japan Research Centre, Australian National University

Titles published by Routledge in association with the PAFTAD International Secretariat and the Australia-Japan Research Centre, Australian National University include:

Business, Markets and Government in the Asia Pacific
Edited by Rong-I Wu and Yun-Peng Chu

Asia Pacific Financial Deregulation
Edited by Gordon De Brouwer and Wisarn Pupphavesa

Asia Pacific Economic Cooperation / APEC: Challenges and Tasks for the 21st Century
Edited by Yippei Yamazawa

Globalization and the Asia Pacific Economy
Edited by Kyung Tae Lee

The New Economy in East Asia and the Pacific
Edited by Peter Drysdale

Competition Policy in East Asia
Edited by Erlinda Medalla

Reshaping the Asia Pacific Economic Order
Edited by Hadi Soesastro and Christopher Findlay

Challenges to the Global Trading System
Adjustment to Globalisation in the Asia-Pacific Region
Edited by Peter A. Petri and Sumner La Croix

Multinational Corporations and the Emerging Network Economy in Asia and the Pacific
Edited by Juan J. Palacios

International Institutions and Asian Development
Edited by Shiro Armstrong and Vo Tri Thanh

The Politics and Economics of Integration in Asia and the Pacific
Edited by Shiro Armstrong

China's New Role in the World Economy
Edited by Yiping Huang and Miaojie Yu

Human Capital Formation and Economic Growth in Asia and the Pacific
Edited by Wendy Dobson

Financial Development and Cooperation in Asia and the Pacific
Edited by Edward K.Y. Chen and Wendy Dobson

Asia and the Middle-Income Trap
Edited by Francis E. Hutchinson and Sanchita Basu Das

Asia and the Middle-Income Trap

Edited by
Francis E. Hutchinson and
Sanchita Basu Das

Routledge
Taylor & Francis Group

LONDON AND NEW YORK

First published 2016 by Routledge

2 Park Square, Milton Park, Abingdon, Oxfordshire OX14 4RN
711 Third Avenue, New York, NY 10017

Routledge is an imprint of the Taylor & Francis Group, an informa business

First issued in paperback 2018

British Library Cataloguing in Publication Data
A catalogue record for this book is available from the British Library

Library of Congress Cataloging in Publication Data
Names: Hutchinson, Francis E., editor. | Basu Das, Sanchita, editor.
Title: Asia and the middle-income trap / edited by Francis E. Hutchinson
& Sanchita Basu Das.
Description: 1 Edition. | New York : Routledge, 2016. | Series: Pacific
trade and development conference series | Includes bibliographical
references and index.
Identifiers: LCCN 2015050289| ISBN 9781138935112 (hardback) |
ISBN 9781315677606 (ebook)
Subjects: LCSH: Economic development—Asia—21st century. | Asia—
Economic policy—21st century. | Asia—Commerce—21st century. |
Technological innovations—Economic aspects—Asia. | Income—Asia.
Classification: LCC HC412 .A71844 2016 | DDC 339.2095—dc23
LC record available at https://lccn.loc.gov/2015050289

ISBN: 978-1-138-93511-2 (hbk)
ISBN: 978-1-138-58067-1 (pbk)

Typeset in Times New Roman
by Florence Production Ltd, Stoodleigh, Devon

Contents

Figures

Tables

Contributors

Shiro Armstrong is Co-Director of the Australia–Japan Research Centre and Fellow at the Crawford School, The Australian National University, Canberra.

Haryo Aswicahyono is a Researcher in the Department of Economics at the Centre for International and Strategic Studies, Jakarta.

Rajesh Chadha is Senior Research Counselor at the National Council of Applied Economic Research, New Delhi.

Sanchita Basu Das is ISEAS Fellow and Lead Researcher for Economic Affairs at the ASEAN Studies Centre, ISEAS-Yusof Ishak Institute, Singapore.

David Dollar is a Senior Fellow at the John L. Thornton China Center at the Brookings Institution, Washington, DC.

Indermit Gill is Director for Development Policy in the Office of the Chief Economist at the World Bank.

Hal Hill is Professor of Economics at The Australian National University, Canberra.

Yiping Huang is Professor of Economics at Peking University, Beijing, and at the China Economy Program, The Australian National University, Canberra.

Francis E. Hutchinson is Coordinator of the Regional Economic Studies Programme at the ISEAS-Yusof Ishak Institute, Singapore.

Emmanuel Jimenez is Director of Public Sector Evaluations at the Independent Evaluation Group, World Bank Group.

Homi Kharas is Senior Fellow and Deputy Director of the Global Economy and Development Program at the Brookings Institution, Washington, DC.

Elizabeth M. King is Director of Education at the World Bank.

Alla Myrvoda is Research Analyst in the Asia and Pacific Department at the International Monetary Fund.

Malhar Nabar is Senior Economist in the Asia and Pacific Department at the International Monetary Fund.

Changyong Rhee is Director of the Asia and Pacific Department at the International Monetary Fund.

Shekhar Shah is Director-General of the National Council of Applied Economic Research, New Delhi.

Tom Westland is Editor of the East Asia Forum at the Crawford School of Public Policy, The Australian National University, Canberra.

Preface

The middle-income trap has been discussed extensively in the Asia-Pacific over the past few years. At the highest levels in Malaysia, China and Vietnam, policymakers have been asking the best way to move from labour- and capital-intensive growth to productivity- and technology-driven growth. The difficulty of this transition is seen in the growing number of middle-income nations that coexist with a limited number of 'exceptional' countries that have been able to reach high-income status. Indeed, the experience of many Latin American and Eastern European nations is that yesterday's boom is no insurance against tomorrow's bust.

While the term 'middle-income trap' has a great deal of resonance for countries in the Asia-Pacific, it has also given rise to a plethora of different definitions, methods of measurement and countries to which it is taken to refer. In addition, there is disagreement about the validity of the concept, the best term to use and whether there are also other traps for countries at other levels of income. The discussion is further complicated by often contradictory advice, formulated on the basis of cross-country regression analysis with different parameters and variables.

The middle-income trap and the debates surrounding it are the focus of this book. The book thus asks the following questions: what is the middle-income trap and how can it best be defined? What can we learn from the countries that have been able to 'escape' the trap to attain high-income status? How are the biggest emerging economies in Asia currently grappling with the challenges of transitioning from factor-intensive to technology- and knowledge-intensive production? Which institutional factors and policies enable the shift to higher and qualitatively better growth?

The conference out of which this book emerged was held in Singapore in 2015 and was the 37th in the Pacific Trade and Development (PAFTAD) series. The host organization was the Institute of South East Asian Studies (ISEAS)-Yusof Ishak Institute, under the leadership of Tan Chin Tiong. We would like to express our appreciation to him for his great trust and leadership. The conference and programme of research work were funded by the ISEAS-Yusof Ishak Institute and the PAFTAD endowment, and the East Asian Bureau of Economic Research (EABER). PAFTAD was an ideal partner institution in organizing the conference, particularly through the collaboration of Peter Drysdale and Wendy Dobson. We would also like to acknowledge the East Asia Bureau of Economic Research for its support for the conference.

A public forum was held on 3 June at the Grand Copthorne Waterfront Hotel. The forum was sponsored by Mitsubishi Corporation in association with the ISEAS-Yusof Ishak Institute and PAFTAD. We were honoured by the presence of George Yeo, Chairman and Executive Director of Kerry Logistics, who delivered the keynote speech. Homi Kharas, Justin Lin and Emmanuel Jimenez participated in the panel discussion at the forum, which was moderated by Hal Hill.

We also acknowledge with great thanks the able assistance of Owen Hutchison, Luke Hurst, Angus Nicholson and Shiro Armstrong and their colleagues at the PAFTAD International Secretariat, as well as the advice given by the PAFTAD International Steering Committee. At ISEAS-Yusof Ishak Institute, we are grateful to the Deputy Director, Ooi Kee Beng. In addition, we are thankful to Y. L. Lee, Ang Swee Loh, Karthi Nair, Betty Tan, May Wong and Loh Joo Yong for their dedication and efficiency in organizing the conference and the public outreach event. Many thanks also go to our Research Officers – Michael Yeo, Kathleen Azali, Danielle Hong, Vanessa Khoo, Reema B. Jagtiani, Veena Nair, Vandana Prakash Nair, Pham Thi Phuong Thao, Ten Leu-Jiun and Gerard Wong – for their efforts in transcribing the entire conference and producing an excellent rapporteurs' report. Tan Keng Jin and Hafidzah Ikbar from the Public Affairs Unit managed the outreach activities masterfully.

May we extend our sincere thanks to the PAFTAD International Secretariat and Jan Borrie for their editorial assistance with finalizing the manuscript.

Most of all, we would also like to express our gratitude to the chapter writers for their extensive work during and after the conference, as well as the discussants and participants.

Francis E. Hutchinson and Sanchita Basu Das
Singapore 2015

Abbreviations

ADB	Asian Development Bank
AEC	ASEAN Economic Community
AFC	Asian Financial Crisis
APEC	Asia-Pacific Economic Cooperation
ASEAN	Association of South East Asian Nations
BI	Bank Indonesia
BJP	Bharatiya Janata Party
ECD	early child development
FDI	foreign direct investment
FTA	free-trade agreement
GFC	Global Financial Crisis
GMM	generalized method of moments
GNI	gross national income
GPN	global production network
GST	goods and services tax
ICT	information and communication technology
IFS	International Financial Statistics
IMF	International Monetary Fund
IP	intellectual property
IPR	intellectual property rights
IT	information technology
ITA	International Technology Agreement
LMI	lower middle-income
MNE	multinational enterprise
NBS	National Bureau of Statistics
NETAP	National Employability through Apprentice Program
NITI	National Institution for Transforming India
PISA	Programme for International Student Assessment
PPP	purchasing power parity
R & D	research and development
REER	real effective exchange rate
SOE	state-owned enterprise
TIMSS	Trends in Mathematics and Science Study

TFP	total factor productivity
TOT	terms of trade
ULC	unit labor cost
UMI	upper middle-income
VTE	vocational and technical education
WDI	World Development Indicator
WEO	World Economic Outlook
WGI	Worldwide Governance Indicator
WTO	World Trade Organization

1 Asia and the middle-income trap

An overview

Francis E. Hutchinson and Sanchita Basu Das

Much has been said about this being the Asian Century, with global growth increasingly being driven by China, India and the South East Asian economies of Indonesia, Malaysia, Thailand and Vietnam. Its dynamism, openness to trade and aggressive export production have shifted the economic 'weight' of the globe towards Asia.

While Asia accounted for a mere 19 per cent of the global economy in 1950, by 2010 it accounted for 28 per cent. This rapid expansion has been due to the widespread adoption of three common policies by countries across the region: export-oriented industrialization; heavy investment in education; and focus on long-term growth (ADB, 2011).

As a result, Asia is on course to regain its historic position as the most important region in the global economy. Looking forward, the Asian Development Bank (ADB) predicts that, if the region retains its competitiveness, by 2050, Asia could generate 52 per cent of global GDP, and its residents could enjoy an average per capita income of $40,800 in purchasing power parity (PPP) terms – a level similar to Europe's current income level (ADB, 2011).

Recent economic trends support this scenario. Indeed, since the turn of the century, the fortunes of emerging Asian economies stand in stark contrast to those of mature economies (Table 1.1). Since 2000, the United States and the European Union have experienced anaemic growth, with growth rates at or below 2 per cent per annum. For its part, China grew at 10.3 per cent per annum from 2000 to 2009 and 8.6 per cent from 2010 to 2014. India grew at 6.9 per cent and 7.3 per cent over the same periods, respectively. Other key economies in the region, such as Indonesia, Malaysia and Vietnam, grew at 5 per cent per annum or more post 2000.

Not only are the average growth rates in the emerging Asian economies significantly higher than the global mean, as well as mature economies in aggregate, but also their growth is more resilient. Having learned the hard lessons of the 1997 Asian Financial Crisis, economies in the region have worked hard to maintain strong economic fundamentals and ensure that macro-prudential policies are in place. In 2009, at the height of the Global Financial Crisis, the world economy contracted 2.1 per cent (Figure 1.1). While the advanced economies of the United States, the European Union and Japan experienced prolonged downturns, the

Table 1.1 GDP growth, 1980–2014 (annual percentage change)

	1980–9	1990–9	2000–9	2010–14
China	9.8	10.0	10.3	8.6
India	5.7	5.8	6.9	7.3
Indonesia	6.4	4.8	5.1	5.8
Malaysia	5.9	7.2	4.8	5.8
Thailand	7.3	5.3	4.1	3.6
Vietnam	4.5	7.4	6.6	5.9
Korea	8.6	6.7	4.7	3.7
Japan	4.4	1.5	0.6	1.5
United States	3.1	3.2	1.8	2.2
European Union	2.3	2.2	1.6	1.0
World	3.1	2.7	2.6	2.8

Source: WDI Online, constant local currency.

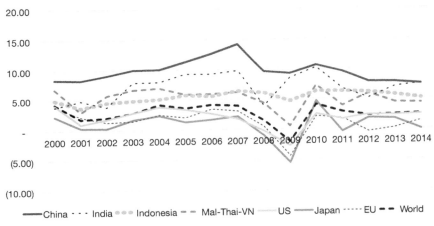

Figure 1.1 GDP growth, 2000–14 (annual percentage change)

Sources: World Bank National Accounts data and OECD National Accounts data files.

emerging economies of China, India and South East Asia largely sustained their growth rates, albeit with a brief dip.

Notwithstanding recent performance, future growth is not guaranteed. Despite high levels of growth, there are indications that these economies are slowing. Although China has averaged growth rates at or near 10 per cent per annum since 1980, its economy's momentum has decreased, with growth falling to less than 8 per cent per annum in 2011–14. India, for its part, has long performed erratically, alternating between growth at 4 per cent and bursts at 8 per cent per annum. And, while the South East Asian 'Tiger' economies of Indonesia, Malaysia and Thailand have also experienced good growth, it has not been at the levels seen before the Asian Financial Crisis. In the period 1990–7, these economies grew at an average of 7.6, 9.2 and 7.4 per cent, respectively. In 2011–14, the respective growth rates for these economies were 5.7, 5.4 and 2.5 per cent (WDI Online).

This has prompted introspection and questioning among policymakers about the way forward. Initially, growth comes from the inter-sectoral reallocation of factors of production, with faster growth of output and employment in industry than in agriculture. This is more productive in aggregate terms, and allows economies of scale through specialization and the acquisition of technological capabilities. Industrial activities have the potential for multiplier effects in the economy, through the demand for downstream and upstream suppliers (Kaldor, 1978).

By basing this industrialization process on export production and an initial focus on low value-added and high-volume assembly operations for export, countries such as Malaysia, Thailand, Indonesia and China become part of production networks across the region. Over time, these countries have been able to make some progress at climbing the value chain through upgrading products and processes (World Bank, 2010). This has been termed the 'easy' phase of growth.

This economic model – referred to as 'Factory Asia' by the ADB (2013b) – has enabled those countries adopting it to benefit from sustained increases in per capita income. In 1980, Malaysia, Thailand and Indonesia had per capita incomes of US$1,803, US$683 and US$536, respectively. By 2014, the corresponding figures were US$10,830 (for Malaysia), US$5,561 (Thailand) and US$3,315 (Indonesia), representing a more than fourfold increase in each case. China, for its part, has done even better, with its per capita income level increasing from US$193 in 1980 to US$7,594 in 2014 (WDI Online).

This stage of growth is, however, finite. At some point, the reserve army of labour in each of these countries is – or will be – exhausted. Wages subsequently rise and, if this is not accompanied by commensurate increases in productivity and technological progress, these countries will become uncompetitive.

Indeed, there are signs that this transition may not be happening. Relative to countries of similar income in other parts of the world – and particularly the high-income Asian economies of Japan, South Korea and Taiwan – innovation levels in the middle-income countries of Asia are below par (World Bank, 2010). There are also concerns about the availability and quality of human capital in China and key South East Asian economies (Fang and Yang, 2013; Jimenez *et al.*, 2013; Raya and Suryadarma, 2013).

This situation is commonly referred to as the 'middle-income trap'. The trap, insofar as it can be so termed, refers to countries that have reached a certain level of per capita income on the basis of labour-intensive tasks and are struggling to transition towards more skill-intensive and sophisticated activities. Unable to compete with lower-cost locations in mature sectors, yet not possessing sufficient skill or technological capabilities to perform high value-added and well-remunerated tasks, they are likely to stagnate economically. This issue is best exemplified by one statistic. According to the World Bank, only 13 of 101 countries classified as middle income in 1960 have subsequently been able to attain high-income status. In East Asia, this group is thus far limited to Japan, South Korea, Taiwan, Hong Kong and Singapore (World Bank, 2013: 12).

Barring these five countries, the rest in the region – including high performers such as Malaysia, Thailand, China and Indonesia – are still in the middle-income bracket. Faced with slowing growth rates, increasing wage levels and below par innovation in these and other countries, policymakers have deliberated intensively about how to make the transition from labour- and capital-intensive growth to productivity- and technology-driven growth. Given the difficulty in attaining high-income status, the debate has arisen about whether there is something qualitatively different about this transition.

Thus, the middle-income trap debate is about the appropriate institutional and policy settings for middle-income countries to enable them to continue to grow past the 'easy' phase of economic growth. However, there is disagreement regarding the validity of the concept, the best term to use and whether there are also other traps for countries at other levels of income. The MIT debate is further complicated by often contradictory advice, formulated on the basis of cross-country regressions with different parameters and variables.

The MIT and the debates surrounding it are the focus of this book. We thus ask the following questions: what is the middle-income trap and how can it best be defined? What can we learn from the countries that have been able to 'escape' the trap to attain high-income status? How are the biggest emerging economies in Asia currently grappling with the challenges of transitioning from labour-intensive to technology- and knowledge-intensive production? Which institutional factors and policies enable the shift to higher and qualitatively better growth?

This book is divided into four parts. The first part looks at the conceptual underpinnings of the MIT, particularly where the concept originated, how it should be defined and to what groups of countries it applies. The second seeks to learn from success, particularly the experience of high-performing Asian economies, and tries to identify distinctive characteristics of their growth experience. The third part looks at the three largest emerging countries in Asia to understand the challenges they face in making the transition towards productivity- and technology-driven growth. The fourth and final part examines the determinants of growth – in particular: institutional quality; the availability and quality of human capital; and policies affecting trade and investment and their implications for innovation.

Conceptual underpinnings

While the term 'middle-income trap' has been successful at attracting the attention of policymakers, it has also given rise to a range of different definitions, methods of measurement and countries to which it is taken to refer. It is thus helpful to look at the origins of the concept and the approaches taken to study it in order to clarify ambiguities.

In 2004, Garrett wrote about globalization's 'missing middle'. He argued that globalization processes have benefited wealthier countries whose institutions and human capital bases encourage innovation, as well as poorer nations that focus on routine tasks and utilize easily available technology at low costs. However, countries in the middle, with higher labour costs and imperfect institutional configurations, have not benefited as much. Trapped between countries at the technological frontier, such as the United States on the one hand and low-cost providers such as China on the other, middle-income countries are faced with decreasing opportunities. In order to survive, they need to implement far-reaching reforms in areas such as finance, government and legal systems in order to encourage innovation.

In their 2007 work, *An East Asian Renaissance*, Gill and Kharas develop the challenges facing the 'missing middle'. They argue that, contrary to expectations, East Asia recovered quickly from the Asian Financial Crisis. The region's capital markets developed quickly, poverty decreased substantially and the middle class expanded substantially. As a result, they contend that East Asia is increasingly a middle-income region and, consequently, has a number of countries that could attain high-income status. However, middle-income countries find it difficult to maintain high growth rates and, consequently, must seek to alter the way they do things. In particular, this group of countries will need to: become more specialized in terms of what it produces; shift from investment-driven to innovation-driven growth; and produce workers able to innovate in the workplace. If this transition does not occur, middle-income countries will be 'squeezed between the low-wage poor-country competitors that dominate in mature industries and the rich-country innovators that dominate in industries undergoing rapid technological change' (Gill and Kharas, 2007: 5).

Perhaps more than any other publication, *An East Asian Renaissance* served to bring the MIT to the attention of policymakers. However, while intuitively appealing, this is not an uncontested concept. *The Economist* (2013) famously labelled the issue as 'claptrap', arguing that policies should just focus on leveraging a country's comparative advantage. The periodical argues not that competitiveness is a dichotomy of labour-intensive or skill-intensive activities, but rather that economies operate along a continuum, and competitiveness is determined at a given price point. Furthermore, the transition from labour-intensive to knowledge-intensive production is a continuous process, but most probably a disruptive one.

This position has considerable merit. Yet, if simply focusing on a given country's comparative advantage were sufficient for growth to occur – albeit at slower rates as it became wealthier – and the transition from labour-intensive to knowledge-intensive production was continuous, surely more countries would have 'graduated' to high-income status over the past five decades. The fact that only a small minority has done so suggests that this process is not automatic, and that growth past a certain threshold is more difficult.

Following widespread discussion of the MIT, a significant volume of research has been carried out to define and measure the concept. In terms of definitions, there are two approaches. First, one can use international income standards to identify those countries that classify as middle income and then try to specify thresholds or performance indicators that indicate whether they have 'graduated' to high-income levels or have failed to do so – thus falling into a 'trap'. Alternatively, one can look at countries seeking to transition from labour-intensive to knowledge-intensive tasks and analyze the policy challenges they face.

With regard to income thresholds, the World Bank sets out low-, middle- and high-income categories (World Bank, 2015a).[1] In 2015, low-income countries referred to those with a per capita income of US$1,045 or less; middle-income economies were those with per capita income of between US$1,045 and US$12,746; and high-income economies included those with per capita income above US$12,746. However, given that the middle-income bracket spans US$1,045 to US$12,746, many have questioned the utility of a category that is so expansive.

Middle-income countries are further split into two at a threshold of US$4,125. Those below this income are lower middle income, and those above it are upper middle income. Many, but not all, of the countries associated with the middle-income trap debate – such as Malaysia, Thailand and China – belong in the upper middle-income category. These countries have enjoyed rapid and more sustained growth than have exemplars of the MIT from other regions. For example, Brazil and Mexico are also said to be in the trap, but they attained middle-income status in the 1980s and have remained there since.

Felipe *et al.* (2012) look at the pace at which countries grow and move from one income category to the other. As with the World Bank, they identify four groups by GDP per capita: low income; lower middle income; upper middle income; and high income. However, unlike the World Bank, which regularly updates its definitions, the specific thresholds are held constant over time. Based on cross-country comparisons, and particularly the trajectory of high-performing economies, Felipe *et al.* then specify how long a given country should take to pass from middle income to high income. Those countries that are unable to 'graduate' to high income within this time frame are taken to be in the middle-income trap. Based on this, they conclude that a country is in the lower middle-income trap if it has been in that category for 28 years or more; and that it is in the upper middle-income trap if it has been in that category for 14 years or more.

Along a similar vein, Eichengreen *et al.* (2013) argue that the middle-income trap can be understood as a slowdown in growth after a specific threshold. This is counter to the conventional convergence hypothesis, which holds that economies will slow gradually as they grow richer and move closer to the technological frontier. Instead, Eichengreen *et al.* contend that there are specific levels of per capita income at which economies slow. Defining a slowdown as a decrease in growth of at least 2 per cent over two consecutive and non-overlapping seven-year periods, they examine episodes of slowdowns in previously rapidly growing middle-income economies. They find that, rather than one specific point, there are two levels – one at approximately US$10–11,000 and another at US$15–16,000 (in 2005 PPP dollars) – where growth slowdowns are more frequent. This means that a larger group of countries is at risk of slowdown and at a lower level of income than previously thought.

While absolute and relative income thresholds are important, another approach is to focus on the structural issues that most middle-income economies face in their transition away from factor-driven growth to innovation-driven growth. Thus, the Commission on Growth and Development (2008) and ADB (2011) refer to the challenges inherent in negotiating a transition from labour-intensive to productivity- and technology-driven growth. In similar fashion, the Organization for Economic Cooperation and Development refers to the transition from 'intrinsic' (based on factor-driven) growth to 'extrinsic' (or productivity-driven) growth (2013: 279). This more expansive definition has enabled the discussion of the middle-income trap to encompass countries that are industrializing quickly but have yet to attain (upper) middle-income status. Thus, policymakers in countries such as Vietnam, Indonesia, India and the Philippines have begun to ask what measures need to be put in place before they exhaust the possibilities of factor-driven growth.

Ohno (2009) focuses more specifically on industrialization and the acquisition of technological capabilities to drive growth and encourage structural transformation. He links growth performance to different levels of industrial capabilities and identifies four stages that countries can transition through. They are: (a) simple manufacturing under foreign guidance; (b) the development of indigenous supporting industries, but still under foreign guidance; (c) the acquisition of leading-edge technology and management practices; and (d) full indigenous capability in innovation and product design. According to this classification, Vietnam is at the first stage, Malaysia and Thailand are at the second, South Korea and Taiwan are at the third, and Japan, the United States and the European Union are at the fourth.

Ohno argues that the transition from the first stage to the last is not guaranteed and, indeed, the stages are progressively more difficult. In particular, he argues that the transition from the second to the third stage is very difficult, and has been a 'glass ceiling' for all South East Asian and many Latin American countries. It is this inability to master fully the technology and management techniques necessary for the production of high-quality manufactured items that constitutes the middle-income trap.

It is within this context that **Indermit Gill** and **Homi Kharas** revisit the MIT concept in **Chapter 2** of this book, tracing its evolution over the past decade, and asking what lessons have been learned regarding its validity and implications.

On the origins of the concept, Gill and Kharas observe that discussions regarding the trap arose due to the lack of an applicable growth strategy for middle-income developing countries. The Solow model was applicable to emerging economies that were about to 'take off' and could do so through promoting low-cost exports, having an external orientation and investing in basic health and education. The endogenous growth model, for its part, was more suited for mature economies, as they sought to maximize their innovative potential. However, there was little at hand that was of relevance to countries between these two stages. Yet, it was this group of countries that accounted for the bulk of the world's population. In addition, while many East Asian countries had been growing strongly and had attained middle-income status in a short time, the economic fortunes of middle-income countries in Latin America and Eastern Europe showed that past performance was not a guarantee of future success.

Gill and Kharas argue that the MIT concept is still valid, and has been very useful for alerting decision makers to the dangers of complacency on the one hand and policy misdiagnosis on the other. This misdiagnosis can take two forms: first, of seeking to retain labour-intensive growth strategies for too long, and second, of seeking to artificially create new and sophisticated industries without the requisite institutional and technological capabilities. The consequences can be growth slowdowns or, simply, growth below potential. In addition, they stress that the concept refers to a trap that middle-income countries can fall into, rather than constituting a generalized phenomenon per se. Gill and Kharas do state that avoiding the trap involves a series of transitions that are unique to middle-income countries. These include: relinquishing labour-intensive production; fostering technological upgrading; creating more efficient and responsive bureaucracies; and moving towards more participatory forms of government.

The authors then examine the policy recommendations they formulated in *An East Asian Renaissance* to see if they are still relevant. They argue that the six propositions that they initially laid out are still valid. These are: leveraging trade and technology to reap scale economies and retain export competitiveness; fostering innovation to generate new products and processes; ensuring the stability and development of financial systems; promoting liveable and connected cities to maximize innovation and agglomeration economies; encouraging inclusive growth and minimizing inequality; and combating corruption and promoting accountability.

Gill and Kharas admit that, in retrospect, they did not give sufficient attention to three issues that recent experience has shown to have implications for middle-income countries and their future growth potential: demographic factors, in particular the ramifications of aging populations; entrepreneurship and start-ups; and regionalism and the implications of external commitments for reform processes.

Lessons from success

Given that only a small number of countries have been able to attain high-income status, and that successfully moving from middle- to higher-income status seems to constitute a qualitatively different challenge to moving from low to middle income, research has sought to examine the growth experience of success stories to identify useful policy choices and transferable lessons.

Much of this research focuses on the ability of countries to engineer successfully the 'structural transformation' of their economies – broadly taken to mean the shift towards undertaking more complex and value-added tasks. According to the ADB (2013a), this process has five constituent parts: the shift of factors of production from agriculture to more productive sectors such as manufacturing and services; the increasing sophistication of production and export 'baskets' underpinned by deepening capabilities and diversification of products; the use of more efficient methods of production; increasing urbanization; and accompanying social changes, such as the increased participation of women in the workforce.

The ADB contends that, in Asia, only the five economies of Japan, South Korea, Taiwan, Singapore and Hong Kong have been able to successfully achieve this transformation. The bank argues that there are a number of factors that shape a country's ability to achieve structural transformation. Demand factors, largely in the form of increasing income levels, generate demand for non-agricultural products; and supply factors, in the form of greater and more relevant skills, as well as more capital stock per worker, are the key. Geographic and demographic characteristics such as natural resource endowments and population density also influence the ability to attain structural transformation. Good organizational and technical capabilities – referring to the tacit knowledge needed to deliver a specific service or produce a good – are also vital to this process. Conversely, the lack of these competencies can result in economic stagnation, as vital skills are not acquired. Last, specific policies, institutional configurations and political contexts play a role in enabling or constraining a given economy's structural transformation (ADB, 2013a: Part I).

Research has attempted to identify causal linkages between different aspects of this argument. For example, using trade data, Felipe *et al.* (2012) evaluate differences in the ability of different countries to undertake structural transformation, which they define as possessing a more diversified export basket and making products that require more sophisticated capabilities. The authors conclude that countries that graduate to upper middle-income status had a diversified, sophisticated and non-standard export basket at the time of their transition vis-à-vis the ones confined to lower middle-income status. In comparing countries in the middle-income bracket with those in the high-income class, the authors find that although the sophistication of the export basket of the two groups of countries is not very different, the product 'mix' of middle-income countries is less diversified and comprises more standard products.

Along this vein, Bulman *et al.* (2014) look at the structural differences between 'escapee' and 'non-escapee' countries. They find that a number of factors are linked to higher rates of growth, including: a more developed industrial sector and, in particular, a faster transition away from agriculture; a more sophisticated export sector; lower rates of inflation; and lower dependency ratios and levels of inequality. Looking at growth rates, they do not find evidence that middle-income countries are more likely to stagnate than those at other income levels. However, they do find that, at higher levels of income, total factor productivity is much more important than at lower income levels – suggesting that growth past middle-income level may need to be qualitatively different than at other income levels.

In their work on incidents of slowdowns, Eichengreen *et al.* (2013) attempt to identify the underlying mechanisms that make them more likely. Looking at 146 countries over the period 1957–2010, they find that slowdowns are positively correlated with an aging population, high investment rates and undervalued currencies. They are also negatively correlated with well-educated populations (secondary and tertiary levels of education) and export baskets comprising high-technology products. As with other research, these findings support the importance of structural transformation, as well as the need to move away from factor-driven growth and promote skill-intensive and export-oriented activity.

The International Monetary Fund (IMF, 2013) carried out a similar exercise, seeking to identify the reasons for growth slowdowns in 138 countries over the period 1955–2010. It finds that there are three broad economic fundamentals that have positive implications for growth: good economic institutions, such as limited government involvement in the economy, a lack of excessive regulation and a strong rule of law; good demographics; and trade structure, including diversified exports, regional commitments and proximity to end markets. And, it is deterioration in these economic fundamentals in a given country that accounts for its slowdowns. In contrast, it finds that large capital inflows are not related to avoiding slowdowns. In general terms, these findings hold for middle-income economies, but with a few differences. With regard to economic institutions, reducing the role of the government in the economy and easing regulation are found to be more important.

It is within this set of debates that **Alla Myrvoda**, **Malhar Nabar** and **Changyong Rhee** examine, in **Chapter 3** of the volume, economic resilience and its implications for escaping development traps. They contend that while a great deal of attention has been placed on encouraging economic growth, relatively little has been focused on understanding the implications of resilience, which is defined as countries 'staying in positive growth states' and minimizing periods in negative or stagnant growth.

The authors assert that the big difference between the current rich and poor countries is not merely that they have grown faster but, rather, that the former group has stayed in positive growth for longer periods and, conversely, that their time in negative growth states has been shorter. Underlying this has been the capacity of high-performing economies to recover faster from downturns.

Myrvoda *et al.* look at a cross-country sample of 105 economies from 1960 to 2010, seeking to identify the determinants of resilient growth. They find that the attributes that help to build economic resilience are: investment in physical capital as well as the quality of human capital, associated with years of schooling; the structure of the economy, especially the share of industrial employment; economic openness in terms of foreign direct investment and portfolio investment flows as opposed to trade flows; financial deepening in order to support investment in physical and human capital; as well as other factors such as low exchange rate volatility and good-quality governance.

They argue that policies to support human capital, economic openness and financial sector development can contribute to more robust economic growth. The implications of these findings are that beyond merely increasing rates per se, policymakers also need to look at the quality of growth.

Individual country experience

While the second part looks at what can be learned from Asia's high-performing economies, the third part focuses on the current challenges faced by China, India and Indonesia, the world's largest, second-largest and fourth-largest countries, respectively, in population terms. In PPP terms, their economies are the largest, third-largest and eighth-largest, respectively, in the world (World Bank, 2014, 2015b).

At present, China is an upper middle-income country, while India and Indonesia are lower middle-income countries. And, although all are yet to reach high-income status, these three countries have enjoyed consistently high rates of growth – albeit from a low base – for extended periods. The World Bank's Commission on Growth and Development (2008) classified China and Indonesia among a group of only 13 countries that were able to attain high rates of growth – held at 7 per cent per annum – for three decades or more in the post-war period. India, having started its economic take-off later, was on course to join this group.

Looking forward, the ADB holds that the economic performance of these three countries will have profound implications for regional and global growth. They are – along with Japan, Korea, Malaysia and Thailand – the seven countries that will account for the overwhelming proportion of the region's growth. According to the ADB, this group of countries will generate 91 per cent of Asia's GDP growth in the period through to 2050 (ADB, 2011). However, for this potential to be reached, a number of underlying challenges must be successfully dealt with.

Yiping Huang looks, in **Chapter 4**, at China's future growth potential, asking whether the country will be able to sustain high rates of growth in the future or remain in the ranks of middle-income countries. He does this by asking three questions. First, is the current growth slowdown a passing phenomenon or the 'new normal'? Huang leans more towards the latter point of view, arguing that there are in fact two slowdowns at work. The first is macroeconomic in nature and temporary. The second is structural and has long-term implications. Historically, domestic consumption has been weak, with growth driven by exports and investment. The underlying drivers for these have been labour-intensive, low-cost manufactures and capital-intensive heavy industry, respectively. Rising costs and shrinking global demand relative to the increasing size of the Chinese economy are undercutting the first. Overcapacity is affecting the second. Thus, the country needs to develop new industries to drive exports and investment.

Second, can the country change its growth model? Huang argues that while the economy has expanded rapidly, it has a deep-seated structural imbalance. This is due to the transition strategy adopted by the country to move away from a command economy – namely, to retain a large state-owned enterprise (SOE) sector, while promoting the growth of the private sector. China has thus created two dual-track economies. The first is between SOEs and the private sector, and the second is between product and factor markets. While there has been some rationalization, many SOEs still enjoy de facto monopolies or implicit subsidies. Second, the implicit subsidies gave rise to free product markets but highly distorted factor markets. Some distortions include: limited labour mobility; financial repression; the setting of artificial energy prices; and depressed input costs. Huang argues that further reforms in these two areas are necessary.

What can be done to improve China's capabilities for technological innovation and industrial upgrading? Huang points to three key areas. First, the country's capacity to innovate must be increased through boosting spending on education and research and development (R & D). This can be achieved through redirecting spending from infrastructure. Second, the financial system needs to be liberalized to enable more effective financial intermediation for entrepreneurship and innovation. This involves developing venture capital and private equity markets, as well as multilayered capital markets. Third, the institutional environment needs to be made more conducive to business creation, information exchange and innovation through lowering the entry barriers to many sectors, as well as protecting labour and property rights.

Haryo Aswicahyono and **Hal Hill** look, in **Chapter 5**, at the case of Indonesia. In reviewing the country's growth experience, they document Indonesia's rapid progress from 1966 until the Asian Financial Crisis, and then its speedy recovery. While overall growth has been good, the authors note that Indonesia's post-crisis growth is some 2 percentage points lower than before. Aswicahyono and Hill hold that the country's overall growth has also been accompanied by good poverty reduction but middling progress at reducing inequality. They note that the country has undergone significant structural change, moving from agriculture to industry, and contest the notion that Indonesia is deindustrializing – because relative to its income level, the industrial sector is quite developed.

With this as a backdrop, they contend that Indonesia's consistent growth since the mid-1960s means that the concept of the middle-income 'trap' is not analytically useful. Rather, the question should be why, despite overall good performance, Indonesia has not grown as fast as the Asian high performers. Aswicahyono and Hill put forward four central reasons for Indonesia's good, but not stellar, performance.

The first is a deep-seated ambivalence towards globalization. Thus, public opinion and, consequently, policymaking have oscillated between openness to trade and investment on the one hand and protectionism on the other. Openness has been put forward by the country's politically insulated technocracy, and sporadically supported by short-lived coalitions for reform. However, economic nationalism has also ebbed and flowed, accounting for episodes of protectionism. This ambivalence has also meant that the country's ability to enter global production networks has been limited, and sets it apart from many of its neighbours.

The second is the country's education system and labour market. Indonesia has made great strides in expanding its basic education system, eliminating illiteracy and establishing minimum levels of expenditure. However, there are serious issues of quality, as seen in high levels of dropouts and attrition, as well as poor performance in international tests of educational achievement. Furthermore, the country's higher education system is underdeveloped, affecting its ability to produce skilled labour. This is coupled with an overly regulated labour market that is characterized by fractious industrial relations and increasing wages.

The third is the state of Indonesia's infrastructure. The country's geographic characteristics make internal transport complicated and expensive, which is further exacerbated by low levels of infrastructure investment, inefficiency and excessive regulation.

The fourth area is the country's institutions. Despite Indonesia's tradition of technocracy and high levels of capacity for macroeconomic management, other parts of the country's institutional context face serious barriers. Of note are: a compromised legal system; a weak bureaucracy; and an increasing number of local governments, many of variable quality.

Aswicahyono and Hill conclude by stating that while there is an argument for developing R & D capabilities further, the four areas outlined above constitute much more fundamental priorities.

Shekhar Shah and **Rajesh Chadha** provide, in **Chapter 6**, an in-depth analysis of the unique challenges that India faces. On the one hand, the country has enjoyed good rates of growth since 1980, which increased markedly in the 2000s. While recent growth has yet to consistently hit the government's target of 7–8 per cent, India's performance enabled it to join the ranks of middle-income countries in 2007. In addition, the country is set to begin enjoying a demographic dividend, with a larger proportion of its population in the workforce. On the other hand, the authors point out that India has the world's largest number of poor people and also has very marked internal disparities in income. Because of this duality, the country must do two things: escape the low-income trap and simultaneously avoid middle-income pitfalls.

On escaping the low-income trap, Chadha and Shah hold that there are a number of pressing issues facing the country. These include: improving the quality and reach of infrastructure; ensuring an enabling environment for investment; and creating jobs. They point to a number of underlying areas for reform, including: streamlining and harmonizing labour laws; amending land acquisition legislation; and reinvigorating the industrial sector. While these policy needs are daunting enough in and of themselves, they must now be dealt with in a context that is more challenging than that faced by the East Asian high performers. Policymakers in India need to: cater to a multiplicity of interest groups; face a more disorderly international trading context; and reconcile growth with the imperatives posed by climate change.

While dealing with these challenges, the country's leaders also need to lay the groundwork for an effective transition to another economic model if growth is to be sustained. This involves measures to maximize productivity and encourage innovation. Key priorities here include: increasing public and private expenditure on R & D; strengthening the country's intellectual property rights regime; improving educational quality; and increasing the participation of women in the workforce.

Chadha and Shah review a number of recent initiatives that have potential to help India deal with these two challenges simultaneously. The Make in India and Skill India campaigns are aimed at fostering the development of a number of higher value-added sectors through: increasing access to finance; facilitating licensing and permits; providing relevant infrastructure; and ensuring the availability of relevant and appropriately skilled labour. Other initiatives seek to maximize the potential of urbanization, further develop the railway sector, and leverage technology to more effectively target social protection mechanisms.

While India's growth rates have increased of late, China has been experiencing a slowing of momentum. After 24 years of an average growth of 9.8 per cent per annum, the country's economic expansion has dropped to 7–8 per cent over the past three years.

Determinants of growth

In identifying lessons from successful cases, the second part of the book examines the linkages between the sectoral composition of GDP, export baskets, the availability and quality of human capital and political institutions on the one hand and growth rates on the other. For its part, the fourth and final part of the book disaggregates factors linked to economic growth and examines them in greater depth, specifically as they relate to the middle-income trap. As a result, this part comprises a chapter each on: institutional quality; human capital; and policy frameworks in respect of trade and financial openness.

While research on the determinants of economic growth has been continuously evolving, institutions represent a relatively new area of research. After the failure of privatization and liberalization reforms in Russia, the high social cost of market reforms in Latin America, and the disruption caused by financial liberalization in Asia, the overwhelming focus of decision makers on macroeconomic stability, privatization and price reform has since given way to an increasing awareness of the institutional underpinnings of market economies. Indeed, while individuals and firms can and do react to price signals, prices function only as incentives within a wider context characterized by secure property rights, protection from corruption and abuse, and political institutions that mediate conflict (Rodrik, 2007).

In *Why Nations Fail* (2012), Acemoglu and Robinson argue cogently for the link between political and economic institutions, and ensuing economic outcomes. They put forward the concepts of inclusive and extractive economic and political institutions, and argue that these different institutional contexts explain the long-term development trajectories of countries. Acemoglu and Robinson argue that inclusive economic institutions, such as those that protect property rights, ensure competition, foster investments in new areas and provide a more enabling context for entrepreneurship and growth. These economic institutions are linked to inclusive political institutions that enable participation but also some degree of central control that can underpin effective markets. Conversely, extractive economic institutions allow a reduced number of people to obtain resources from the populace at large, and do not protect property rights or reward innovation. These economic institutions are, for their part, linked to political institutions that disenfranchise the bulk of the population, allowing political power to be exercised by a few and to their benefit. Following an exhaustive analysis of institutional contexts in different geographic settings and at different points in time, the authors argue that more inclusive economic and political institutions engender more innovative and productive activities through providing better incentives.

In **Chapter 7**, **David Dollar** explores the link between institutions and economic outcomes in relation to income level, seeking to understand whether there are specific institutional issues and challenges facing middle-income countries. Using growth rates for 146 countries over the course of the 1990s and 2000s, this chapter looks at the link between accelerations and decelerations in growth and a country's institutional 'quality'. Among other questions, the chapter seeks to answer the riddle: if certain institutions are positively linked to growth and they are slow to change, what explains the low rate of growth in recent years of countries with well-developed institutions?

Dollar argues that there is no discernible tendency for the growth of middle-income countries to slow more frequently than growth in other income groups. However, he finds that the best predictor of future economic performance is the quality of a country's economic institutions – measured by the rule of law, anti-corruption measures and government effectiveness – at the beginning of a given period. That said, while a given country may start out with high-quality institutions relative to its income level, this is not permanent. During the early phases of growth, protecting property rights and ensuring the rule of law may be sufficient. However, at higher levels of income, other institutional contexts may be necessary. Ease of firm entry and exit, availability of capital and reduced regulation may be more important. Dollar finds that high-performing countries show continual improvements in institutional quality. Indeed, if institutional quality lags relative to economic growth, a given country may find its growth prospects compromised in the future. This is a trap of sorts that can hinder the progress of countries at any income level.

Dollar then looks at political institutions and, in particular, the link with economic institutions, examining the link between the rule of law and civil liberties, and then authoritarianism, democratization and economic growth. He argues that at lower income levels, countries with authoritarian political systems grew, on average, more quickly than those with more democratic systems. Dollar argues that, at early stages of development, growth tends to be due to capital accumulation rather than driven by increases in productivity or knowledge. However, this relationship reverses at a given income threshold, after which countries with democratic political systems grow more rapidly. He holds that political freedoms and civil liberties are vital for innovation-driven economies.

While economic activity is shaped by the institutional context within which it takes place, its potential and productivity are also influenced by the availability and quality of human capital. The work of Lucas (1988) on the 'mechanics' of economic growth and Romer (1986) on endogenous growth theory has demonstrated the centrality of human capital formation in driving growth. They have demonstrated that growth comes from an economy having not just a greater quantity of workers, but also better qualified ones with more skills.

With regard to the high-income East Asian economies, the importance of high levels of education expenditure and the generation of large quantities of trained workers – due, in part, to a demographic dividend – has been well researched. For example, *The East Asian Miracle* (World Bank, 1993) comprehensively documents the long-standing commitment of countries in the region to human capital development. It argues that Hong Kong, South Korea and Singapore developed their primary education systems rapidly in the 1960s and, by the 1980s, had largely universal access to secondary education. It was this rapid development of human capital along with physical capital that accounted for the bulk of the region's high rates of growth. This was further bolstered by a demographic dividend that accrued to many countries in East Asia (Bloom *et al.*, 1999).

In **Chapter 8**, **Emmanuel Jimenez** and **Elizabeth M. King** re-examine the role of human capital and long-term economic development, but with a focus on the transition from middle- to high-income levels. In this chapter, they compare the human capital base of the high-performing countries in the region, the so-called Asian Tigers, with middle-income countries. The chapter seeks to identify crucial policy choices that enabled the first group of countries to grow faster.

In so doing, Jimenez and King make three central arguments. First, an adequate stock of human capital is central for long-term prospects for economic development. Not only does it contribute directly to growth, but also it aids growth indirectly through positive externalities such as increasing learning among workers and enabling the acquisition of technological capabilities. Since *The East Asian Miracle*, subsequent research has driven home the importance of post-primary education in developing the human capital base. While the Asian Tigers did develop primary education, this was part of a phased approach to expand access to education progressively that then encompassed secondary and tertiary education. Beyond education, demographic trends are also important, as the demographic dividend must be capitalized on. If countries are unable to attain high-income levels before they age, this could constitute a middle-income trap of sorts.

Second, human capital formation consists of the development of three types of skills: cognitive, non-cognitive and creative. The successful East Asian development stories demonstrate that, beyond simply expanding the capacity of education systems, the quality of education is the key. Coupled with expanded access to education, high-quality instruction enabled workers to successfully acquire the necessary cognitive skills for the countries' structural transformation. In addition, this was accompanied by efforts to develop non-cognitive skills, which look to be increasingly important in the future as economies shift towards greater service sector activities. And, despite their emphasis on basic skills, results in creative problem-solving tests demonstrate that students in high-performing East Asian countries are well equipped.

Third, with regard to the measures that need to be put in place by current middle-income countries, there is broad agreement on what needs to be done. Current priorities include the need to: increase the quantity and quality of human capital, particularly at the post-secondary level; expand the availability of early childhood development; increase the range of educational opportunities; and strengthen regulation of education provision. These overarching priorities need to be tailored, of course, to the contexts of specific countries and also supported by rigorous evaluation.

Having looked at the large 'building blocks' of institutional quality and human capital, the last chapter of the book turns to policy settings. In **Chapter 9**, **Shiro Armstrong** and **Tom Westland** examine the role of openness to trade and investment in encouraging growth in middle-income countries. In particular, they examine the relationship between growth rates from 69 countries from 1973 to 2005 and openness and repression of financial markets.

The authors argue that the recent experience of East Asia has shown that openness to trade and investment was a vital component of the growth strategy of high-performing economies. Lacking in natural resources, they specialized first in labour-intensive exports, before moving to capital- and then technology-intensive production. Low tariffs and a receptiveness to foreign capital were critical, as this allowed local firms to acquire technological know-how, exposed them to international competition and encouraged specialization in activities where they enjoyed a comparative advantage.

However, in many Asian countries, this openness to trade and investment also coexisted with considerable protection for local firms and privileged access to credit. This was due to the use of 'second-best' institutions to help compensate for the lack of well-developed markets in the early stages of economic development. Indeed, without this protection, there is a question as to whether fledgling entrepreneurs would have had the necessary incentives to invest in new ventures or acquire additional capabilities.

That said, as countries get closer to the technology frontier, policies and institutions that are helpful in the early stages of growth need to be reworked and adapted to growth that is based on innovation. In particular, firms need incentives to innovate, rather than simply adopting or replicating products and processes. This requires a deepening of liberalization measures, including institutions that enable firm entry and exit, financial markets that apportion capital quickly and effectively, and competitive local markets for products and inputs.

Armstrong and Westland provide interesting empirical evidence of the importance of different institutional and policy settings to performance at different relative income levels and the importance of capital market openness to advanced-economy performance. Countries that are unable to effectively make the transition between the two modes of growth by reworking their institutional and policy contexts can be said to be in the middle-income trap, and may face declining competitiveness in sectors of existing comparative advantage.

Conclusions

The middle-income trap is a relatively new concept, and research findings are still being generated. While the contours and implications of the concept are still under debate, the idea has considerable policy traction.

The MIT debate has certainly focused attention on the policy needs of a growing group of countries. Forty years ago, when development economics was at its apex, the bulk of the world's population was poor. It was thus appropriate that attention focused on kick-starting growth and creating jobs. Now, the majority of people live in countries that are classified as middle income. In these countries, the industrialization process is under way or established, inroads have been made into key overseas markets, some sectors are integrated into regional production networks, and pockets of expertise have emerged.

The question is when this easy phase of growth stops and the transition to more value-added sources of growth begins. While the jury is out on whether middle-income countries are more likely to experience growth slowdowns than are those countries at other income levels, the key lesson learned from the closing decades of the past century is that while many countries have been able to attain middle-income status, relatively few go on to higher income levels. Complacency is dangerous, because previous growth does not necessarily translate into consistent growth in the future – as the examples of Latin America and Eastern Europe, in particular, demonstrate.

In addition, much of the detailed work in the research behind this book strongly suggests that growth past middle income entails a qualitative difference in growth – a transition of sorts – away from labour-intensive and resource-intensive growth, and towards productivity- and technology-driven growth. This implies looking at institutions and the incentives they offer for innovation, learning and experimentation. Rather than directing credit to preferred industrial activities, ensuring a basic level of education for all and lowering barriers to trade and investment, this next step implies a more diverse set of policies to encourage entrepreneurship, investment in new sectors and high-end skills and to foster innovation.

Whether we call it the middle-income trap, enabling transitions for middle-income countries or avoiding slowdowns, this is the policy need that this emerging area of research seeks to address.

Note

1　A variant of this approach is to look at income relative to a frontier economy, usually the United States (for example, Im and Rosenblatt, 2013; Lee, 2013).

References

Acemoglu, D and Robinson, JA 2012. *Why Nations Fail: The Origins of Power, Prosperity and Poverty*. New York: Crown.

Asian Development Bank (ADB) 2011. *Asia 2050: Realising the Asian Century*. Manila: Asian Development Bank.

Asian Development Bank (ADB) 2013a. *Asia's Economic Transformation: Where to, How, and How Fast?* Manila: Asian Development Bank.

Asian Development Bank (ADB) 2013b. *Beyond Factory Asia: Fuelling Growth in a Changing World*. Manila: Asian Development Bank.

Bloom, DE, Canning, D and Malaney, PN 1999. *Demographic change and economic growth in Asia*. CID Working Paper No. 15. Cambridge, MA: Center for International Development, Harvard University.

Bulman, D, Eden, M and Nguyen, H 2014. *Transitioning from low-income growth to high-income growth: Is there a middle income trap?* Policy Research Working Paper No. 7104. Washington, DC: The World Bank.

Commission on Growth and Development 2008. *The Growth Report: Strategies for Sustained Growth and Inclusive Development.* Washington, DC: The World Bank.

The Economist 2013. Middle income claptrap: Do countries get trapped between poverty and prosperity? *The Economist,* 16 February.

Eichengreen, B, Park, D and Shin, K 2013. *Growth slowdowns redux: New evidence on the middle-income trap.* NBER Working Paper No. 18673. Cambridge, MA: National Bureau of Economic Research.

Fang, C and Yang, D 2013. The changing demand for human capital at China's new stage of development. In W Dobson (ed.), *Human Capital Formation and Economic Growth in Asia and the Pacific.* New York: Routledge.

Felipe, J, Abdon, A and Kumar, U 2012. *Tracking the middle-income trap: What is it, who is in it, and why?* Working Paper No. 715. New York: Levy Economics Institute of Bard College.

Garrett, G 2004. Globalization's missing middle. *Foreign Affairs,* 83(6), 84–96.

Gill, I and Kharas, H 2007. *An East Asian Renaissance: Ideas for Economic Growth.* Washington, DC: The World Bank.

Im, FG and Rosenblatt, D 2013. *Middle-income traps: A conceptual and empirical survey.* Policy Research Working Paper No. 6594. Washington, DC: The World Bank.

International Monetary Fund (IMF) 2013. *Regional Economic Outlook: Asia and Pacific.* Washington, DC: International Monetary Fund.

Jimenez, E, Nguyen, VT and Patrinos, HA 2013. Human capital development and economic growth in Malaysia and Thailand: Stuck in the middle? In W Dobson (ed.), *Human Capital Formation and Economic Growth in Asia and the Pacific.* New York: Routledge.

Kaldor, N 1978. *Further Essays on Economic Theory.* New York: Holmes & Meier.

Lee, K 2013. *Schumpeterian Analysis of Economic Catch-Up: Knowledge, Path-Creation, and the Middle-Income Trap.* Cambridge: Cambridge University Press.

Lucas, RE 1988. On the mechanics of economic development. *Journal of Monetary Economics,* 22(1), 3–42.

Ohno, K 2009. *The Middle Income Trap: Implications for Industrialisation Strategies in East Asia and Africa.* Tokyo: GRIPS Development Forum. Available online at: www.grips.ac.jp/forum/pdf09/MIT.pdf (accessed 16 July 2015).

Organization for Economic Cooperation and Development (OECD) 2013. *Economic Outlook for Southeast Asia, China, and India 2014: Beyond the Middle-Income Trap.* Paris: OECD Publishing.

Raya, UR and Suryadarma, D 2013. Human capital and Indonesia's economic development. In W Dobson (ed.), *Human Capital Formation and Economic Growth in Asia and the Pacific.* New York: Routledge.

Rodrik, D 2007. *One Economics, Many Recipes: Globalization, Institutions, and Economic Growth.* Princeton, NJ: Princeton University Press.

Romer, PM 1986. Increasing returns and long-run growth. *The Journal of Political Economy,* 94(5), 1002–37.

World Bank 1993. *The East Asian Miracle: Economic Growth and Public Policy.* New York: Oxford University Press.

World Bank 2010. *East Asia and Pacific Economic Update 2010, Volumes 1 and 2.* Washington, DC: The World Bank.

World Bank 2013. *China 2030: Building a Modern, Harmonious, and Creative Society.* Washington, DC: The World Bank and the Development Research Centre of the State Council.

World Bank 2014. *Gross Domestic Product, PPP*. Washington, DC: The World Bank. Available at: http://databank.worldbank.org/data/download/GDP_PPP.pdf (accessed 17 August 2015).

World Bank 2015a. *New Country Classifications*. Washington, DC: The World Bank. Available at: http://data.worldbank.org/about/country-and-lending-groups#Lower_middle_income (accessed 8 August 2015).

World Bank 2015b. *Total Population in Number of People*. Washington, DC: The World Bank. Available at: http://data.worldbank.org/indicator/SP.POP.TOTL (accessed 14 August 2015).

World Development Indicators Online (WDI Online). Available online at: http://data.worldbank.org/data-catalog/world-development-indicators (accessed 13 July 2015).

Part I

Conceptualizing the middle-income trap

2 The middle-income trap turns 10

Indermit Gill and Homi Kharas[1]

The origins of the middle-income trap

About a decade ago, in 2005, while researching economic development in East Asia, we observed that there was no easily communicable growth strategy we could recommend to policymakers in the middle-income economies in the region. The prevailing economic development literature had its intellectual foundation in an augmented Solow growth model that emphasized efficient physical and human capital accumulation as the main drivers of growth. At the World Bank, this was operationalized by prescribing a focus on export-led manufacturing to take advantage of comparatively cheap labour, coupled with health and education programmes to improve skills. The outward orientation would ensure investment was allocated based on internationally set market prices, and improved skills would create growth with equity. This basic model worked well for low-income countries. We did not, however, find it was generating a productive policy dialogue in East Asia in 2005.

The difficulty, of course, was that the China export juggernaut was accelerating, and other middle-income countries in East Asia, particularly those in the Association of South East Asian Nations (ASEAN), were concerned that they could not sustain exports in the face of Chinese competition. With wage levels that had already risen as a result of a successful transition from low-income to middle-income status, countries such as the Philippines, Malaysia and Thailand were simply uncompetitive with China in labour-intensive manufacturing. By 2005, the three-year phase-out period for restrictions on foreign investors contained in China's World Trade Organization (WTO) accession agreement was ending and foreign direct investment (FDI) was being diverted from South East Asia to China.

The Agreement on Textiles and Clothing also terminated all restrictions on the global garment trade that had been subject to quotas since the Multifibre Arrangement of 1974. East Asian economies had used these quotas to build up their export industries. But by 2005 they had realized that this strategy would need a drastic overhaul. They were right. From 2006 to 2013, the value of garment exports from Malaysia, the Philippines and Thailand decreased by 2 per cent,

8 per cent and 4 per cent annually, respectively, on average (UN, 2015). In this environment, recommending a growth strategy based on labour-intensive exports was neither credible nor useful to the middle-income countries of the region.

About the same time, theories of endogenous growth had entered the mainstream of policy debates. After the pioneering work by Romer (1986), Lucas (1988) and, a decade later, Aghion and Howitt (1996a, 1996b), economists had started to unpack the technological black box of the Solow growth model. Competition, science and scalable technologies entered the mainstream of growth theory. These models seemed to better explain the phenomenon of 'club convergence' (Baumol, 1986), where a select group of advanced countries appeared to converge (at least in terms of economic growth rates, if not in terms of per capita income levels), while low- and middle-income countries, with only a few exceptions, were left ever further behind (Pritchett, 1997). And of course, technological breakthroughs and soaring valuations of technology companies suggested a new economics with important scale economies was at play in the twenty-first century.

There was considerable interest within ASEAN about transitioning to 'knowledge economies'. South Korea had done this successfully after the Asian Financial Crisis in 1997–8. But we concluded that this would be premature for most of the middle-income ASEAN countries, given the mediocre quality of their higher education systems and low enrolment rates, the lack of domestic patents, low levels of innovation and technological diffusion, an absent venture capital environment and assembly-type firms that were not moving rapidly up the value chain.

The annual meetings of the World Bank and International Monetary Fund (IMF) being held in Singapore in 2006 provided an opportunity to reassess the issues faced by middle-income countries in the region, primarily those in ASEAN. So, in early 2005, we started work that would be published in 2007 as *An East Asian Renaissance* (Gill and Kharas, 2007). This was the first time the concept of the 'middle-income trap' was introduced into the development literature.

This concept was influenced by our experiences working in Latin America, where, although in different contexts and social and economic environments, rapidly growing economies such as Brazil had suddenly stagnated. Empirical work by Easterly *et al.* (1993) suggested mean reversion of growth rates was common, so East Asia's past successful growth could not be projected forward in a mechanical fashion. Figure 2.1, which is an updated version of a graph in Gill and Kharas (2007), shows how five economies in Latin America – Argentina, Brazil, Chile, Colombia and Mexico – that had grown reasonably rapidly from 1950 to the mid-1970s then stagnated. We contrasted this experience with the growth pattern of the four East Asian newly industrializing economies and Japan, which showed continuous steady growth, and asked which path the five middle-income South East Asian (EA5) countries would follow. In Figure 2.1, we have also added, for reasons that will become obvious, the seven largest new member states of the European Union, who are the latest set of countries to sustain rapid growth at middle-income levels and – in the case of many of them – attain high-income status.

The key point is that unlike the EA5 high-growth economies, the middle-income countries in all three other groups – developing East Asia, Central Europe and Latin America – have shown divergent experiences. The best performers have continued to grow rapidly, with several Eastern European and Latin American countries graduating to become high-income economies in the 2000s, while the worst performers have grown slowly or stagnated, appearing to be trapped in the middle-income range.

It was against this theoretical and empirical background that we coined the term the 'middle-income trap' to describe economies that were being 'squeezed between the low-wage poor-country competitors that dominate in mature industries and the rich-country innovators that dominate in industries undergoing rapid technological change' (Gill and Kharas, 2007: 5).[2] Our advice at the time was: 'For middle-income countries, it seems the trick is to straddle both strategies.'

Ten years on, we are again writing about the middle-income trap in Asia. While there has been progress in many countries, growth has been slower than rates before the Asian Financial Crisis. China has continued to grow rapidly, providing both an opportunity for neighbours and a threat to their export industries. The jury

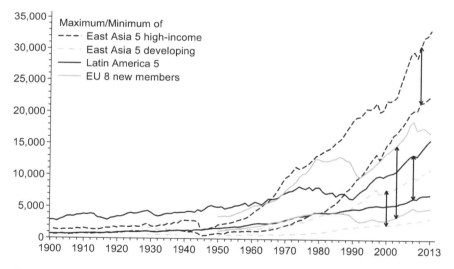

Figure 2.1 Per capita income levels, East Asia, Latin America and Central Europe

Note: The figure shows the development in the range of per capita incomes within four groups of economies: the high-income East Asia Five (Hong Kong [China], Japan, the Republic of Korea, Singapore and Taiwan [China] – maximum and minimum); the middle-income East Asia Five (China, Indonesia, Malaysia, Philippines and Thailand – maximum and minimum); the large, middle-income Latin America Five (Argentina, Brazil, Chile, Colombia and Mexico – maximum and minimum); and the EU Eight New Members (Bulgaria, Croatia, the Czech Republic, Hungary, Poland, Romania, the Slovak Republic and Slovenia – maximum and minimum). In the last group, prior to 1985, data for Czechoslovakia are shown, instead of for the Czech and Slovak Republics.

Sources: Bolt and van Zanden (2014); Conference Board Total Economy Database; Maddison (2003).

is still out as to whether middle-income ASEAN countries such as Indonesia, Malaysia, the Philippines, Thailand or Vietnam can expect to replicate the growth experience of the Asian Tigers or of Latin America.

In this brief retrospective of the developments since 2005, we would like to emphasize three things.

- First, to us, the middle-income trap was more the absence of a satisfactory growth theory that could inform development policy in middle-income economies than the articulation of a generalized development phenomenon. It was a trap of ignorance about the nature of economic growth in middle-income countries: endogenous growth theories addressed the problem in high-income economies (where about one billion people live today), and the Solow growth model was still the workhorse for understanding the growth problem in low-income countries (where another one billion live), but neither is satisfactory for understanding what to do in countries where the remaining five billion people in the world live – in middle-income countries.
- Second, the trap was meant to convey an empirical regularity that past success was no guarantee of future success. In the wake of daily articles on 'the Asian Century', there was a real risk that countries in the region could become trapped by complacency. The trap was meant to warn policymakers that lack of vigilance could trigger a long period of below-potential growth. (We leave until later the meaning of a 'long' period, but Yegor Gaidar, the eminent Russian reformer, allegedly asserted that his country had been trapped in middle income for two centuries. The same could be said of Belarus and the Ukraine.)
- Third, the trap was a device to spark a discussion of policy choices in middle-income countries. It was not intended to be a statement of determinism that low growth rates were a matter of destiny for middle-income countries. As we will see below, this is more than a matter of semantics. For us, the 'middle-income trap' was shorthand for 'a trap that can catch middle-income countries'. It was not a statement that middle-income countries are more likely to be trapped than other countries. In fact, we were silent on low-income countries and high-income countries because the focus of our attention was on policymaking in middle-income countries. In retrospect, it would have been helpful to clarify this.

The middle-income trap since 2005

We were not the first to comment on the slow growth in middle-income countries. Garrett (2004) had talked about 'globalization's missing middle' and warned that middle-income countries might stagnate. In his words:

[T]he challenge for the middle-income world is to find ways to 'tech up' and enter the global knowledge economy, so as to escape the trap of having to dumb down to compete in standardized manufacturing and, increasingly, standardized services . . . the countries of Latin America and eastern Europe are not likely to be able to achieve [the transformation] on their own. The transition to democracy has not itself proved the necessary catalyst. Instead, it has raised popular expectations that politicians find increasingly difficult to satisfy.

Garrett's focus was on the distribution of the benefits of globalization and what rich countries could do to help middle-income countries, by moderating free trade and capital account liberalization. He, too, was disappointed that theoretical political economy constructs – that democracy would lead to stronger economic performance – did not seem to be supported by the evidence. But unlike our analysis, he did not venture into the policy debate of what middle-income countries themselves could do – other than warn about the perils of trade liberalization, a warning that in retrospect was alarmist.

We introduced the term 'middle-income trap' while writing a report to assess economic developments in East Asia since the crisis of the 1990s. We did so with modesty, because we had not rigorously established its prevalence. To our surprise, the phrase immediately became popular among policymakers and development specialists. In East Asia, the great recession of 2008 rocked the confidence of economic policymakers and triggered a big debate on what to do next. By mid-2009, Malaysian policymakers, including Prime Minister Najib Razak, had started to use the phrase in speeches (Chance and Peng, 2009; Lopez, 2014) and even launched a National Economic Advisory Council to elaborate a plan on how to escape the trap. In Vietnam, the Deputy Prime Minister, Nguyen Thien Nhan, had used the concept in 2009, also influenced by Kenichi Ohno (2009a), who was writing about his own version of the trap, referring to the lack of industrial upgrading in the economy. In China, from 2010 onwards, officials in charge of the preparation of the Twelfth Five-Year Plan 2011–16, including Liu He, started to actively debate whether China was becoming vulnerable to the middle-income trap (Shuli *et al.*, 2010).

As government leaders repeatedly referred to the term, first academics and then the mainstream media started to adopt it (Figure 2.2). By mid-2011, there were enough newspaper headlines per month using 'middle-income trap' for the term to register in Google trends. Following the launch of the World Bank's China 2030 report in February 2012, which also referred to the middle-income trap, the level of media interest increased further. Since 2012, there has been a steady stream of monthly headlines using the term, as reflected in Google searches.

Academics also became interested in the subject. By May 2015, a search of Google Scholar returned more than 3,000 articles including the term 'middle-income trap' and close to 300 articles with the term in the title.[3] However, these papers do not use a common definition. Instead, the term has been used loosely to describe situations where a growth slowdown results from bad policies in middle-income countries that prove difficult to change in the short run (hence,

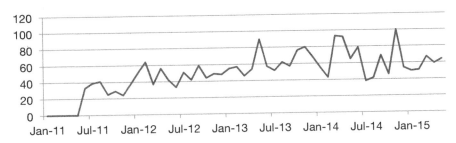

Figure 2.2 Graph of middle income trap news headlines (Google Trends)

Note: "Numbers represent search interest relative to the highest point on the chart. If at most 10% of searches for the given region and time frame were for ['middle income trap', it is considered] 100. This doesn't convey absolute search volume."

Source: Google Trends, retrieved 17 June 2015.

'trap'). A small selection of academic papers on the middle-income trap is: Egawa (2013); Eichengreen *et al.* (2013); Huang (2014); Islam (2014); Kharas and Kohli (2011); Kumagai (2014); Liu *et al.* (2013); Spence (2011); Vivarelli (2014); Wu (2014); and Yilmaz (2014).

The majority of international institutions have also conducted their own research on the topic. Not surprisingly, the organization that uses the term the most is the World Bank – for example: Agenor and Canuto (2012, 2014); Agenor and Dinh (2013a, 2013b); Agenor *et al.* (2012); Bulman *et al.* (2014); Flaaen *et al.* (2014); Gill and Kharas (2007); Gill and Raiser (2012); Im and Rosenblatt (2013); Jimenez *et al.* (2012a, 2012b); Lin and Treichel (2012); Ohno (2009b); Robertson and Ye (2013). The institution with the second most frequent usage of the middle-income trap concept is the Asian Development Bank (Felipe 2012a, 2012b; Felipe *et al.* 2014). The Organization for Economic Cooperation and Development (OECD) (Gurria, 2013; Jankowska *et al.*, 2012a, 2012b; Koen *et al.*, 2013; Pezzini, 2014; Tanaka *et al.*, 2014) and the IMF (Aiyar *et al.*, 2013) have also analyzed the middle-income trap, and the IMF has used it in numerous country concluding statements and briefs (such as IMF, 2014b).

The middle-income trap has also been used by the African Development Bank (Brixiova and Kangoye, 2013; Fraser-Moleketi, 2013; Kaberuka, 2013a, 2013b, 2013c), the European Commission (Bogumił and Wielądek, 2014), the European Bank for Reconstruction and Development (Berglof, 2013, 2014), the Inter-Development American Bank (Devlin, 2014) and the United Nations (UN, 2013).

In the rest of this chapter, we look back on this explosion of literature and use of the term middle-income trap. We review alternative definitions, the empirical evidence, the criticisms of the concept itself, and the policy implications that have been advanced. We close with personal reflections on what, with the benefit of hindsight, we think we got right and what we missed.

Definitions and evidence

As it has evolved, we can discern three broad definitions of the middle-income trap in the literature. First, there are a number of authors who focus on how policy and institutional change must adapt to structural characteristics of middle-income countries. Our own initial definition falls into this category: the middle-income trap that we described was a trap of policy misdiagnosis when countries failed to match their growth strategies with the prevailing structural characteristics of their economies. We identified two types of common traps that middle-income countries could fall into. At one end, we observed middle-income countries trying to sustain labour-intensive manufacturing export-led growth, despite the competitive disadvantage caused by higher wages. We came across many cases where policymakers who had observed the growing diversification of the economy as it transitioned from low- to middle-income status sought to continue that process by artificially encouraging new industries (most commonly information technology industries) with no economic foundation. The important lesson of Imbs and Wacziarg (2003) – that more advanced countries tend to specialize – was ignored. These countries became trapped when they failed to identify alternative sources of demand to replace exports.

At the other end, we also saw countries trying to leapfrog prematurely into 'knowledge economies', with none of the institutional infrastructure in place to accomplish this. Poor-quality universities, low levels of human capital, limited venture capital, regulatory barriers and incomplete rule of law present significant barriers to becoming an innovation-driven economy. Middle-income countries that invest heavily and prematurely in trying to become 'knowledge economies' can find low returns to such investments. The combination of wasted fiscal spending and a faulty growth diagnostic can lead to substandard performance – another example of the middle-income trap.

Ohno (2009b) and, before him, Garrett (2004) are others who have taken a descriptive approach to defining the middle-income trap. Ohno focuses on the need for middle-income countries to move up the value chain and describes the trap as being a reliance on growth strategies that have natural limits, such as those based on natural resources or FDI inflows. He advocates for a proactive industrial policy, with technocratic government teams and strategic alliances with business driving progress forward. In this construct, the middle-income trap is about the microeconomic underpinnings of growth. It puts an emphasis on active government industrial policy.

Garrett's focus is somewhat different, although he too puts emphasis on the need for technological progress and the difficulties that could be caused by globalization and trade liberalization for middle-income countries in trying to move up the value chain. What is common in all the descriptive definitions is that they recognize that structural features of economies can be important drivers of total factor productivity growth, and that once initial gains from the structural transformation of the labour force from low-productivity agriculture to higher productivity manufacturing and services have run their course, new sources of growth will be needed.

A second definition of the middle-income trap is empirical. It is based on the observation that many countries remain in a narrow income band for long periods. Spence (2011) has the clearest exposition of this. He shows that there are few countries that have managed to achieve per capita income levels above $10,000 (2005 purchasing power parity, PPP) since 1975. As a result, there is a clustering of countries with income levels between $5,000 and $10,000 (Figure 2.3).

Felipe *et al.* (2012a) have developed a variant of Spence's analysis. They identify two middle-income bands: one with a range of $2,000 to $7,500, and the other with a range of $7,500 to $11,500 (1990 PPP). If a country stays in the first range for longer than 28 years or in the second range for longer than 14 years, it is classified as being stuck in a middle-income trap. Felipe *et al.* (2012a) identify 35 middle-income countries that are stuck, out of a sample of 52 countries that they looked at.

The bands of income levels set by Spence and Felipe where middle-income countries could potentially become trapped are heuristic. Others have taken an econometric approach. Eichengreen *et al.* (2013) ask whether middle-income countries are more likely than others to experience a growth slowdown, which is defined as a decline of at least 2 percentage points relative to a seven-year moving

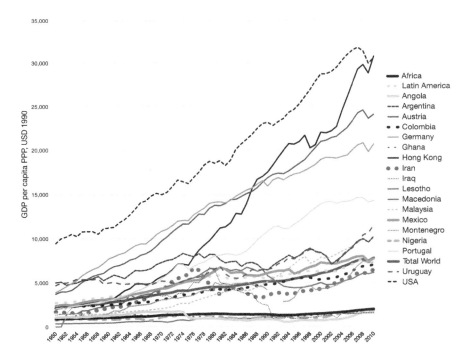

Figure 2.3 Long-term economic growth, selected countries

Sources: Authors' elaboration; the Maddison Project (2013); Penn World Table (2015); World Bank (2015).

average.[4] They conclude that there appear to be two ranges of growth slowdowns: one between $10,000 and $11,000, and the other between $15,000 and $16,000. The implication is that countries may find themselves slowing at lower income levels than previously believed, and may decelerate in steps rather than smoothly or at a single point in time. They also emphasize the importance of moving up the technology ladder in order to avoid such a secular slowdown.

Aiyar *et al.* (2013) take a similar approach, differing from Eichengreen in the counterfactual against which a growth slowdown is measured. Aiyar *et al.* use the predictions of a Solow growth model. They identify and examine 123 episodes of growth slowdowns since 1960 and find that middle-income countries (defined as those with income levels between $1,000 and $12,000) do indeed have a greater frequency of slowdowns than either advanced or low-income countries.[5] They also find that some of the explanatory variables for growth slowdowns differ between middle-income countries and the full sample: middle-income countries with low levels of infrastructure and limited regional integration are more likely to have slowdowns. This evidence is consistent with the authors' prior belief that, in practice, anxiety over growth slowdowns has been particularly acute in middle-income countries.

A third definition of the middle-income trap is based on the absence of convergence to a benchmark advanced country, typically the United States. Im and Rosenblatt (2013) are a good example. They create a set of thresholds based on a country's GDP per capita relative to that of the United States, and look at the probability of a country transitioning to a higher category. They find that the probability of countries with middle incomes transitioning to a higher category is quite low – in other words, there is evidence of a middle-income trap where convergence with the United States stops.

Agenor and Canuto (2012) reach the same conclusion. They plot GDP per capita relative to the United States in 1960 against the same relative income measure in 2008. Updating this analysis, Figure 2.4 shows that most middle-income countries are indeed stuck; they are either on or below a 45-degree line, meaning there has been no convergence with the United States over a 50-year period.

Several other studies also focus on convergence. Hawksworth (2014) designed an ESCAPE index by combining 20 different indicators that are taken from cross-country regressions of growth and convergence, including economic, social, political and regulatory infrastructure and environmental sustainability variables. Based on this, he identifies a 'fragile five' group of countries that could become stuck because they do not display the policy and structural characteristics to sustain rapid growth. Hawksworth does not, however, attempt any statistical validation of his methodology.

But there are more sceptics than supporters. *The Economist* magazine challenged the notion of the middle-income trap by charting decadal growth rates against initial income for 160 countries (except oil exporters) between 1950 and 2010. It found that per capita income growth in middle-income economies was actually higher than in other countries. It further looked at episodes of growth slowdowns,

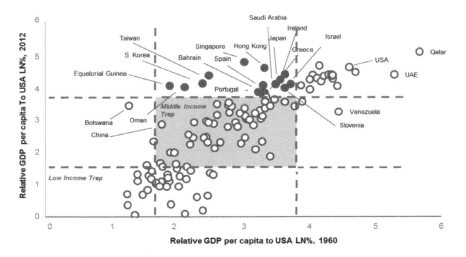

Figure 2.4 Evidence of a middle-income trap, 1960–2012

Sources: Bolt and van Zanden (2014); World Bank (2013).

following the Eichengreen *et al.* methodology, and found that the probability of a growth slowdown did not appear to increase at middle-income levels. It concluded the whole debate was pointless (*The Economist* 2013b).

What can we conclude from these various definitions, and what can be generalized? Probably the most widely accepted proposition is that a 'trap' is characterized by a context where growth is below potential. Such traps can exist at all income levels, from low to upper income, but may well be different in nature at different income levels. If the purpose of defining a middle-income trap is to help policymakers in middle-income countries frame policy choices in the right way, then it is useful to describe those choices that are particularly pertinent to middle-income countries.

If one agrees that in order for growth to reach its potential it is essential to continuously reform and to sustain reforms over time, then the middle-income trap can simply be redefined in terms of middle-income countries growing below potential. Even this, however, is not fully satisfactory. It leaves open the question of how to define potential growth. Some analysts have used comparisons with other countries at similar income levels, but it is not clear that countries at different periods would have the same potential growth rate. In fact, academics like Rodrik (2015) have suggested that as a result of 'premature de-industrialization' it is now harder for developing countries to grow rapidly.

Other questions about growth potential relate to the risk involved in different growth strategies. If observed growth in one country is high, it could be related to a high-risk strategy. Other countries may voluntarily choose to pursue slower, but steadier growth. Or countries might trade-off slower growth for higher-quality growth – for example, if it entails lower environmental and health-related costs or if it involves less inequality.

Potential growth would also have to be defined in a historical context. Some periods may be conducive to high growth; others (like today) may reflect a global context of sluggish growth, greater risk of external shocks and a complicated political environment for policy implementation.

In other words, defining the middle-income trap as growth below potential does not resolve the difficult question of identifying which countries are trapped. Instead, we are left with a loose sense that governments must play an active role in middle-income countries if undesirably low growth is to be avoided, and this means identifying appropriate reforms to maintain growth momentum in the long run.

Middle-income transitions

What is new about the middle-income trap is the framing of the key transitions that middle-income economies (and not countries at other income levels) pass through, which must be managed by public policy. If there is a generalization to be made, it is that all middle-income countries need to pass through these transitions. Those that adapt policies and institutions successfully to their circumstances avoid the middle-income trap; those that do not, risk becoming trapped.

To understand these transitions, we can revert back to theory. The original Solow model suggests that differences in observed growth across countries stem from factor accumulation, especially capital investment. Efficient capital investment requires that an economy be relatively open to international trade and that market forces drive the sectoral allocation of capital. Empirical evidence continues to confirm these basic findings. Open economies, at all levels, grow faster and achieve higher income levels than closed economies.[6]

One transition that middle-income countries face is a Lewis turning point, when unskilled labour released from agriculture is exhausted, and agricultural and urban unskilled wages start to rise rapidly. During this transition, economies must move away from labour-intensive technologies. At the same time, the productivity gains due to inter-sectoral factor reallocations start to slow. For many countries, the Lewis turning point occurs at middle-income levels.

In our original formulation of the middle-income trap, we focused on the financial sector and trade openness as key determinants of the efficiency of investment to which policymakers should pay close attention in managing this transition. The financial sector needs to both support the emergence of new sectors, particularly services, and push firms to exit from sectors where comparative advantage has been lost.

A second transition has to do with technological upgrading. At middle-income levels, the intra-industry reallocation of resources becomes more significant than inter-industry reallocations. Rajan and Zingales (1998) show that sectors that are more in need of external finance grow disproportionately faster in countries with better developed financial markets. They argue that the initial phase of relationship banking must give rise to more formalized capital markets in order to spur growth in finance-reliant sectors.

There is some support for the notion that industrial policy becomes more important in middle-income countries in managing the transition to greater technological sophistication. This should not be interpreted as 'picking winners'. It can mean understanding how different policy choices can have different impacts depending on a country's initial conditions. For example, entrepreneurship and high rates of entry and exit are required to boost productivity in any sector. As Acemoglu *et al.* (2006) show, catch-up adoption of technologies (a middle-income country priority) tends to favour incumbents, and demands a natural selection of firms and managers, while the need for innovation (a high-income country priority) favours new entrants.

Technological upgrading is also associated with a transition to higher levels of skilled labour. Skilled labour has been incorporated into 'augmented' Solow growth models, but those continue to treat the technology frontier as given: the same for all countries. In practice, however, there may be a close relationship between a country's endowment of skilled labour and new technologies. Managing this endogeneity is not straightforward. Is the appropriate strategy to increase the supply of higher education with the prior belief that better jobs will follow, or to create jobs and hope that supply adapts to labour market conditions?

This issue is particularly acute in middle-income countries. In low-income countries, the focus should be on basic education. In high-income countries, there has often been sufficient learning and experience to get skilled labour markets into balance. But for middle-income countries, the workings of the market for skilled labour are less clear. In some countries, governments have taken a strong position. For example, Singapore invested heavily in polytechnics, while limiting the number of university students. Emphasis was given to technical degrees and on-the-job learning. But this is no panacea. Cross-country evidence on the impact of government training programmes, for example, is quite negative. Nevertheless, it seems clear that getting the transition wrong can create a trap where skilled labour markets exhibit a significant skills mismatch that can take years to unravel.

We noted that much catch-up technology was embodied in trade policy, specifically through the import of capital goods and intermediates to permit firms to participate in regional supply chains. Beyond this, however, we also noted the importance of cities and liveability to create spaces where skilled talent would choose to live and where agglomeration economies could accrue. We documented the close links between a skilled workforce and the creation of a science and technology establishment that could help in the adaptation and diffusion of modern technology throughout the economy.

A third transition concerns the move from authoritarian to democratic regimes. In his chapter in this volume, David Dollar argues that the 'optimal' transition time is about $8,000 per capita – squarely in the middle-income country range. The argument is that at low income levels, authoritarianism can be better for growth because leadership is decisive (of course, it can also be worse for growth with the wrong kind of leadership), but that as an economy becomes more complex it requires greater institutional stability than can be provided by an authoritarian government, and a move to democracy can prove beneficial.

One of the institutional problems we highlighted in our original work was the need to have a 'fair' distribution of national income. In the early stages of growth based on exports of labour-intensive manufacturing, it is possible to generate 'growth with equity'. But recent experience suggests that globalization and technology are moving to reduce wages and raise the returns to entrepreneurs and managers of large corporations. Most governments today in middle- and high-income economies are faced with the task of managing the distribution of the benefits of national growth through an appropriate mix of taxes, safety nets and subsidized public delivery of social services (health, education, low-cost housing). The policy choices to be made in this area are often better done through democratic and decentralized governments, rather than by authoritarian governments. As the Arab Spring has shown, popular satisfaction with the economy does not always track economic growth. The extent to which growth is inclusive is also important.

Another institutional transition is about ensuring effective and responsive government bureaucracies. In middle-income economies, the government sector, broadly defined, starts to become a very sizeable share of the whole economy, so government effectiveness is paramount in determining economic growth. This is true for traditional government sectors (including justice, administration, health and education) as well as for state-owned enterprises. Government also regulates the extent of 'economic rents' in the economy. As an economy develops, the scale of rents can increase, but as markets mature, the scope for rents can decline. Because total rents are a combination of scale and scope, they are potentially at their maximum level for middle-income countries.[7]

What we got right, and what we missed: evidence from the past 10 years

With the benefit of 10 years of hindsight, we are even more convinced today that there is a 'practice gap' between the Solow and the endogenous growth models. The former appears suitable for describing the growth problem and guiding policymaking in low-income countries, but one of its central features – the exogeneity of technology – is a clear defect in any discussion about middle-income country prospects. Endogenous growth models seek to unpack the technological discussion, but relate more to creating new technology for frontier economies than to the process of adapting and diffusing technology in a way that allows firms in middle-income countries to catch up to the frontier. So policymakers in middle-income countries must straddle both models. They must ensure that capital investments remain efficient even after an economy transitions through the Lewis turning point. They must focus on the transition from productivity growth stemming from inter-sectoral resource reallocations to intra-sectoral catch-up technological growth (moving up the value chain). And they must manage a transition to more mature institutions.

What does this mean in practice? We think that the six propositions we elaborated on 10 years ago are still reasonable. They are the following:

1 *Trade and technology*. We argued that middle-income countries were likely to retain export competitiveness in a few sectors where they could reap scale economies. Scale economies are to be found in selected products, such as scientific instruments, electrical machinery, non-electrical machinery, iron and steel, and pharmaceuticals. They can also be created through services such as efficient logistics that are needed for firms to be competitive in global value chains – often benefiting even more from agglomeration effects in cities. These principles still seem valid. Global trade is increasingly intra-firm; parts and components have been the most rapidly rising components of global trade. Firms participating in global value chains also see substantial productivity gains as a result.

   The evidence on the importance of the link between trade and growth is stronger than ever, but globally, the elasticity of trade with respect to growth appears to have slowed in recent years. Partly this is cyclical, but structural factors are also at play (World Bank 2015a). There has been greater protectionism in major economies, although the WTO estimates that only about 4 per cent of merchandise exports have been affected. There has also been a consolidation of regional supply chains in East Asia, with China substituting more domestic parts for foreign components in its exports; the domestic value added in China's exports has risen by about 30 per cent since 2000.

   As the case study on Indonesia in this volume shows, ambivalence towards trade is one reason why Indonesia has not grown faster. Continued problems with customs bureaucracy as well as poor infrastructure have led to Indonesia slipping steadily, from 43rd to 53rd in the World Bank's Logistics Performance Index. Malaysia, meanwhile, has improved its ranking, now standing at 25th globally.

2 *Ideas and innovation*. We highlighted the role of competition, especially through openness to foreign markets and investments in creating an environment for innovation, following Aghion and Howitt (1996a, 1996b). The empirical literature since then seems to bear out the importance of this. We also highlighted the role played by new capital investments and R & D as a means of diffusing technology domestically. Comin and Mestieri (2013) have recently documented the links between R & D intensity and technological adoption. And if the focus on science and technology in the negotiations for the new Sustainable Development Goals is any guide, there has been a steady increase in the interest from middle-income countries on access to and diffusion of new technologies.

   Indonesia is an example of a country that perhaps underinvests in R & D. It spends only 0.1 per cent of GDP on R & D and only 0.3 per cent of GDP on higher education. Meanwhile, South Korea, a country that has escaped the middle-income trap, spends about 4.4 per cent of its GDP on R & D, ranking first among OECD countries in R & D intensity. Of course, spending is no guarantee that innovation will follow: Japan also has a comparatively high share of R & D spending (more than 3 per cent), but little innovation to show for it. Japan has low entry and exit of firms, as well as low levels of entrepreneurship.

3 *Finance and risk.* Many middle-income country governments had based policy on the belief that deep involvement in global supply chains required fixed exchange rates. But they discovered that international finance followed supply chains, creating two sources of vulnerability: currency risk and balance sheet risk associated with plentiful external liquidity being made available for investments throughout the economy, including non-tradable activities such as real estate. Our recommendation was to move towards more flexible exchange rates, while developing local financial markets to permit firms more opportunities to hedge the foreign exchange (forex) risk. Indeed, middle-income countries have been moving steadily in this direction, recovering monetary policy as an instrument of macroeconomic management.

According to the IMF (2014a), many countries have revised prudential requirements to improve the liquidity, solvency and risk management of the financial sector. At the same time, despite bouts of capital flow volatility stemming from the tapering of quantitative easing by the US Federal Reserve, there has been a trend towards the overall liberalization of capital transactions, notably on capital and money market instruments. Globally, the world is roughly evenly split between countries relying on an exchange rate anchor for monetary policy (mostly small islands and members of currency unions in Africa, for example) and those with more independent monetary policy (including most high-income countries).

4 *Cities and liveability.* Apart from the economic arguments suggesting that agglomeration economies can be significant, 'smart cities' have become a dominant theme in the recent economic development literature. Fuller and Romer (2014) argue that nothing other than the urbanization project 'will create as many opportunities for social and economic progress'. The New Climate Economy Report 2014 argues that cities are crucial for sustainable development and that 'the stakes for growth, quality of life and carbon emissions could not be higher'.

Glaeser (2010) shows a strong link between area density and per capita gross metropolitan product at all income levels. Density is strongly correlated with wages and productivity, as well as with future housing price growth. This seems to reflect the benefits accruing from labour market pooling and the exchange of ideas, rather than from the benefit of reduced transport costs of goods between, for example, suppliers, manufacturers and customers. Skilled labour pooling seems to be particularly important. Unfortunately, East Asian countries have paid scant attention to cities. Among developing East Asia cities, Bangkok is ranked at 117th, Beijing at 118th, Manila at 136th, Ho Chi Minh at 152nd and Hanoi at 153rd in the Mercer 2015 City Rankings. Only Kuala Lumpur, at 84th, among all cities in developing Asia, breaks into the top-100 global cities.

5   *Cohesion and inequality.* We had argued that middle-income countries would need to pay special attention to inequality because the shifting growth and urbanization strategies would likely worsen the distribution of labour income, and suggested that fiscal transfers to reduce unequal access to social services would be a good instrument. The past few years have been marked by an escalation of concerns about inequality. Even the IMF has begun to emphasize the links between inequality and growth (Ostry *et al.*, 2014).

In the past decade, there has been a rapid rise in most indices of country inequality across the world, including in, but not restricted to, middle-income countries. The exception has been in Latin America, where already very high levels of inequality have slowly started to decline. In high-income countries, the concern has been with the slow wage growth for blue-collar workers. In many middle-income countries there is concern with graduate unemployment and the difficulties faced by young people in finding their first job. In some Arab middle-income economies, unemployment rates for graduates are even higher than the national average.

6   *Corruption and accountability.* Middle-income countries face a particular challenge in tackling corruption because many of them are moving towards democracy and decentralization, but have not developed the institutional structures to make these transitions effective. For example, the move towards decentralization (in small and large countries) has promised closer attention to local demands, but can also lead to capture by local elites and to more rather than less corruption. Control of corruption, of course, has become a central pillar of Chinese President Xi Jinping's reforms. But it has also exposed the contradictions inherent in the attempts to end corruption without disciplining government by making political power contestable.

Three case studies in this volume – on China, India and Indonesia – all highlight the challenges of government effectiveness and institutional development. But they also show that it is necessary to break down general country-wide indices into more granular components to understand better the needs for institutional reform. For example, Indonesia's good performance on institutionalizing sound macroeconomic performance and tackling corruption stands in contrast with far less success in enhancing local level governance. Both Indonesia and India suffer from entrenched bureaucratic inefficiencies. Legal reform is an issue in all three cases. The glimmer of hope is that many small changes in institutions appear to be taking place and these could, over time, have a large cumulative impact.

The experience in Asia and Latin America has validated this list of concerns. But there are areas that we missed. In retrospect, we would give more attention to these three.

1   *Demography and aging.* Many middle-income countries, like Nigeria or India, are hoping that a generation of young people entering the labour force will provide them with a demographic dividend; others worry that the dividend

has now run its course. The danger for all middle-income countries is that of growing old before they get rich, which would give a demographic dimension to the middle-income trap. Each case requires specific policies and, as the saying goes, demography is not destiny. The problem is particularly acute for middle-income countries because they are where the demographic transition is happening most rapidly. Some studies suggest that one-quarter of China's growth in the past three decades has been the result of its demography. We did not give any prominence to demography in our research, missing the clues from the developments in countries such as Japan, South Korea and Bulgaria. In hindsight, we missed an important driver of economic performance. We think it is far more important to the policy discourse than we had imagined.

The case study of India provides an illustration of the power of demographic forces. India is set to reap a demographic dividend, with a rising share of the working-age population in total population. This dividend could be even larger if female labour force participation, which is very low in India, picks up. But there is an open discussion as to whether enough jobs will be created and how to adapt policies to ensure the demographic dividend is as large as possible. Indeed, some recent research (Bloom *et al.*, 2010) even suggests that aging populations do not necessarily have to experience increasing dependency ratios or lower productivity.

2   *Entrepreneurship and start-ups.* In our discussion of innovation, we did not look at the supply of entrepreneurs and the environment in which they were operating – something that Baumol had been emphasizing for more than a decade when we began our work. Lazear *et al.* (2014) have looked at the links between entrepreneurship and demographics, noting that younger workers may have more creativity, but experience in management is required to get the business acumen necessary for entrepreneurs. Separately, Lazear (2005) has also shown that entrepreneurs tend to have varied educational backgrounds with a balanced set of skills. By contrast, many middle-income countries have been obsessed with science and technology, often focusing narrowly on producing science, technology, engineering and mathematics students. We underestimated the importance of start-ups to the process of growth and innovation, and ignored the necessary entrepreneurial climate. We had almost no discussion of intellectual property rights – something that has come to dominate today's trade negotiations involving middle-income countries.

Metrics like the Global Entrepreneurial Index provide a body of useful empirical benchmarks that could now make this a fruitful avenue to explore. It makes for sombrer reading for many Asian countries. Indonesia (120th), India (104th), the Philippines (95th) and Thailand (68th) all rank below levels that would inspire optimism. Malaysia (53rd) has also slipped in the rankings in recent years.

3   *External commitment and regionalism.* We were conscious of neighbourhood effects and the impact of China on East Asian economies, but we mainly saw this operating through the channels identified in the literature on economic

geography – on 'regionalization' rather than 'regionalism'. As a result, we neglected the value of regional institutions and organizations in pre-committing middle-income countries to a long-term reform trajectory and the impact this could have on economic development. In a world where the WTO and other global rules have stalled, these external commitments are likely to be regional in nature. The added advantage of that is it could be easier for groups of countries within a region to escape the middle-income trap together than for individual countries to do so on their own.

The economic success of countries integrating into the European Union has persuaded us that external commitments have a far more significant role to play than we thought. In fact, convergence within Europe has been one of the extraordinary stories of growth in this century. A recent assessment of the European economic model (Gill and Raiser, 2012: 25) provides clues about how this might have happened: 'If you can be a part of the formidable European convergence machine, you do not need to be extraordinarily fortunate [in terms of finding natural resources] to become prosperous nor – like the East Asian Tigers – do you have to be ferocious. You just have to be disciplined.'

Of the countries that have grown quickly from middle-income to high-income status, half – Croatia, Cyprus, the Czech Republic, Estonia, Greece, Hungary, Latvia, Malta, Poland, Portugal, the Slovak Republic and Slovenia – are in Europe. Joining the European Union has allowed countries to take a systematic approach to convergence, dealing with all the issues above, except for liveable cities. This is why we are optimistic about the prospects of countries such as Bulgaria and Romania, which are already part of the European Union, and even those of middle-income Albania, Georgia, Macedonia and Serbia, which might one day belong to an expanded European Union.

Even though there have been setbacks recently in several European countries, the lesson is still that a deep and wide institutional anchor provides the best way for middle-income countries to converge with high-income countries at a rapid pace.

External institutional anchors cannot be created by one country alone. They are the product of international collaboration, globally or regionally. In Asia, both ASEAN and Asia-Pacific Economic Cooperation provide some anchoring, but it does not seem that the agreements being reached under these auspices are strong enough or go deep enough to bind countries to reform faster than they otherwise would.

Returning to its origins, the idea of the middle-income trap was to serve as an entry point for a policy dialogue that is not being well served by economic theory. By combining a commitment to trade and globalization with a focus on finding areas of comparative advantage that derive from scale economies rather than factor endowments, we believe that a discussion about the six old themes and the three proposed new themes would be useful in any middle-income country.

Concluding remarks

We believe that there are predictable economic transitions that middle-income countries must manage. Forewarned, policymakers can make adjustments so that passage through transitions becomes an opportunity for continued rapid growth. Several countries have demonstrated an ability to do this and to converge rapidly with high-income countries. Some have found their own way; others have used the external environment, or integration with their neighbourhood, to bind themselves to policy and institutional reforms that support higher income levels. Unfortunately, this has been the exception rather than the rule. The need for constant reform and adaptation to new challenges posed by changing economic structures as development proceeds, and by globalization, demographic and technological change, has often not been satisfied. And of course, the reform that is needed is not just about passing new legislation, but also about implementation of regulations – something that requires bureaucratic and institutional capacity-building that cannot be achieved through 'stroke-of-the-pen' actions, but which takes time and effort to become effective.

In middle-income countries the incentives for inaction can be strong. These incentives can be political (the short-termism of politicians in a democratic system), technical (the concentration of costs and the diffusion of reform benefits) or social (rent-seeking by elites). The result is policy drift and subpar economic performance. Countries can all too easily become trapped in such states.

Our review of East Asian countries suggests some reasons for optimism. Outward orientation, financial deepening and a focus on technology and innovation are becoming policy norms. These have been helped by a historical focus on infrastructure investments to connect East Asian economies to the rest of the world. But there are also reasons for pessimism. The development of efficient cities, of social safety nets and of institutional reforms to establish the rule of law is mostly subpar in the region. Demography is now working against most countries. Entrepreneurship is low (one sign of this is that bankruptcy is still stigmatized in the region). External commitments – now largely regional rather than global – are only potentially effective in some areas, and even there they now carry a risk of trade diversion, distortionary patents and other inefficiencies. Asian governments seeking to avoid the middle-income trap will need to look to their own domestic political and institutional reform processes, however hard that may be, rather than relying on external commitments as much as they could in the past.

As a final observation, we are disappointed that the economics profession has yet to provide a reliable theory of growth to help policymakers in middle-income economies navigate the transition from low- to high-income status. A crudely constructed hybrid of Solow–Swan and Lucas–Romer models is not unhelpful, but it is a poor substitute for a well-constructed analytical framework to inform policymaking in the countries where close to three-quarters of the world's people now live.

Notes

1 Paper presented at the 37th Pacific Trade and Development Conference, Institute of South East Asian Studies, National University of Singapore, Singapore, 3–5 June 2015. The authors are grateful to the participants at the conference, especially our discussants Cassey Lee and James Riedel, for very constructive comments. We would also like to thank Kamil Pruchnik, Naotaka Sugawara and Lorenz Noe for their help.
2 While our contribution has always been recognized within the World Bank, it was only the publication of an article in *The Economist* that established for the rest of the world that our work was the first to propose the idea of the middle-income trap.
3 Google Scholar, retrieved 17 June 2015.
4 Eichengreen *et al.* (2013) also limit the sample to those countries that had growth rates higher than 3.5 per cent per annum, and whose income levels exceeded $10,000 in PPP terms.
5 A growth slowdown is defined as occurring by looking at the residual of actual growth less predicted growth. When this difference is less than the twentieth percentile of the difference in residuals over all countries and all periods (and continues for two continuous periods), there is a growth slowdown.
6 Bruce Riedel, comments at 37th PAFTAD Workshop, Singapore, June 2015.
7 Ibid.

References

Acemoglu, D, Aghion, P and Zilibotti, F 2006. Distance to frontier, selection, and economic growth. *Journal of the European Economic Association*, 37–74.

Agenor, P and Canuto, O 2012. *Middle-income growth traps*. Research Working Paper No. 6210. Washington, DC: The World Bank.

Agenor, P and Canuto, O 2014. *Access to finance, product innovation and middle-income traps*. Policy Research Working Paper No. 6767. Washington, DC: The World Bank.

Agenor, P and Dinh H 2013a. *From imitation to innovation: Public policy for industrial transformation*. Other Operational Studies No. 17024. Washington, DC: The World Bank.

Agenor, P and Dinh H 2013b. *Public policy and industrial transformation in the process of development*. Policy Research Working Paper No. 6405. Washington, DC: The World Bank.

Agenor, P, Canuto, O and Jelenic, M 2012. Avoiding middle-income growth traps. Other Operational Studies No. 16954. Washington, DC: The World Bank.

Aghion, P and Howitt, P 1996a. Research and development in the growth process. *Journal of Economic Growth*, 1(1) (March), 49–73.

Aghion, P and Howitt, P 1996b. The observational implications of Schumpeterian growth theory. *Empirical Economics*, 21(1), 13–25.

Aiyar, S, Duval, R, Puy, D, Wu, Y and Zhang, L 2013. *Growth slowdowns and the middle-income trap*. IMF Working Paper No. 13/71. Washington, DC: International Monetary Fund.

Baumol, WJ 1986. Productivity growth, convergence, and welfare: What the long-run data show. *American Economic Review*, 76(5), 1072–85.

Berglof, E 2013. *Stuck in Transition? Transition Report 2013*. London: European Bank for Reconstruction and Development.

Berglof, E 2014. *Innovation in Transition. Transition Report 2014*. London: European Bank for Reconstruction and Development.

Bloom, DE, Canning, D and Fink, G 2010. Implications of population ageing for economic growth. *Oxford Review of Economic Policy*, 26(4), 583–612.

Bogumił, P and Wielądek, R 2014. Securing Poland's economic success: A good time for reforms. *ECFIN Country Focus*, 10(9).

Bolt, J and van Zanden, JL 2014. The Maddison Project: collaborative research on historical national accounts. *The Economic History Review*, 67(3), 627–651. Available online at: www.ggdc.net/maddison/maddison-project/home.htm (accessed 4 June 2015).

Brixiova, Z and Kangoye, T 2013. *Youth employment in Africa: New evidence and policies from Swaziland*. Working Paper No. 175. Tunis: African Development Bank.

Bulman, D, Eden, M and Nguyen, H 2014. *Transitioning from low-income growth to high-income growth: Is there a middle income trap?* Policy Research Working Paper No. 7104. Washington, DC: The World Bank.

Chance, D and Peng, SA 2009. Malaysia PM sets big reforms to boost investment. *Reuters*, 30 June. Available online at: http://in.reuters.com/article/2009/06/30/idINIndia-40688420090630.

Comin, DA and Mestieri, M 2013. *Technology diffusion: Measurement, causes and consequence*. NBER Working Paper No. 19052. Cambridge, MA: National Bureau of Economic Research.

Devlin, R 2014. *Towards good governance of public-private alliance councils supporting industrial policies in Latin America*. Technical Note No. IDB-TN-615. Washington, DC: Inter-American Development Bank.

Easterly, W, Kremer, M, Pritchett, L and Summers, LH 1993. *Good policy or good luck? Country growth performance and temporary shocks*. NBER Working Paper No. 4474. Cambridge, MA: National Bureau of Economic Research.

The Economist 2013b. Middle-income claptrap: Do countries get 'trapped' between poverty and prosperity? *The Economist*, 16 February. Available online at: www.economist.com/news/finance-and-economics/21571863-do-countries-get-trapped-between-poverty-and-prosperity-middle-income-claptrap.

Egawa, A 2013. *Will income inequality cause a middle-income trap in Asia?* Bruegel Working Paper No. 2013/06. Brussels: Bruegel.

Eichengreen, B, Park, D and Shin, K 2013. *Growth slowdowns redux: New evidence on the middle-income trap*. NBER Working Paper No. 18673. Cambridge, MA: National Bureau of Economic Research.

Felipe, J 2012a. *Tracking the middle-income trap: What is it, who is in it, and why? Part 1.* ADB Economics Working Paper Series No. 306. Manila: Asian Development Bank.

Felipe, J 2012b. *Tracking the middle-income trap: What is it, who is in it, and why? Part 2.* ADB Economics Working Paper Series No. 307. Manila: Asian Development Bank.

Felipe, J, Kumar, U and Galope, R 2014. *Middle-income transitions: Trap or myth?* Economics Working Paper Series No. 421. Manila: Asian Development Bank.

Flaaen, A, Ghani, E and Mishra, S 2014. *How to avoid middle-income traps? Evidence from Malaysia*. Policy Research Working Paper No. 6427. Washington, DC: The World Bank.

Fraser-Moleketi, G 2013. The next ten years of Africa's economic growth: What does it mean for women? Keynote Address, African Development Bank.

Fuller, B and Romer, P 2014. *Urbanization as opportunity*. World Bank Policy Research Working Paper No. 6874. Washington, DC: The World Bank.

Garrett, G 2004. Globalization's missing middle. *Foreign Affairs*, 83(6), 84–96. Available online at: http://yaleglobal.yale.edu/content/globalizations-missing-middle.

Gill, I and Kharas, H 2007. *An East Asian Renaissance: Ideas for Economic Growth.* Washington, DC: The World Bank.

Gill, I and Raiser, H 2012. *Golden Growth: Restoring the Lustre of the European Economic Model.* Washington, DC: The World Bank.

Glaeser, EL 2010. *Agglomeration Economics.* NBER Conference Report. Chicago: University of Chicago Press.

Gurria, A 2013. *The People's Republic of China: Avoiding the Middle-Income Trap – Policies for Sustained and Inclusive Growth.* Paris: OECD Publishing.

Hawksworth, J 2014. Escaping the middle income trap: What's holding back the Fragile Five? *pwc blogs,* 8 August.

Huang, Y 2014. What's next for the Chinese economy? *MIT Sloan Management Review Magazine,* 17 June.

Im, FG and Rosenblatt, D 2013. *Middle-income traps: A conceptual and empirical survey.* Policy Research Working Paper No. 6594. Washington, DC: The World Bank.

Imbs, J and Wacziarg, R 2003. Stages of diversification. *American Economic Review,* 93(1), 63–86.

International Monetary Fund (IMF) 2014a. *Annual Report on Exchange Arrangements.* Washington, DC: International Monetary Fund.

International Monetary Fund (IMF) 2014b. *Turkey: Concluding Statement of the 2014 Article IV Mission.* Washington, DC: International Monetary Fund.

Islam, N 2014. Will inequality lead China to the middle income trap? *Frontiers of Economics in China,* 9(3), 398–437.

Jankowska, A, Nagengast, A and Ramon, JR 2012a. *The middle-income trap: Comparing Asian and Latin American experiences.* OECD Development Centre Policy Insights No. 96. Paris: OECD Publishing.

Jankowska, A, Nagengast, A and Ramon, JR 2012b. *The product space and the middle-income trap: Comparing Asian and Latin American experiences.* OECD Development Centre Policy Insights No. 311. Paris: OECD Publishing.

Jimenez, E, Nguyen, V and Patrinos, H 2012a. *Stuck in the middle? Human capital development and economic growth in Malaysia and Thailand.* World Bank Policy Research Working Paper No. 6283. Washington, DC: The World Bank.

Jimenez, E, Nguyen, V and Patrinos, H 2012b. *Transitioning from low-income growth to high-income growth: Is there a middle income trap?* World Bank Policy Research Working Paper No. 7104. Washington, DC: The World Bank.

Kaberuka, D 2013a. Is Africa's growth reaching the people? Transcript. Tunis: African Development Bank.

Kaberuka, D 2013b. Second Meeting of ADF 13 Replenishment, closing remarks. Transcript. Tunis: African Development Bank.

Kaberuka, D 2013c. Sustaining Africa's economic growth: The challenges of inclusion and financing infrastructure, closing remarks. Transcript. Tunis: African Development Bank.

Kharas, H and Kohli, H 2011. What is the middle income trap, why do countries fall into it, and how can it be avoided? *Global Journal of Emerging Market Economies,* 3(3), 281–9.

Koen, V, Herd, R and Hill, S 2013. *China's march to prosperity: Reforms to avoid the middle-income trap.* OECD Economics Department Working Paper No. 1093. Paris: OECD Publishing.

Kumagai, S 2014. *The middle-income trap from the viewpoint of trade structures.* IDE Discussion Paper No. 482. Chiba, Japan: Institute of Developing Economies.

Lazear, EP 2005. Entrepreneurship. *Journal of Labour Economics*, 23(4), 649–80.

Lazear, EP, Liang, J and Wang, H 2014. *Demographics and entrepreneurship*. NBER Working Paper No. 20506. Cambridge, MA: National Bureau of Economic Research.

Lin, J and Treichel, V 2012. *Learning from China's rise to escape the middle-income trap: A new structural economics approach to Latin America*. Policy Research Working Paper Series No. 6165. Washington, DC: The World Bank.

Liu, C, Luo, R, Rozelle, S, Yi, H and Zhang, L 2013. The human capital roots of the middle income trap: The case of China. *Agricultural Economics*, 44(s1), 151–62.

Lopez, G 2014. Malaysia struggles to escape the middle-income trap. *The Malaysian Insider*, 20 June. Available online at: www.themalaysianinsider.com/sideviews/article/malaysia-struggles-to-escape-the-middle-income-trap-greg-lopez.

Lucas, RE, jr 1988. On the mechanics of economic development. *Journal of Monetary Economics*, 22, 3–42.

The Maddison Project 2013. *Maddison Project Data*. Groningen: University of Groningen. Available online at: www.ggdc.net/maddison/maddison-project/home.htm.

Ohno, K 2009a. Avoiding the middle income trap: Renovating industrial policy formulation in Vietnam. *ASEAN Economic Bulletin*, 26(1), 25–43.

Ohno, K 2009b. *The Middle Income Trap: Implications for Industrialization Strategies in East Asia and Africa*. Tokyo: GRIPS Development Forum.

Ostry, JD, Berg, A and Tsangarides, CG 2014. *Redistribution, inequality, and growth*. IMF Staff Discussion Note SDN14/02, April. Washington, DC: International Monetary Fund.

Penn World Table 2015. *Penn World Table*. Groningen: University of Groningen. Available online at: www.rug.nl/research/ggdc/data/pwt/?lang=en.

Pezzini, M 2014. Trapped in the middle? Why middle income countries need our continuous attention. Global Partnership for Effective Development Cooperation Blog.

Pritchett, L 1997. Divergence, big time. *The Journal of Economic Perspectives*, 11(3), 3–17.

Rajan, RG and Zingales, L 1998. Financial dependence and growth. *American Economic Review*, 88(3), 559–86.

Robertson, P and Ye, L 2013. *On the existence of a middle income trap*. Economics Discussion Paper No. 13.12. Perth: Department of Economics, University of Western Australia.

Rodrik, D 2015. *Premature deindustrialization*. Working Paper No. 107. Princeton, NJ: School of Social Science Institute for Advanced Study.

Romer, PM 1986. Increasing returns and long-run growth. *Journal of Political Economy*, 94(5), 1002–37.

Shuli, H, Changzheng, Z and Zheyu, Y 2010. Liu He on China's new transformation trail. *Caixin Online*, 11 August. Available online at: http://english.caixin.com/2010–11–08/100196829.html.

Spence, M 2011. *The Next Convergence: The Future of Economic Growth in a Multispeed World*. New York: Farrar, Straus & Giroux.

Tanaka, K and Pezzini, M 2014. *Economic Outlook for Southeast Asia, China and India 2014: Beyond the Middle-Income Trap*. Paris: OECD Publishing.

United Nations (UN) 2013. *Development Cooperation with Middle-Income Countries: Report of the Secretary-General*. New York: United Nations.

United Nations (UN) 2015. *UN Comtrade: International Trade Statistics Database*. New York: United Nations. Available online at: http://comtrade.un.org/data.

Vivarelli, M 2014. *Structural change and innovation as exit strategies from the middle income trap*. IZA Discussion Papers 8148. Bonn: Institute for the Study of Labour.

World Bank 2013. *China 2030: Building a Modern, Harmonious, and Creative Society.* Washington, DC: The World Bank and the Development Research Centre of the State Council.

World Bank 2015a. *Global Economic Prospects*. January. Washington, DC: The World Bank.

World Bank 2015b. *World Development Indicators*. Washington, DC: The World Bank.

Wu, Y 2014. Productivity, economic growth and the middle income trap: Implications for China. *Frontiers of Economics in China*, 9(3), 460–83.

Yilmaz, G 2014. *Turkish middle income trap and less skilled human capital.* Working Papers No. 1430. Ankara: Research and Monetary Policy Department, Central Bank of the Republic of Turkey.

Part II

Lessons from success

3 Resilience and escaping development traps

Lessons for Asian-Pacific economies

Alla Myrvoda, Malhar Nabar and
Changyong Rhee[1]

Introduction

Sustaining growth and escaping traps – low income, middle income or even advanced economy secular stagnation – are once again top priorities at all levels of global income distribution. In Asia, as growth in China slows, policymakers are increasingly asking what this means for their economies. Some prominent commentators and academics outside the region have raised the prospects of a 'middle-income trap' (Eichengreen *et al.*, 2013), while others have argued that high growth rates in Asia are due for reversion to a more modest global mean (Pritchett and Summers, 2014). Against this backdrop, the key question now for Asia's emerging and frontier economies is what can be done to maintain the pace of convergence to higher per capita income.

This chapter has a simple message. Rather than focusing exclusively on boosting average growth rates, Asian-Pacific economies should also focus on building 'resilience' – staying in positive per capita income growth states and minimizing negative growth states. This message is not meant to minimize the importance of boosting average growth. Rather, our sense is that there has been a comparative neglect in the academic literature and policy discourse of the importance of resilience itself (regardless of the actual magnitude of the positive growth).

Average growth and resilience are two different concepts. While measures that boost growth may often also boost resilience, sometimes they can work in different directions. Take steps to boost credit growth, for example. Financial deepening and extending credit to those not previously able to access the formal financial system could raise average growth by transferring resources to factors with higher marginal productivity. But very rapid credit growth without adequate prudential oversight could also lead to misallocation and souring of loans, with the potential for adverse feedback to real activity.

We document a positive long-run association between average per capita income growth and resilience. Countries that stay in positive per capita income growth states for larger fractions of time also tend to have higher average growth rates of per capita income over the long run. We document that this is true not just in the broader global sample, but also within subgroups by continent and by income level. We show with a simple example that the positive association is not simply tautological, and that one does not automatically imply the other. In line with previous studies (North *et al.*, 2009; Winters *et al.*, 2010), we establish that a big difference separating currently rich from currently poor countries is that the former group has stayed in positive growth states for a larger fraction of time and, when they experience negative growth, the magnitude of the decline is relatively small compared with the poor countries. Finally, based on cross-country evidence, we establish some 'universals' – determinants of resilience that apply regardless of the level of income per capita.

Staying in positive growth in per capita terms for a larger fraction of time will arithmetically translate into sustained increases in income per capita (and, for the most part, better living standards for an ever wider cross-section of society). Along the way, it will mean escape from the so-called development traps: low income and middle income. Very few countries have actually managed to do this since the Industrial Revolution fundamentally altered the nature of a small set of European economies and set them on the path of sustained growth. But increasingly now, especially in Asia and Latin America, a widening set of economies appears to be on its way to breaking out of the development traps. It is important to ascertain if there are any general attributes – for example, production and employment structure, outward orientation and financial development – that allow them to do so.

Our main findings are the following:

- In terms of proximate factors, both investment in physical capital and the accumulated stock of human capital (proxied by years of schooling) are positively associated with higher resilience.
- The structure of the economy also matters for resilience. We find evidence of a positive association between industrial employment share and the fraction of time spent in positive growth.
- Openness matters for resilience, but more along the dimension of capital flows (foreign direct investment [FDI] and portfolio investment) than trade flows.
- Financial deepening is important for resilience to the extent that it supports investment in physical capital and education spending. Once these channels are accounted for, we find evidence of a negative direct impact of higher leverage on resilience. We also document that higher external real effective exchange rate (REER) volatility is negatively associated with resilience.
- Fiscal policy prudence (represented by positive average cyclically adjusted and structural balances) and low debt ratios help raise resilience.
- Finally, on 'fundamental factors' underlying economic performance, our results indicate that improvements in the quality of governance are associated with higher resilience.

The chapter is organized as follows. The first section presents the data on resilience and patterns of growth. The second section looks at the determinants of resilience. The third section discusses the policy implications, and the fourth section concludes.

Resilience and growth

Resilience and long-run average growth rates across countries

Going back at least to the early 1990s, much attention has been focused on the question of differences in long-run average growth rates across countries (Barro, 1991; Levine and Renelt, 1992; Mankiw *et al.*, 1992). Far less light has been shed on the question of differences across countries in time spent in positive growth.

At the outset, it is important to clarify that these are not the same thing. We might be tempted to say that one automatically follows the other: higher average growth over a long interval necessarily implies that a country has spent a larger fraction of time in positive growth. And, in the other direction, the longer a country spends in positive growth, the higher will be its average growth. But a simple example illustrates that there need not be a simple mapping in this way.

Suppose that in a 10-year interval, a country experiences six years of growth at 5 per cent per year and four years of negative 5 per cent growth per year. Its average growth over the 10 years is 1 per cent. In that same 10-year interval, suppose another country experiences eight years of positive growth at 2 per cent per year and two years of negative growth at negative 10 per cent per year. The average growth rate for this country will be –0.4 per cent.

The simple example illustrates that it is not obvious that spending more years in positive growth immediately translates into higher average growth over the long run. Put differently, a positive association between average growth and years spent in positive growth is not necessarily a given, and we should not automatically expect it to hold over a large sample of countries. The fact that it does suggests that understanding sources of resilience can help advance our understanding of how to break out of traps, be they low income or middle income.

To appreciate the importance of resilience, consider the example of Malaya (later Malaysia) and Nigeria. The Federation of Malaya became independent from the United Kingdom in 1957. The Federation of Nigeria became independent from the United Kingdom in 1960. These two countries emerged from the rule of a common colonizer at roughly the same time, with their economies both heavily dependent on commodities. At the time of Nigeria's independence, the country's income per capita was slightly *above* that of the part of Malaya that later became Malaysia. Over the next 50 years, they took vastly different paths. After starting off slightly below Nigeria in terms of per capita income, by 1980 Malaysia's income per capita was almost three times as large as Nigeria's; by 2010, it was seven times as large.

It is of course straightforward to surmise that behind this divergence in levels is a large gap in the average growth rates of the two countries. Perhaps what is less well known is that in the 50 years from 1960 to 2010, Malaysia experienced only six years of negative growth in per capita income, at well-spaced intervals. Nigeria, on the other hand, experienced 25 years of negative growth in per capita income, often in multi-year spells. Not only has Nigeria been more vulnerable to negative growth episodes, but it has also found it more difficult to bounce out of phases of negative growth. By contrast, Malaysia has proven more resilient to shocks and quicker at bouncing back.

What is true in bilateral comparisons also holds more generally: there is a positive association between average per capita income growth and years spent in positive growth. Countries that pull away from the pack and rise up the income ladder have tended to do so in sustained fashion, experiencing more years in positive growth than countries that have not. And when they experience growth reversals, they tend to bounce back more quickly as well. North *et al.* (2009) point out that rich countries are differentiated from poor countries not so much by the average growth rates during periods of positive growth, but because the richer economies spend less time in negative growth and also experience higher average growth during negative growth periods than the poor countries do during their negative growth intervals.

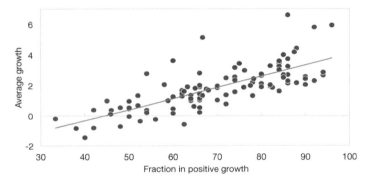

Figure 3.1A Resilience and average growth (per cent)

Source: IMF staff estimates and calculation
Note: Sample includes 105 economies. Data cover 1960–2010, varies by country based on data availability. Growth defined as real GDP per capita in PPP dollars.

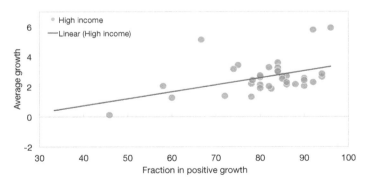

Figure 3.1B Resilience and average growth: high income economies (per cent)

Source: IMF staff estimates and calculation
Note: Sample includes 35 economies. Data cover 1960–2010, varies by country based on data availability. Growth defined as real GDP per capita in PPP dollars. World Bank country classification by income level

Figure 3.1 plots fractions of years spent in positive growth against the average growth rate for large cross-sections of countries for the period 1960–2010. The upper left chart covers the entire sample, whereas the other three are subsamples by income level. All four charts display positive correlations: high average growth countries also tend to spend larger fractions of time in positive growth.

This correlation holds within a sample of Asian economies as well (Figure 3.2). Comparing the Asian plot with the one above for the general sample, clear differences emerge from the extremes of the distribution. More familiarly, at the top end, rapidly growing Asian economies such as China, Korea and Taiwan Province of China have experienced must faster average growth rates than the world average and have also spent longer fractions of time in positive growth.

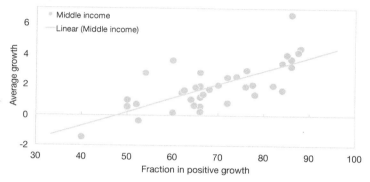

Figure 3.1C Resilience and average growth: middle income economies (per cent)

Source: IMF staff estimates and calculation
Note: Sample includes 40 economies. Data cover 1960–2010, varies by country based on data availability. Growth defined as real GDP per capita in PPP dollars. World Bank country classification by income level

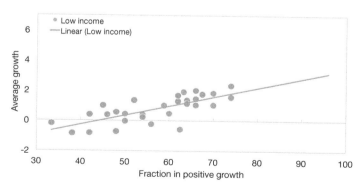

Figure 3.1D Resilience and average growth: low income economies (per cent)

Source: IMF staff estimates and calculation
Note: Sample includes 30 economies. Data cover 1960–2010, varies by country based on data availability. Growth defined as real GDP per capita in PPP dollars. World Bank country classification by income level

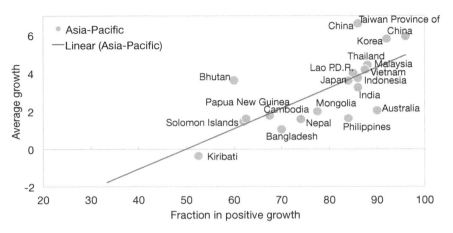

Figure 3.2 Resilience and average growth, Asia-Pacific (per cent)

Source: IMF staff estimates and calculation.

Perhaps less familiar is the bottom end of the distribution: the weaker performing Asian economies have not experienced an average growth rate as negative as the weaker performing economies from the broader world sample. At the same time, weak Asian performers have spent more time in positive growth than the world sample as a whole.

While these scatter plots are not intended to make any statements about causality from time spent in positive growth to average growth rates, clearly the positive association in the data points to a key attribute of economies that maintain positive growth and build resilience: such economies also tend to have higher average growth rates of per capita income over the long run. Two economies (such as Nigeria and Malaysia, cited in the example above) starting from the same initial level of income per capita will end up with very different levels of income if one manages to stay in positive growth for a long time and the other does not. A useful illustration of this feature is a simulation by Winters *et al.* (2010), which shows that the mechanical impact of reducing negative growth states over time is to double (and in some cases nearly triple) the period-end level of income per capita.

More broadly, the data on growth experiences for 1960–2010 indicate that currently rich countries are distinguished from currently poor countries along two important dimensions. The rich countries have tended to stay in positive growth states for a larger fraction of time than poor countries. And the rich countries' experience of negative growth has been less damaging than that of poor countries – average growth rates during negative states tend to be *less* negative in magnitude for the currently rich countries than for the currently poor.

The accompanying table (Table 3.1) summarizes growth experiences in the overall sample of 105 countries over 1960–2010 (with countries classified into groups using the World Bank income classification of high, middle and low income) as well as three subgroups: Asia-Pacific, Africa and the rest of the world.

Table 3.1 Years in positive/negative growth and average growth over 1960–2010 (in per capita terms)

	Income level[1]			
	High	Middle	Low	Total
World				
Number of countries	35	40	30	105
Years in positive growth (% of total)	83	70	57	70
Average growth rate (%)	2.7	2.0	0.8	1.9
In years with positive growth	*3.9*	*4.8*	*5.0*	*4.5*
In years with negative growth	*–3.1*	*–4.5*	*–4.9*	*–4.4*
Asia-Pacific				
Number of countries	5	13	3	21
Years in positive growth (% of total)	87	78	71	79
Average growth rate (%)	3.7	3.2	1.4	3.1
In years with positive growth	*4.7*	*5.5*	*3.8*	*5.0*
In years with negative growth	*–2.5*	*–4.9*	*–4.3*	*–4.4*
Middle East and Africa[2]				
Number of countries	3	15	25	43
Years in positive growth (% of total)	68	62	56	59
Average growth rate (%)	2.7	1.3	0.7	1.0
In years with positive growth	*5.4*	*5.0*	*5.1*	*5.1*
In years with negative growth	*–3.1*	*–4.6*	*–4.9*	*–4.7*
Rest				
Number of countries	27	12	2	41
Years in positive growth (% of total)	83	72	52	78
Average growth rate (%)	2.5	1.6	0.2	2.1
In years with positive growth	*3.6*	*3.8*	*5.3*	*3.7*
In years with negative growth	*–3.2*	*–3.9*	*–5.4*	*–3.7*

Sources: IMF staff estimates and calculations.
[1] Based on World Bank country classification for 2015FY.
[2] Include Middle East and North Africa and Subsaharan Africa categories.

For each group shown, Table 3.1 calculates the fraction of positive growth years by adding the number of years of positive growth across all countries in that group and dividing by the total number of country-years spanning 1960–2010 for which data are available. The average growth rates shown within each category are simple arithmetic averages of growth for all years of that category.

For the world sample (top panel, final column), 70 per cent of the country-year observations recorded positive growth in income per capita. During those years, the average growth rate of per capita income was 4.5 per cent per annum. In the remaining 30 per cent of country-year observations with negative growth, the average growth rate of per capita income was –4.4 per cent per annum. Breaking the world sample into income groups, we see that the high-income countries (column 1) spent more time in positive growth than those belonging to the other two groups (83 per cent for high income versus 70 and 57 per cent respectively for the other two). We also see that the high-income countries, when they experienced negative growth, incurred smaller losses than the other two groups: in years with negative growth, the average growth rate was –3.1 per cent per annum for the high-income countries compared with –4.5 for middle income and –4.9 for low income.

As shown in the second and third panels, similar patterns emerge in Asia-Pacific, the Middle East and Africa: within each group, the high-income countries spend more years in positive growth than countries in the other two groups, and their average growth rate in negative growth years is not as weak as the average growth rate in negative growth years for the other two groups.

Comparing Asian-Pacific economies (panel 2) with the Middle East and Africa (panel 3), the Asian-Pacific economies have spent more time in positive growth than the countries from the latter group (79 per cent versus 59 per cent), and their average growth rate in negative growth years is not as weak (–4.4 per cent per annum in Asia-Pacific versus –4.7 per cent for the Middle East and Africa). The average growth rate in positive growth years is broadly similar across the two groups (5 per cent per annum for Asia-Pacific, 5.1 for the Middle East and Africa). The big difference across the two groups of economies is that Asian-Pacific economies have proven more resilient.

What is interesting about the correlation shown in Figures 3.1 and 3.2 and the data presented in Table 3.1 is that the pattern holds across the distribution of world income, covering all ranges of income. It is not a feature only of low-income economies or of middle-income economies, or, for that matter, of high-income economies. As such, understanding sources of resilience will be key for all countries, not just those trying to break out of low- or middle-income traps.

Features of resilient economies

What are some of the features of more resilient economies? As a first cut, consider a simple comparison of economies with above-median levels of resilience (Group A) versus those with below-median levels (Group B), where the median is calculated for the world distribution of resilience across countries during 1960–2010. Clearly, there are selection issues involved if we slice the sample this way and look for differences after separating countries based on resilience or growth rates. Nevertheless, the simple comparison can shed some light on how attributes accumulate over time if we look back over the entire sample for 1960–2010 to tease out differences across these two groups of economies.

Figure 3.3 shows the panel charts for the world and Asian samples split by median resilience. In both samples, the more resilient economies have been those with output shares concentrated more in services and industry than in agriculture. Less resilient economies are those with higher output shares concentrated in agriculture. In terms of employment shares, more resilient economies tend to employ the largest fraction of their workforce in services, followed by industry and agriculture, in that order. Less resilient economies tend to employ their largest fraction of workers in agriculture, followed by services and industry, in that order.

Comparing the Asian sample with the world sample, some key differences are the following:

- Agricultural value-added share of GDP is higher among Asian high-resilience economies than in the world sample, while the reverse is true when comparing the services value-added share of GDP. The industry value-added share is similar across the high-resilience economies in the two samples.
- Asian high-resilience economies have a smaller share of the workforce employed in industry and services compared with the high-resilience economies in the world sample, whereas they have a higher share of the workforce in agriculture compared with world high-resilience economies.
- Similarly, comparing the low-resilience economies in the two samples, Asian low-resilience economies employ a smaller fraction of workers in services and industry compared with low-resilience economies in the overall world sample.

Results

We draw our data from the World Bank's World Development Indicators (WDI) and World Governance Indicators, the International Monetary Fund (IMF), World Economic Outlook (WEO) and International Financial Statistics (IFS), Polity IV dataset and Barro–Lee data on years of schooling. We construct a panel data set from annual data on 105 countries for 1960–2010 by taking five-year averages for all variables to smooth out business-cycle fluctuations. Volatility indicators are taken as standard deviations within five-year intervals. Our measure of resilience is the fraction of the five-year interval spent in positive growth. Data sources are summarized in Table 1 in Appendix 3.1.

One immediate question is, why not use as the dependent variable growth spells, as in Hausmann *et al.* (2005), or regimes of growth, as in Jerzmanowski (2006)? For one, this approach has been studied extensively. Second, the measures of growth spells in these studies are usually subject to some minimum average growth threshold (average growth rate of x per cent over minimum z years). Our view is that regardless of the magnitude of growth, understanding why some countries spend a larger fraction of years in positive growth than others (separate from the cross-country differences in propensity to experience long spells of high average growth) is important.

At the outset, we do not want to prejudge and restrict ourselves only to countries at certain ranges of the income distribution; rather we want to include countries at all levels of income and all continents to the extent possible to achieve as broad a sample as we can. Indeed, focusing only on middle- or low-income countries to understand differences in resilience leaves the exercise vulnerable to missing relevant information.

Our objective is to identify 'universals' that underpin resilience. The determining variables included in the regression are therefore based on inputs in the aggregate production function (investment, schooling); the structure of output (services and industry share of gross value added); structure of the labour market (employment shares of services and industry); the degree of openness (gross trade and capital

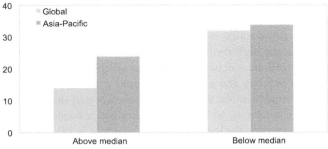

Figure 3.3A Value added: agriculture (per cent of GDP)

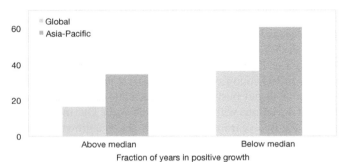

Figure 3.3B Employment: agriculture (per cent of total employment)

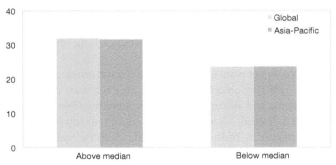

Figure 3.3C Value added: industry (per cent of GDP)

Source: IMF staff estimates and calculations
Note: Sample covers 105 economies, of which 20 are in the Asia–Pacific. Data cover 1960–2010, varies by country based on data availability

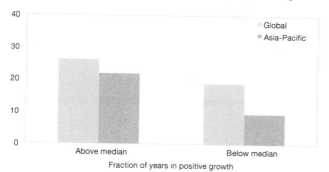

Figure 3.3D Employment: industry (per cent of total employment)

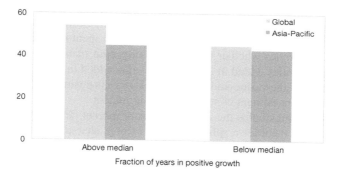

Figure 3.3E Value added: services (per cent of GDP)

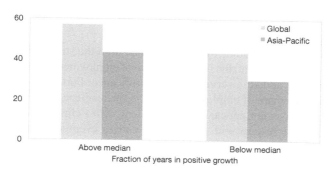

Figure 3.3F Employment: services (per cent of total employment)

Source: IMF staff estimates and calculations
Note: Sample covers 105 economies, of which 20 are in the Asia–Pacific. Data cover 1960–2010, varies
by country based on data availability

flows); financial development and net dependence on foreign financing; aggregate volatility (proxied by variability in the REER and in the terms of trade); and, finally, fundamentals (governance). Descriptive statistics for the variables used in this analysis are summarized in Table 2 in Appendix 3.1.

Results: physical and human capital, basic structure of output and employment

Table 3 in Appendix 3.1 reports results of fixed-effects panel regressions that examine whether proximate factors (inputs in the production function) and the structure of the economy have an impact on resilience. The regressions control for initial income and for unobserved country-specific time-invariant factors (such as topography, disease environment, location, soil quality and deep historical legacies).

Column 1 reports the basic specification with investment in physical capital and years of schooling (to proxy for human capital). The investment share of GDP is significant, with a 1 percentage point increase in investment associated with a 0.75 percentage point increase in the fraction of time spent in positive growth.

Column 2 examines whether the structure of output matters for resilience by adding shares of value added in industry and value added in services to the basic specification. A higher value-added share of services is positively associated with resilience, while investment continues to be significant.

The third column studies the impact of labour market structure on resilience. The specification includes a split by labour income shares across industry and services. Here, the employment share in industry is associated positively with resilience whereas the employment share in services is not. One possible interpretation is that since services include both high and low value-added activities (high end/low end), simply boosting the overall share of service sector employment may not have any impact on resilience if the bulk of the increase is at the low value-added end. Industrial share of employment, on the other hand, represents activities that include manufacturing, construction and so on – which may contribute more by way of value added while also raising the demand for higher value-added services.

Indeed, in the final column, where we include both the structure of output and the structure of employment, the industrial share of employment remains significant whereas the value added in services loses significance. Furthermore, the finding that the industrial share of employment matters for resilience, whereas industrial share of output does not appear to, is consistent with Felipe *et al.* (2014), who establish a similar pattern with regard to countries eventually achieving high-income status.

Across all specifications, the level of initial income is not significant, suggesting no systematic relationship between level of income and degree of resilience, once the unobservable time-invariant factors are controlled for.

Investment/GDP is significant across all specifications, suggesting that higher investment spending is associated with more resilience – possibly indicating that an environment that facilitates higher investment spending and guides long-term decision-making by firms (mobilizes the funding, matches funding to projects) also fosters greater resilience.

Finally, average years of schooling are statistically significant in the final column when both the structure of output and the structure of employment are included as additional controls. Raising the average years of schooling by one unit increases the fraction of time spent in positive growth by 3.5 percentage points.

Since resilience (or lack thereof) may be persistent over time, the regressions in Table 4 in Appendix 3.1 include lagged fraction of time spent in positive growth – that is, over the preceding five-year interval. The introduction of the lagged dependent variable biases the fixed-effects estimates. Instead, the specification used in Table 4 in Appendix 3.1 is an Arellano-Bond panel generalized method of moments (GMM) estimation, which allows for the inclusion of the lagged resilience measure along with other regressors. By using lagged levels of the right-hand side variables as instruments, the GMM corrects the bias in estimates introduced by endogeneity, measurement error and omitted variables.

The sample size drops because of insufficient data on some countries to generate enough lags as instruments. The results in Table 4 in Appendix 3.1 indicate that years of schooling and investment are positively associated with resilience. Industrial share of employment is positively associated with resilience when only the structure of the labour market is included as an additional control (column 3).

Degree of openness

Tables 5 and 6 in Appendix 3.1 examine whether the degree of openness matters for resilience. We study three dimensions of openness: to trade flows, to FDI and to portfolio flows.

Across both the fixed-effects regressions (Table 5 in Appendix 3.1) and the GMM (Table 6 in Appendix 3.1), we find no evidence of a systematic relationship between trade openness and resilience. By contrast, the evidence suggests openness to capital flows is associated positively with resilience. The fixed-effects specification (Table 5 in Appendix 3.1, columns 2 and 4) indicates that openness to FDI is statistically significant – with a 1 percentage point increase in the ratio of FDI/GDP associated with an increase in the fraction of time spent in positive growth ranging between 0.5 and 0.6 percentage points.

The GMM specifications reported in Table 6 in Appendix 3.1 indicate that portfolio flows are positively associated with a larger fraction of time spent in positive growth. An immediate concern is that this may simply reflect reverse causality: more resilient economies attract higher portfolio flows. To the extent that the GMM method corrects for this through the use of relevant lags as instruments, the reported coefficients are purged of any bias introduced by reverse causality.

As in the basic specifications reported earlier, the investment share of GDP continues to remain positively associated with resilience while the level of initial income is not statistically significant.

Financing

Tables 7 and 8 in Appendix 3.1 examine the relationship between resilience and financing, including the impact of the current account balance (to proxy for reliance on foreign funding).

The results in Table 7 in Appendix 3.1(fixed effects) indicate that investment spending remains statistically significant and positively associated with resilience.

Table 8 in Appendix 3.1 reports results of the GMM specifications. As seen across all three columns, both investment spending and years of schooling are statistically signi-ficant. We also find that financial deepening (proxied by the ratio of credit/GDP) is negatively associated with resilience. One interpretation of this finding is that once the degree of financing needed to support investment and education spending is accounted for, any further direct impact of higher leverage tends to be associated with rising fragilities and lower resilience.

The current account balance itself is not statistically significant in any of the specifications across Tables 7 and 8 in Appendix 3.1.

Volatility

Table 9 in Appendix 3.1 looks at the relationship between volatility and persistence. Volatility is measured using REER and terms of trade (TOT) volatility. We focus only on fixed-effects specifications as we do not have enough lagged data for several countries to do this with GMM.

In the fixed effects, we find a negative association between volatility (REER and TOT) and resilience when each is included as a separate regressor. When both are included together, only REER volatility matters (Table 9 in Appendix 3.1, column 3). The coefficient indicates that a 1 percentage point increase in the standard deviation of REER growth is associated with a 1.7 percentage point decrease in the fraction of time spent in positive per capita income growth.

Investment continues to be positively associated with resilience across these specifications.

Fiscal policy and space

Table 10 in Appendix 3.1 reports regression results using different indicators of fiscal policy stance: net lending and borrowing as a percentage of GDP; cyclically adjusted balance and structural balance, both as a percentage of GDP; and gross general government debt as a percentage of GDP to reflect fiscal space. All fiscal variables are averaged over five-year intervals.

As Table 10 in Appendix 3.1 indicates, greater fiscal prudence (represented by more positive net lending and borrowing, cyclically adjusted, and structural balances) and higher fiscal space (reflected in low debt ratios) are associated with higher resilience.

Governance

Table 11 in Appendix 3.1 looks at deeper determinants of economic performance by including governance indicators in the regression. The particular measures used here are from the Worldwide Governance Indicators (WGI) project of the World Bank (Kaufmann *et al.*, 2010). The WGI reports governance indicators for 215 economies over the period 1996–2013, based on multiple individual data sources compiled by survey institutes, think tanks, non-governmental organizations, international organizations and private sector firms.

The evidence suggests that a higher degree of corruption control and greater government effectiveness are associated with higher resilience. The interpretation of magnitude is difficult since the indicators run on a scale of –2.5 (weak) to +2.5 (strong), but the signs on the coefficients point towards a positive association.

Results: summary

Although we examine the impact of factors usually considered in cross-country growth regressions, and some of our findings on their relevance for resilience are similar to what has been found by researchers studying drivers of cross-country variation in growth, there are a couple of important nuances. First, our result on credit/GDP suggests that financial deepening is important for boosting resilience to the extent that its influence works through physical and human capital accumulation. Beyond this, we find a negative association between leverage and resilience. Second, while the growth literature has typically found that openness to trade is positively associated with growth (Frankel and Romer, 1999), here we do not see a similar association between trade flows and resilience.

These distinctions are not intended as statements about the benefits or costs of leverage or trade openness, but rather to point out that policy implications for growth and for resilience are not always fully overlapping. The next section turns to a more detailed discussion of policy implications that follow from the regression results.

Policy implications

The results in the previous section indicated that factors such as the investment share of GDP, schooling, industrial share of employment, lower volatility and greater openness to FDI, portfolio flows and fiscal prudence are all positively associated with higher resilience. From Asia's perspective, what policies will help?

Past IMF work (Nabar and Syed, 2011) documented that the investment share of GDP for emerging and developing Asia (outside China) is relatively low, while in China, Japan and the newly industrializing economies investment is directed towards export-oriented manufacturing and less towards services and non-tradables.

A number of policies would help raise *investment* in areas where it is relatively low and shift its composition towards non-tradables where it is currently skewed towards export-oriented manufacturing, including: lowering uncertainty related to the corporate tax code and providing cyclically appropriate macro policy support; further improvements in the ease of doing business (echoing the positive association in the current empirical exercise between, on the one hand, two dimensions of governance – control of corruption and government effectiveness – and, on the other, resilience); raising infrastructure spending (the Asian Development Bank estimated emerging Asia's total infrastructure needs at approximately US$7.5 trillion for this current decade; ADB, 2009).

Besides boosting the investment share of GDP, these measures could also help attract *FDI and portfolio flows* – factors positively associated with resilience.

Our results also indicate that the structure of the economy matters for resilience – specifically, a higher *share of industrial employment* is positively associated with spending longer fractions of time in positive growth. The policy recommendations listed above for boosting investment as a share of GDP would carry over to raising the industrial share of employment. We deliberately avoid getting into a discussion of which specific industries matter for resilience since the formula that worked in a particular set of countries at a particular point in time will not necessarily carry over to the next generation of frontier and developing economies attempting to boost resilience. Rather, doing the small things right, such as reducing search and matching costs through job agencies and credit registries – to increase the efficiency of pairing vacancies with jobseekers, financiers with projects and manufacturers with distributors – would reduce hold-up costs and incentivize industrial growth.

The measure we have in mind is industrial employment (as defined by the World Bank *WDI* database, the category includes manufacturing, construction, mining and utilities such as electricity, water and gas), not the narrower category of manufacturing employment. As Rodrik (2013) has pointed out, manufacturing is becoming increasingly capital intensive and automated, so that countries' shares of manufacturing employment are peaking at lower levels than used to be the case. The lesson for Asia's frontier and developing economies is clear in this regard. Pursuing a larger manufacturing base itself (without also considering broader development objectives, including making conditions conducive for construction, utilities provision and services in general) may not be the optimal strategy to pursue, given the risks of wasteful overcapacity creation, potential weakening of asset quality and the diminished scope for manufacturing to absorb labour (for detailed studies of future growth areas for 'Factory Asia', see Choi and Rhee, 2014).

The other proximate factor in the production function, *human capital* (as proxied by the years of schooling), has increasingly become an object of policy interest in recent years. The obvious macro policy implication is redirecting public expenditure from wasteful areas (such as poorly targeted subsidies) to financing education infrastructure and teacher training. But attention will also need to be paid to the demand side and take-up, especially for frontier and developing economies. As the World Bank (2015: 88) has documented, the timing of conditional cash transfers over the course of the year can affect school re-enrolment rates and therefore, over time, the educational attainment of the workforce.

Our results also indicate that *fiscal prudence* and maintaining low debt-to-GDP ratios help raise resilience. With larger fiscal buffers to work with, governments can provide countercyclical support to activity as needed and help maintain positive growth in per capita income for a larger fraction of the time.

Finally, from a long-horizon perspective, reforming *institutions of economic and political governance* to enhance control of corruption and boost government effectiveness will have a first-order impact on raising resilience. In the terminology of Acemoglu and Robinson (2012), this involves shifting from extractive to inclusive institutions. In the terminology of North *et al.* (2009), this means moving from 'natural order/limited access' states to 'open access' states. These transitions – from a governance system that favours a narrow elite at the expense of others, to a more meritocratic, equal-opportunity system – take a very long time and are rare. But to the extent that incremental steps can be taken by changes to the legal framework so as to introduce more checks and balances, while reducing barriers to entry into protected sectors, our empirical results suggest they will contribute to raising resilience.

Conclusion

Escaping traps – be they middle income, low income or advanced economy secular stagnation – is ultimately about boosting resilience, sustaining growth and maintaining improvements in living standards over time. As countries have made these transitions in the past, they have faced different challenges at various stages of history and have therefore been offered different policy prescriptions: tight controls over capital flows versus liberalization; import substitution versus export-oriented manufacturing; and heavy industry promotion versus lighter consumer-oriented industry and services. One common thread that has run through all of these phases over the years is that more resilient countries have also tended to end up with higher levels of income per capita over the long run.

For Asian economies looking to sustain convergence, achieving a larger fraction of years spent in positive growth (remaining resilient) will play an important role in the process. Based on estimates from a broad cross-country sample of 105 economies over the period 1960–2010, the factors associated with greater resilience include the investment share of GDP, years of schooling, FDI and portfolio flows as a percentage of GDP, lower external volatility, fiscal prudence and better governance. We also find evidence of a positive association between industrial employment share and resilience. Financial deepening (increasing credit as a share of GDP) is found to have no direct influence on resilience beyond its impact through the channels of facilitating physical and human capital accumulation. Indeed, a challenge for the region's economies will be to ensure a 'safe' financial deepening that limits vulnerabilities by matching the risk appetite of investors with the risk profile of underlying projects. Policy efforts directed towards the factors identified here as contributing to resilience would benefit countries across the income distribution seeking to avoid stagnation at their particular levels of development – regardless of whether they have low-, middle- or high-income status.

Appendix 3.1

The data sources for the variables used in the empirical analysis are listed in Table 1 and descriptive statistics are summarized in Table 2.

The World Bank's World Development Indicators (WDI) database defines industry as corresponding to International Standard Industrial Classification (ISIC) divisions 10–45, including manufacturing (ISIC divisions 15–37), mining, construction, electricity, water and gas. The value added for a sector is calculated as aggregate output for that sector, net of intermediate inputs. No deductions are made for depreciation of machinery or loss of non-renewable natural resources.

Table 1 Tables for the Empirical Analysis

Variable	Definition	Scale	Unit	Source
PPP GDP per capita	PPP GDP per capita at 2005 constant prices		PPP dollars per person	Penn World Tables
Investment	Gross fixed capital formation, current prices	Billion	National currency	IMF, World Economic Outlook
GDP	GDP, current prices	Billion	National currency	IMF, World Economic Outlook and IFS
GDP	GDP, current prices	Billion	US dollars	IMF, World Economic Outlook
Exports	Exports of goods and services, current prices	Billion	National currency	IMF, World Economic Outlook
Imports	Imports of goods and services, current prices	Billion	National currency	IMF, World Economic Outlook
Current account	Balance on current account	Billion	National currency	IMF, World Economic Outlook and IFS
FDI inflows	FDI inflows	Billion	US dollars	IMF, World Economic Outlook
FDI outflows	FDI outflows	Billion	US dollars	IMF, World Economic Outlook
Portfolio investment assets	Portfolio investment assets	Billion	US dollars	IMF, World Economic Outlook
Portfolio investment liabilities	Portfolio investment liabilities	Billion	US dollars	IMF, World Economic Outlook
Terms of trade	Terms of trade	Index	2010=100	IMF, World Economic Outlook
Years of schooling	Average years of total schooling		Years	Barrow and Lee dataset
REER	Real effective exchange rate, CPI based	Index	2005=100	GDS
Credit to private sector	Domestic credit to private sector		percent of GDP	World Bank, World Development Indicators
Value added in agriculture	Agriculture, value added (% GDP)		percent of GDP	World Bank, World Development Indicators
Value added in industry	Industry, value added (% GDP)		percent of GDP	World Bank, World Development Indicators
Value added in services	Services, value added (% GDP)		percent of GDP	World Bank, World Development Indicators
Employment share of agriculture	Employment in agriculture (% of total employment)		percent of total employment	World Bank, World Development Indicators
Employment share of industry	Employment in industry (% of total employment)		percent of total employment	World Bank, World Development Indicators
Employment share services	Employment in services (% of total employment)		percent of total employment	World Bank, World Development Indicators
Rule of law	Reflects perceptions of the extent to which agents have confidence in and abide by the rules of society, and in particular the quality of contract enforcement, property rights, the police, and the courts, as well as the likelihood of crime and violence.	Index	Estimate ranges from approximately -2.5 (weak) to 2.5 (strong)	World Bank, World Governance Indicators
Regulatory quality	Reflects perceptions of the ability of the government to formulate and implement sound policies and regulations that permit and promote private sector development.	Index	Estimate ranges from approximately -2.5 (weak) to 2.5 (strong)	World Bank, World Governance Indicators
Control of corruption	Reflects perceptions of the extent to which public power is exercised for private gain, including both petty and grand forms of corruption, as well as 'capture' of the state by elites and private interests.	Index	Estimate ranges from approximately -2.5 (weak) to 2.5 (strong)	World Bank, World Governance Indicators
Government effectiveness	Reflects perceptions of the quality of public services, the quality of the civil service and the degree of its independence from political pressures, the quality of policy formulation and implementation, and the credibility of the government's commitment to such policies.	Index	Estimate ranges from approximately -2.5 (weak) to 2.5 (strong)	World Bank, World Governance Indicators
Polity indicator	Combined polity score	Index	Estimate ranges form -10 to 10	Polity IV: Regime authority Characteristics and transitions dataset
Binomial variables				
High income economies	World bank classification			
Middle income economies	World bank classification			
Low income economies	World bank classification			
Advanced economies	IMF, World Economic Outlook classification			
Emerging and developing economies	IMF, World Economic Outlook classification			
Asia Pacific economies	IMF, World Economic Outlook classification			

Table 2 Descriptive statistics

	Units	Average	Standard deviation
Log of initial income	Level	8.1	1.5
Investment-to-GDP	percent of GDP	21.3	9.1
Years of schooling	years	5.8	3.4
Value added in agriculture	percent of GDP	23.1	17.4
Value added in industry	percent of GDP	27.7	10.8
Value added in services	percent of GDP	49.3	13.2
Employment share of agriculture	percent of employment	20.3	20.7
Employment share of industry	percent of employment	24.8	7.9
Employment share services	percent of employment	54.4	16.4
Trade openness	percent of GDP	70.2	45.7
FDI openness	percent of GDP	7.3	52.2
Portfo investment openness	percent of GDP	9.8	62.9
Current account	percent of GDP	-3.4	10.6
REER volatility	Index	6.4	5.2
Terms of trade volatility	Index	11.5	38.3
Government effectiveness 1/	Index	0.0	1.1
Regulatory quality 1/	Index	0.0	1.1
Rule of law 1/	Index	-0.1	1.1
Control of corruption 1/	Index	0.0	1.1
Share in positive growth (%)	percent	69.8	14.9
Average real growth (PPP terms)	percent	1.9	1.5

Source: IMF staff estimates and calculations.

1/ Scale ranges from -2.5 (weak) to +2.5 (strong).

Table 3 Structure of economy

Log Initial Income	-0.303	-1.042	1.615	1.444
	(1.997)	(2.261)	(3.011)	(2.961)
Investment / GDP	0.746***	0.814***	0.845**	0.877**
	(0.194)	(0.198)	(0.361)	(0.401)
Years of Schooling	0.860	-1.592	2.932	3.519*
	(0.756)	(1.191)	(1.866)	(1.948)
Value Added in Industry		0.0623		-0.646
		(0.305)		(0.490)
Value Added in Services		0.760**		0.264
		(0.297)		(0.413)
Employment Share in Industry			0.847*	1.244***
			(0.432)	(0.451)
Employment Share in Services			0.150	-0.389
			(0.386)	(0.361)
SAMPLE YEARS	1965-2010	1965-2010	1965-2010	1965-2010
Number of countries	84	78	75	70
Observations	518	465	281	260
R-Squared	0.055	0.090	0.09	0.1

Sources: IMF staff estimates and calculations.
Notes: Dependent Variable: Fraction of positive growth states
Robust Standard Errors in parentheses. *** p<0.01, ** p<0.05, * p<0.1
Fixed Effects Estimation

Table 4 Structure of economy (GMM)

Lagged Fraction of Positive Growth Years	0.0263	0.000150	-0.252**	-0.442***
	(0.0917)	(0.0934)	(0.107)	(0.110)
Log Initial Income	0.774	-0.266	1.745	2.493
	(2.469)	(2.502)	(2.471)	(2.311)
Investment / GDP	0.726***	0.858***	0.264	1.057**
	(0.244)	(0.281)	(0.367)	(0.464)
Years of Schooling	2.961*	0.689	7.585***	9.489***
	(1.566)	(1.827)	(2.926)	(3.531)
Value Added in Industry		0.554		-0.229
		(0.441)		(0.990)
Value Added in Services		0.728		-1.096
		(0.474)		(0.726)
Employment Share in Industry			1.196**	0.597
			(0.466)	(0.623)
Employment Share in Services			-0.630	-0.497
			(0.597)	(0.694)
SAMPLE YEARS	1965-2010	1965-2010	1965-2010	1965-2010
Number of countries	74	68	53	48
Observations	332	302	176	163
Arellano Bond test of no second order autocorrelation in first-differenced errors (p-value)	0.88	0.86	0.15	0.08

Sources: IMF staff estimates and calculations.

Notes: Dependent Variable: Fraction of positive growth states

Robust Standard Errors in parentheses. *** p<0.01, ** p<0.05, * p<0.1

Panel GMM Estimation

Table 5 Openness

Log Initial Income	-0.101	-0.320	0.461	0.376
	(2.155)	(2.104)	(2.344)	(2.374)
Investment / GDP	0.735***	0.726***	0.947***	0.908***
	(0.200)	(0.206)	(0.180)	(0.200)
Years of Schooling	1.018	-0.0509	1.114	0.620
	(0.867)	(0.897)	(0.923)	(1.086)
Trade Openness: (X+M)/GDP	0.0221			0.0377
	(0.0400)			(0.0442)
FDI Openness: (Inflow +Outflow)/GDP		0.634**		0.512*
		(0.274)		(0.284)
Portfolio Flows Openness: (Inflow+Outflow)/GDP			0.0776	0.0408
			(0.0609)	(0.0885)
SAMPLE YEARS	1965-2010	1965-2010	1965-2010	1965-2010
Number of countries	82	83	78	76
Observations	494	487	443	421
R-Squared	0.06	0.07	0.07	0.08

Sources: IMF staff estimates and calculations.

Notes: Dependent Variable: Fraction of positive growth states

Robust Standard Errors in parentheses. *** $p<0.01$, ** $p<0.05$, * $p<0.1$

Fixed Effects Estimation

Table 6 Openness (GMM)

Lagged Fraction of Positive Growth Years	0.0260 (0.0901)	0.0202 (0.0898)	-0.0392 (0.0969)	-0.0378 (0.0958)
Log Initial Income	0.998 (2.527)	0.671 (2.580)	1.831 (2.425)	1.999 (2.487)
Investment / GDP	0.755*** (0.245)	0.708*** (0.262)	0.862** (0.354)	0.834** (0.379)
Years of Schooling	3.208* (1.682)	2.021 (1.654)	2.868* (1.688)	2.175 (1.902)
Trade Openness: (X+M)/GDP	0.0528 (0.0698)			0.131 (0.0823)
FDI Openness: (Inflow+Outflow)/GDP		0.481* (0.285)		0.325 (0.225)
Portfolio Flows Openness: (Inflow+Outflow)/GDP			0.198*** (0.0434)	0.195*** (0.0543)
SAMPLE YEARS	1965-2010	1965-2010	1965-2010	1965-2010
Number of countries	73	72	68	67
Observations	322	312	288	278
Arellano Bond test of no second order autocorrelation in first-differenced errors (p-value)	0.79	0.83	0.53	0.64

Sources: IMF staff estimates and calculations.

Notes: Dependent Variable: Fraction of positive growth states

Robust Standard Errors in parentheses. *** $p<0.01$, ** $p<0.05$, * $p<0.1$

Panel GMM Estimation

Table 7 Financing

Log Initial Income	-0.202	-0.327	-0.0986
	(2.313)	(2.042)	(2.363)
Investment / GDP	0.867***	0.758***	0.891***
	(0.183)	(0.206)	(0.191)
Years of Schooling	0.826	0.797	0.819
	(0.811)	(0.801)	(0.854)
Credit to private sector / GDP	0.00216		0.00215
	(0.00327)		(0.00325)
CA / GDP		0.0691	0.112
		(0.205)	(0.226)
SAMPLE YEARS	1965-2010	1965-2010	1965-2010
Number of countries	82	84	82
Observations	483	511	478
R-Squared	0.06	0.05	0.06

Sources: IMF staff estimates and calculations.
Notes: Dependent Variable: Fraction of positive growth states
Robust Standard Errors in parentheses. *** $p<0.01$, ** $p<0.05$, * $p<0.1$
Fixed Effects Estimation

Table 8 Financing (GMM)

Lagged Fraction of Positive Growth Years	-0.0272	0.0393	-0.0230
	(0.0939)	(0.0920)	(0.0944)
Log Initial Income	-0.550	1.094	-0.455
	(2.163)	(2.553)	(2.312)
Investment / GDP	0.908***	0.838***	0.955***
	(0.295)	(0.312)	(0.361)
Years of Schooling	8.292***	2.688*	8.073***
	(1.913)	(1.581)	(1.951)
Credit to private sector / GDP	-0.378***		-0.376***
	(0.0777)		(0.0778)
CA / GDP		0.385	0.153
		(0.338)	(0.338)
SAMPLE YEARS	1965-2010	1965-2010	1965-2010
Number of countries	312	327	308
Observations	71	74	71
Arellano Bond test of no second order autocorrelation in first-differenced errors (p-value)	0.76	0.99	0.68

Sources: IMF staff estimates and calculations.
Notes: Dependent Variable: Fraction of positive growth states
Robust Standard Errors in parentheses. *** p<0.01, ** p<0.05, * p<0.1
Panel GMM Estimation

Table 9 Volatility

Log Initial Income	-0.682	-0.753	-1.219
	(4.102)	(2.054)	(4.101)
Investment / GDP	0.759*	0.767***	0.628*
	(0.407)	(0.230)	(0.377)
Years of Schooling	-4.193	0.387	-4.707
	(2.874)	(0.801)	(2.865)
REER Volatility	-1.464***		-1.667***
	(0.485)		(0.463)
Terms of Trade Volatility		-0.293*	0.0831
		(0.147)	(0.222)
SAMPLE YEARS	1965-2010	1965-2010	1965-2010
Number of countries	78	81	77
Observations	187	472	184
R-Squared	0.12	0.06	0.13

Sources: IMF staff estimates and calculations.
Notes: Dependent Variable: Fraction of positive growth states
Robust Standard Errors in parentheses. *** $p<0.01$, ** $p<0.05$, * $p<0.1$
Fixed Effects Estimation

Table 10 Fiscal policy and space

Log Initial Income	1.898	-0.399	-0.200	-1.459
	(2.919)	(3.261)	(3.162)	(3.402)
Investment / GDP	1.211***	1.280***	0.924*	0.830**
	(0.388)	(0.475)	(0.466)	(0.387)
Years of Schooling	0.460	-3.488**	-3.268*	-0.330
	(1.299)	(1.627)	(1.796)	(1.092)
Net Lending and Borrowing (per cent of GDP)	1.398*** (0.376)			
General Government Cyclically Adjusted Balance (per cent of potential GDP)		1.796*** (0.556)		
General Government Structural Balance (per cent of potential GDP)			2.080*** (0.614)	
General Government Gross Debt (per cent of GDP)				-0.1000* (0.0547)
SAMPLE YEARS	1965-2010	1965-2010	1965-2010	1965-2010
Number of countries	75	46	46	79
Observations	265	146	149	258
R-Squared	0.151	0.153	0.179	0.083

Sources: IMF staff estimates and calculations.
Notes: Dependent Variable: Fraction of positive growth states
Robust Standard Errors in parentheses. *** $p<0.01$, ** $p<0.05$, * $p<0.1$
Fixed Effects Estimation

Table 11 Governance

Log Initial Income	-1.224 (4.458)	-1.011 (4.408)	-1.328 (4.568)	-2.497 (4.226)
Investment / GDP	0.905** (0.365)	1.037*** (0.368)	0.798** (0.347)	0.718** (0.346)
Years of Schooling	-3.027 (3.216)	-3.123 (3.160)	-2.042 (3.188)	-2.520 (2.850)
Rule of Law	9.233 (13.93)			
Regulatory Quality		-6.108 (11.44)		
Control of Corruption			18.92** (9.405)	
Government Effectiveness				34.23*** (9.949)
SAMPLE YEARS	1996-2010	1996-2010	1996-2010	1996-2010
Number of countries	80	80	80	80
Observations	189	189	189	189
R-Squared	0.05	0.05	0.08	0.13

Sources: IMF staff estimates and calculations.
Notes: Dependent Variable: Fraction of positive growth states
Robust Standard Errors in parentheses. *** $p<0.01$, ** $p<0.05$, * $p<0.1$
Fixed Effects Estimation

Note

1 This chapter should not be reported as representing the views of the International Monetary Fund (IMF). The views expressed in this chapter are those of the authors and do not necessarily represent those of the IMF or IMF policy. The authors are grateful to the discussants, Professor Wong Poh Kam and Dr Chien-Fu Lin, and to conference participants for their comments.

References

Acemoglu, D and Robinson, JA 2012. *Why Nations Fail: The Origins of Power, Prosperity and Poverty*. New York: Crown.

Asian Development Bank (ADB) 2009. *Infrastructure for a Seamless Asia*. Manila: Asian Development Bank.

Barro, RJ 1991. Economic growth in a cross section of countries. *Quarterly Journal of Economics*, 106(2), 407–43.

Choi, B and Rhee, C (eds) 2014. *Future of Factory Asia*. Manila: Asian Development Bank and Korea Economic Research Institute.

Eichengreen, B, Park, D and Shin, K 2013. *Growth slowdowns redux: New evidence on the middle-income trap*. NBER Working Paper No. 18673. Cambridge, MA: National Bureau of Economic Research.

Felipe, J, Mehta, A and Rhee, C 2014. *Manufacturing matters . . . but it's the jobs that count*. ADB Economics Working Paper Series No. 450. Manila: Asian Development Bank.

Frankel, J and Romer, D 1999. Does trade cause growth? *American Economic Review*, 89(3), 379–99.

Hausmann, R, Pritchett, L and Rodrik, D 2005. Growth accelerations. *The Journal of Economic Growth*, 10, 303–29.

Jerzmanowski, M 2006. Empirics of hills, plateaus, mountains and plains: A Markov-switching approach to growth. *The Journal of Development Economics*, 81, 357–85.

Kaufmann, D, Kraay, A and Mastruzzi, M 2010. *The worldwide governance indicators: A summary of methodology, data and analytical issues*. World Bank Policy Research Working Paper No. 5430. Washington, DC: The World Bank.

Levine, R and Renelt, D 1992. A sensitivity analysis of cross-country growth regressions. *American Economic Review*, 82(4), 942–63.

Mankiw, NG, Romer, D and Weil, DN 1992. A contribution to the empirics of economic growth. *Quarterly Journal of Economics*, 107(2), 407–37.

Nabar, M and Syed, M 2011. *The great rebalancing act: Can investment be a lever?* IMF Working Paper No. 11/35. Washington, DC: International Monetary Fund.

North, D, Wallis, J and Weingast, B 2009. *Violence and Social Orders*. Cambridge: Cambridge University Press.

Pritchett, L and Summers, LH 2014. *Asiaphoria meets regression to the mean*. NBER Working Paper No. 20573. Cambridge, MA: National Bureau of Economic Research.

Rodrik, D 2013. Structural change, fundamentals, and growth: An overview. Mimeo.

Winters, LA, Lim, W, Hanmer, L and Augustin, S 2010. Economic growth in the low income countries: How the G20 can help to raise and sustain it. Background concept paper for the Seoul G20 Development Consensus.

World Bank 2015. *World Development Report: Mind, Society, and Behavior*. Washington, DC: The World Bank.

Part III

Country cases

4 Can China rise to high income?

Yiping Huang[1]

Introduction

In 2014, China's GDP per capita reached US$7,500, but its GDP growth decelerated to 7.4 per cent from 7.7 per cent a year earlier. The combination of these two indicators raises the question of whether China will be able to continue its steady economic growth, avoid the 'middle-income trap' and become a high-income economy in the coming decade. The sustainability of Chinese growth has always been a contentious subject, but the challenge has never appeared more real than it is now because, historically, most other countries failed to graduate into high-income status after reaching a similar stage of development. And, more alarmingly, Chinese growth has been slowing quite visibly and persistently for the past several years.

The issue of the middle-income trap started to attract nationwide attention in China following publication of the report *China 2030* prepared jointly by the World Bank and the Development Research Center of the State Council in early 2012 (World Bank, 2012). The report reveals a pretty downbeat fact: of 101 middle-income economies in 1960, only 13 became high income by 2008. Later, in 2012, the Asian Development Bank (ADB) and the National School of Development of Peking University also published a joint report, Growing Beyond the Low-Cost Advantage, exploring the same issue (Zhuang *et al.*, 2012).

Whether or not China is able to avoid the middle-income trap is probably one of the most important economic questions facing the world today. Success would lift the living standards of 1.4 billion people, but failure might lead to economic and social instability in China. If China succeeds, it will most likely replace the United States to become the world's largest economy, which should have important implications for global economic structure and international economic governance. If China fails, the world will lose one-third of its global economic engine, and many commodity exporters might dive further in the current economic downturn.

Economists are divided on the subject. On the one hand, Justin Lin and Fan Zhang (2015) believe that the growth potential of the Chinese economy is probably still about 8 per cent, given its large technological gap from the advanced economies, large-scale infrastructure investment and continuous structural readjustment. It is possible for China to achieve an average of above 7 per cent growth in the coming decade. Lin and Zhang identify at least four preconditions for sustaining China's long-term growth: well-functioning markets, a minimum amount of investment, continuous structural upgrading and effective government (Lin and Zhang, 2015). Conditional on these assumptions, Lin and Zhang predict that China will join the high-income club by about 2020.

On the other hand, in a recent joint paper, Lant Pritchett and Larry Summers point out that the correlation across decades in national growth rates is surprisingly low, with coefficients typically in the range of 0.2 to 0.3. This is also inconsistent with many prevailing theories of growth that seek to explain growth performance in terms of highly stable national features such as culture, institutional quality or the degree of openness. They suggest that the prevailing pattern of regression to the mean in growth rates should create substantial doubt about extrapolative forecasts of China's growth. They believe that there is a significant risk of a major growth slowdown in China at some point over the next decade (Pritchett and Summers, 2014).

While Lin and Zhang arrive at completely opposite conclusions to those of Pritchett and Summers about China's growth outlook, the logic of their analyses is not that different. For instance, on the surface, Lin and Zhang make an extrapolative prediction, while Pritchett and Summers emphasize mean reversion. But Lin and Zhang's reasoning about the 'advantage of backwardness' can be viewed as a broad process of regression to the mean: China's growth potential is being lowered over time, although the growth rate can still be relatively high given its income level (Lin and Zhang, 2015; Pritchett and Summers, 2014). Perhaps a more fundamental difference between Lin and Zhang's analysis and that of Pritchett and Summers is about whether one should make a prediction for a single country's growth outlook based on the experiences of a large group of countries. The fact that 13 of 101 middle-income economies in 1960 actually rose to high-income status suggests that there are important economy-specific stories to tell.

Given that most countries will not be able to avoid the middle-income trap, the more relevant question is what makes an economy perform more like the successful 13 mentioned above, and not the remaining 88? In essence, the middle-income trap is about an economy's ability to continue to grow more rapidly than the most advanced economy of the world, the United States at the moment, after reaching middle-income status. A low-income economy can successfully engineer a take-off by taking advantage of its low costs, such as cheap labour. As it reaches the middle-income level, income levels and the cost base become much higher. Therefore, a critical test for the middle-income challenge is the economy's ability to build new industries with higher levels of technology and value added. All the 13 economies mentioned above succeeded in upgrading their industrial structure, while the other 88 economies were stuck in either resources or low value-added manufacturing and services.

Clearly the keywords are 'technological innovation' and 'industrial upgrading'. Both the World Bank and the ADB reports made some important policy recommendations (Table 4.1). The two sets of recommendations have significant overlaps. Both highlight the importance of supporting innovation and industrial

Table 4.1 Some policy prescriptions for China's middle-income transition

World Bank & Development Research Center	Asian Development Bank & Peking University
Accelerating the pace of innovation and creating an open innovation system	Stepping up innovation and industrial upgrading
Implementing structural reforms to strengthen the foundations for a market-based economy	Deepening structural reform, especially reforms of enterprises, labour and land markets Developing services and scaling up urbanization Reducing income inequality
Expanding opportunities and promoting social security for all	
Strengthening the fiscal system	Maintaining macroeconomic and financial stability
Seizing the opportunity to 'go green'	Promoting green growth to conserve resources and protect the environment
Seeking mutually beneficial relations with the world	Strengthening international and regional economic cooperation

Source: World Bank (2012); Zhuang *et al.* (2012).

upgrading. They also focus on measures of structural reform to improve the functioning of markets, macroeconomic policy reforms, greening of the economy and maintaining good relations with the rest of the world. The World Bank also singles out social security for all, while the ADB emphasizes the importance of services, urbanization and equality.

The central policy question of this chapter concerns the critical reforms necessary for China to continue its relatively rapid, albeit slower than before, economic growth in the coming decade. We do not intend to provide a comprehensive analysis of the middle-income trap question. Instead, we want to shed light on three important issues related to this subject. First, is the current growth slowdown temporary or permanent? An important issue to explore is where the new growth rate trend settles once the influence of cyclical factors fades. Second, can China transform its growth model, which is often characterized as rapid growth performance and serious structural imbalances? It is critical to nail down the policy strategies that underpin this unique economic pattern. And, finally, what does China need to do to foster its capability for technological innovation and industrial upgrading? The role played by the government versus the market is often at the centre of such policy discussions.

The rest of the chapter is organized as follows: the next section tries to explain the key reasons for the recent slowdown of Chinese economic growth. The section after that analyzes the current growth model and triggers for change. The penultimate section discusses the policy actions needed to foster China's ability in technological innovation and industrial upgrading. This is followed by some concluding remarks in the final section.

Understanding the recent slowing of Chinese growth

Between 1980 and 2014, China's real GDP grew by an average of 9.8 per cent a year and its GDP per capita rose from US$200 to US$7,500 (Figure 4.1). Economic growth experienced a downturn several times, especially in 1989–90 and 1998–9. In 2012, GDP growth slowed again, to 7.7 per cent from 9.3 per cent a year earlier. This time, however, the growth slowdown looks to be more persistent, staying at 7.7 per cent in 2013 and edging down to 7.4 per cent in 2014. At the start of 2015, there was further evidence of weakening economic activity. The National Bureau of Statistics (NBS) put first-quarter GDP growth at 7 per cent, but several market institutions estimated it at only 5 per cent or less.[2]

An important question is whether the current growth slowdown is cyclical or structural. In a recent study, Dwight Perkins (2015) points out that the reasons for the slowdown are not yet well understood. On the supply side, this is happening because total factor productivity (TFP) is slowing. On the demand side, a low share of household income in GDP has required the country to maintain an unusually high rate of investment in transport infrastructure and housing, but the rapid growth in both of these areas is coming to an end. And, finally, China has reached the point where the manufacturing share of GDP has peaked and will begin to decline as the economy becomes increasingly service based, but services seldom grow at the double-digit rates that manufacturing is sometimes capable of.

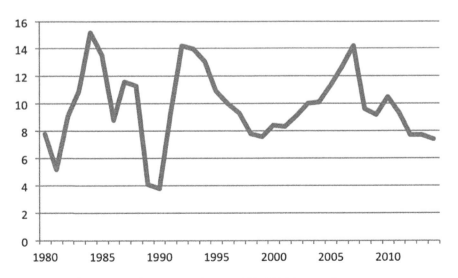

Figure 4.1 China's annual GDP growth rate, 1980–2014 (per cent)

Source: National Bureau of Statistics of China and CEIC Data Company.

Perkins is apparently of the view that the current growth slowdown is driven mainly by structural factors, although some factors might be overcome fully or partially. For instance, slowing investment in infrastructure projects could be compensated by investment in environmental protection. Most Chinese economists share Perkins' assessment that future growth will be slower. In addition to the reasons outlined by Perkins (2015), there is an important ongoing demographic transition (Cai and Lu, 2013). During the Asian Financial Crisis, when the Chinese government first proposed that 8 per cent GDP was necessary for maintaining full employment, the labour force was increasing by eight million a year. Now it is falling by five million a year. This is clearly a negative factor for economic growth.

Most forecasts of China's future growth potential point to steadily lower levels over time. The World Bank and the ADB reports expect growth to fall to 5–6 per cent by 2030 (Table 4.2). It is interesting to note that even the relatively pessimistic predictions, such as those in the ADB report (Zhuang *et al.*, 2012) and in Cai and Lu (2013), assume that China should be able to achieve high-income status by 2020. Justin Lin's prediction is more upbeat, as he believes the current growth slowdown is mainly a cyclical phenomenon, driven primarily by weakening external demand (Lin and Zhang, 2015). Even Lin admits that growth potential is coming down as development reaches a higher level.

Beyond the downward trend in growth, policymakers and market participants are also concerned about the possible bottoming out of economic growth. It is important to understand that currently there are two economic cycles at work, forcing down the growth rate. A short-term cycle is a typical macroeconomic one: as external demand weakens, growth slows. This cycle can be affected by traditional macroeconomic policies, such as monetary and fiscal expansion. An increasing amount of evidence points to possible bottoming out during the second or third quarter of 2015, including improvement in production, bank lending and de-stocking, following repeated easing of monetary policies from the beginning of the year.

But this bottoming out will likely be temporary and short-lived. In fact, this has happened before. For instance, when the government saw 7.4 per cent growth recorded for the first quarter of 2014, it stepped up efforts of so-called mini-stimulus and targeted easing in order to stabilize growth. Growth stabilized in the second quarter of 2014 at 7.5 per cent, but slipped to 7.3 per cent again in the third

Table 4.2 Some estimates of China's growth potential (per cent)

Economists/institutions	*Predictions*
World Bank/Development Research Center	2011–15: 8.6; 2016–20: 7; 2021–5: 5.9; 2026–30: 5.0
Asian Development Bank and Peking University	2011–20: 8.0; 2021–30: 6.0
Fang Cai and Yang Lu	2011–20: 7.2; 2016–20: 6.1
Justin Lin and Fan Zhang	2011–30: 8.0 (actual performance: >7.0)

Source: Compiled by the author; Cai and Lu (2013); Lin and Zhang (2015).

and fourth quarters. The reason why bottoming out of growth during the second quarter of 2014 and, again, possibly during the second/third quarter of 2015 is temporary is that there exists another, longer-term cycle: the transition of industrial structure. In short, while the old leading industries are rapidly losing competitiveness, the new leading industries are yet to take the stage to lead the economy forward.

Economists often divide an economy into three key parts – consumption, investment and exports – based on expenditure-side definitions of GDP. Two engines have powered most of China's economic growth for the past three decades: export and investment. Consumption has been relatively weak. Supporting these two growth engines is a rapidly expanding manufacturing industry. One part of the manufacturing industry – mainly labour intensive and low value added – supported export growth. And the other part – mainly heavy machinery and investment goods – facilitated investment expansion. The combination of these two formed the foundation of the global manufacturing centre and underwrote the so-called 'China miracle'.

Unfortunately, both of these engines are now losing steam. The export sector has already weakened significantly. Chinese exports used to expand at a pace of 20–30 per cent; now they barely increase by 5 per cent. Obviously, export performance may improve if the global economy recovers more strongly. It is, however, almost impossible for Chinese growth to repeat the 20–30 per cent average growth. China has turned from being a small-economy country into a large-country economy in the global market. As it now accounts for 12 per cent of the global export market, any adjustment to its supply and demand is likely to trigger significant changes in the rest of the world, illustrated by the popular phrase 'whatever China buys becomes more expensive, and whatever China sells becomes cheaper'.

More importantly, the traditional Chinese export industries are all built on low costs, which have risen dramatically for the past decade or two. For instance, migrant workers' wages have been growing by about 15 per cent a year for more than 10 years. Such drastic changes in the costs of labour and many other inputs are quickly putting many industries out of business. The coastal economy, which is more export oriented, used to be the most dynamic part of the Chinese economy. Much of it is now in deep trouble. But in a way, this is a result of past success: rapid economic growth lifts the cost of production. This, in turn, erodes the competitiveness of many existing industries.

The other part of the dynamic manufacturing industry is also in trouble. Heavy industries producing investment goods suffer from high overcapacity rates, averaging 40 per cent. China's investment rate was only about 30 per cent at the start of the economic reform. It rose to close to 40 per cent just before the Global Financial Crisis. As a response to the significant growth slowdown in 2008–9, the Chinese government adopted its 4 trillion yuan stimulus package, focusing mainly on infrastructure projects. This quickly lifted the investment rate to 48.5 per cent in 2009. The unusual investment boom not only underscored Chinese economic growth but also supported the so-called super-cycle of the global commodity market. However, the boom may be behind us; both moderating GDP growth and a falling investment rate point to secular weakening demand for investment goods.

Therefore, the cyclical downturn of the economy will continue. Any near-term growth bottoming out will likely be temporary, until new leading industries are solidly established, replacing labour-intensive manufacturing and heavy industries, to carry Chinese growth forward. Of course, many new industries are already forming, such as online shopping, internet finance, express delivery, computer and telecommunications software and hardware, large machinery equipment, heavy trucks, electrical and construction machinery, and so on. These are all expanding rapidly, with some already taking significant roles in the world market. But it will take at least one to two years before these new industries can fill the gaps left by labour-intensive and heavy industries and become the cornerstone of Chinese growth.

Transforming the Chinese growth model

More worrying than the growth slowdown is weakening productivity. Harry Wu (2014) demonstrated recently that TFP growth decelerated steadily from 1.5 per cent a year during 1992–2001 to 1.2 per cent during 2002–7, and further to 0.2 per cent during 2008–10 (Table 4.3). The Domar estimates of TFP fell even faster, from 5 per cent to 2.3 per cent and to –2.3 per cent, during the same period. Recent disappointing productivity performance is probably related to the aftermath of the 4 trillion yuan stimulus package introduced in 2008. But the weakening trend also shows the unsustainability of the growth model. Therefore, improvement of the growth model should be the first step towards avoiding the middle-income trap.

In order to change the growth model, one needs first to understand how it was formed. And one of the most important determining factors for China's current growth model is its reform strategy. In the literature, economists have developed diverse analytical frameworks to explain changes in the Chinese economy during the past decades. Justin Lin, Fang Cai and Zhou Li argue that the key to this success was the transition from a heavy industry-oriented to a comparative advantage-oriented development strategy (Lin *et al.*, 1995). Barry Naughton coined the term 'growing out of the plan' to describe China's incremental growth in the market-oriented private sector, while maintaining support for the old, state-owned

Table 4.3 Estimates of total factor productivity of Chinese industry (per cent)

	1980–91	1992–2001	2002–7	2008–10
Output	8.6	12.7	18.8	13.3
Labour	0.3	0.0	0.3	0.1
Capital	2.4	1.8	2.2	2.5
Material	6.7	9.4	15.1	10.5
TFP	–0.8	1.5	1.2	0.2

Source: Wu (2014).

enterprises (Naughton, 1995). Jeffery Sachs and Wing Thye Woo, however, point out that Chinese economic success can be explained mainly by its convergence with the typical market system of East Asia (Sachs and Woo, 2000).

Despite the differences in their perspectives, these economists all agree that the essence of the Chinese economic reform is the transition from a centrally planned system to a free market system. However, China actually adopted a very unique transition strategy during the reform period: the two dual-track approaches – one between state and privately owned enterprises, and the other between product and factor markets.

When economic reform started in the late 1970s, the Chinese government maintained its support for state-owned enterprises (SOEs) but encouraged private firms to grow. In contrast to the 'shock therapy' later adopted by the former Soviet Union, this gradual dual-track approach ensured economic and social stability during the transition period, since no worker was fired and no firm was shut down. The intention was for the non-state sector to grow more rapidly, making the state sector increasingly less important over time (Naughton, 1994).

This strategy worked quite well for a while, evidenced by strong growth performance. Entering the 1990s, however, the Chinese economy encountered three major crises – all caused fully or partially by financial problems of the SOEs. The first was the fiscal crisis, as government revenues as a share of GDP dropped from 36 per cent at the start of reform to close to 10 per cent at the beginning of the 1990s. The government had to implement a series of fiscal reforms in order to increase government revenues. The second was the SOE crisis, as the state sector as a whole made net losses in the mid-1990s. The government then adopted a drastic reform strategy of 'grasping the big and letting go the small' – essentially privatizing about half a million SOEs within a couple of years. And the third was the banking crisis, as the average non-performing loan ratio reached 30–40 per cent at the height of the Asian Financial Crisis. The authorities then introduced a series of banking reform steps, including cleaning up bad assets, injecting state capital, introducing foreign strategic investors and listing in capital markets.

After a series of reforms in the 1990s, the state sector made significant progress. The number of SOEs was substantially reduced, leaving only about 120 gigantic SOEs at the central government level, while the average size ballooned dramatically. Most of the SOEs are now in strategic industries, such as telecommunications, banking, airlines, railways and hospitals. Many of them are, in fact, incredibly profitable. However, most economists believe that these SOEs are profitable mainly because they either are in monopoly industries or receive implicit subsidies. This is why the government's latest comprehensive reform programme, announced in late 2013, still identifies SOEs as a key area for reform.

The 'implicit subsidy' relates to the second dual-track approach adopted by the Chinese government. Since the government intended to continue to support SOEs, it had to intervene in factor markets in order to provide inputs to inefficient SOEs. This gave rise to the dual-track strategy between product and factor markets. Free markets for products ensure that production decisions are based on supply and demand conditions in the economy. Distortions in factor markets are a way of providing incentives for economic entities and, sometimes, for overcoming market failures (Huang, 2010; Huang and Tao, 2010; Huang and Wang, 2010).

Factor market distortions include the household registration system, which limits labour mobility between rural and urban areas; direct controls of bank deposits and lending rates; the setting of energy, especially oil, prices by state agencies; and offering discounted land-use fees to investors. In most cases, these distortions depress input costs. Labour is a special case, however, as it is unclear whether labour market segmentation lowers or increases labour costs. But labour costs were low for a long time because of abundant agricultural labour or unlimited labour supply, in a typical Lewis dual economy. Taking financial repression as an example, the authorities not only depressed the bank deposit and lending rate but also guided credit allocation, mostly in favour of the SOEs.

Low input costs are like subsidies to companies but taxes on households. They boost production profits, increase returns on investment and improve the international competitiveness of Chinese exports. Low input costs also serve as a mechanism for redistribution of income from households to companies. Over the years, corporate profits grew much faster than household income, as household income was largely capped by stagnant wage rates. This income 'redistribution' was also behind the rapidly growing saving rate during past decades as the corporate saving rate is much higher than the household saving rate. Going one step further, we find that factor market distortions also redistribute income from small and medium enterprises to large corporations, and from low-income to high-income households.

Depressed input costs contributed to rapid economic growth. Over time, however, they also cause some structural problems. First, extraordinary incentives lead to a continuous rise in the shares of exports and investment in GDP. Second, a rise of the share of corporate profit in national income increases the national saving rate, as the corporate saving rate is generally higher than the household saving rate. Third, income inequality among households deteriorates, because low-income households rely more on wage income while high-income households rely more on corporate profits and investment returns. Fourth, the consumption share of GDP declines over time because household income grows more slowly than GDP. And fifth, the unusually low costs of energy, capital and other resources have also resulted in wasteful behaviour on the part of producers.

The good news is that low production costs are already starting to rise and some distortions are beginning to change (Huang *et al.*, 2011). For instance, the labour market shows clear signs of a supply shortage, which is evidenced by accelerating wage increases in recent years (Figure 4.2). The so-called Lewis turning point (LTP) – the transition of the labour market from surplus to shortage – has important implications for China's macroeconomy (Huang and Cai, 2010). Rapid wage growth, especially at the lower end of the market, cuts into profit margins. Therefore, it reverses past redistribution of income from households to corporates. As these implicit subsidies for Chinese companies are reduced, export and investment activities soften and, therefore, the economy rebalances.

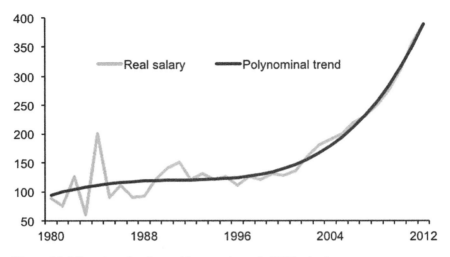

Figure 4.2 Migrant workers' monthly wage (yuan in 1978 prices)
Source: National Bureau of Statistics of China and CEIC Data Company.

It is a universal phenomenon that growth slows as an economy develops; this is because the reduced distance from the technological frontier of the developed world means the economy benefits less from backwardness (Lin, 2012). But the growth slowdown is probably magnified in China by changing demographics, including labour shortages and a diminishing working-age population. For the same reason, rapidly increasing wages could create inflation pressure over time, as rising costs can only be absorbed by higher output prices, narrower profit margins or faster productivity growth, or a combination of the above.

So, increases in household income as a result of changes in the labour market have also contributed to a rising consumption share of GDP in recent years. When an 'unlimited labour supply' exists, rapid industrialization is accompanied by a stable wage rate and, therefore, a declining share of wage income in GDP. This is reversed when a labour shortage emerges: wages rise rapidly and the share of wage income in GDP starts to grow. In fact, labour income also increased, from 41 per cent in 2007 to 47.1 per cent in 2009, which, in turn, has boosted consumption relative to GDP. This is also what happened in Korea and Taiwan in the mid-1980s, when their consumption shares started to recover following their respective LTPs.

Rapid wage growth was probably also behind the recent improvements in income distribution highlighted by the NBS, since low-income households rely more on wage income, and high-income households rely on investment returns or corporate profits (Figure 4.3). If the past trend was households subsidizing corporations, the new trend is redistribution of income from corporations to households, as rising labour costs increase wage income but squeeze corporate profits. This is probably why, in rapidly developing economies, the so-called

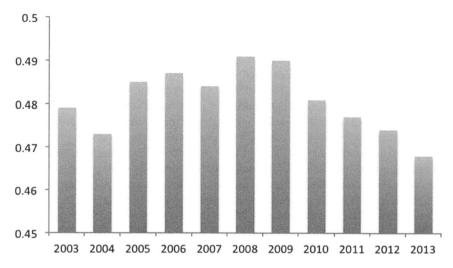

Figure 4.3 Official estimates of Gini coefficient, 2003–13

Source: National Bureau of Statistics of China and CEIC Data Company.

Kuznets turning point (when income distribution shifts from deteriorating to improving) often follows the LTP (Huang and Cai, 2010).

Other changes in factor markets are also taking place. For instance, rapid growth of shadow banking transactions led to the disintermediation of the banking sector and contributed to the 'back-door liberalization of interest rates'. All these changes are behind the emergence of a 'new normal' for the Chinese economy: slower growth, accelerating industrial upgrading and rebalancing of economic structure. But this is only the beginning. Further changes require implementation of a more comprehensive reform agenda, such as the one announced at the Third Plenum of the Eighteenth Party Congress, which contains reform measures in 60 areas. But the key, really, is to complete the transition to the market system by eliminating the two dual-track strategies. And this means further reform of the SOEs and the removal of remaining distortions in factor markets.

Fostering innovation capability and upgrading

Rebalancing the economy is only the first step towards avoiding the middle-income trap. A more important step is to continuously move up the technological ladder and achieve productivity improvement. The real challenge of the middle-income trap is an economy's capability for repeatedly developing new competitive industries and companies after reaching the middle-income level. Countries failing to do that will be stuck in the middle-income range, unable to compete with either more advanced economies (because of lower efficiency) or less developed economies (because of higher costs).

In a recent study, Yingjie Feng and Yang Yao (2014) review descriptive characteristics of a large group of economies. They find that economies successfully rising to high income are often characterized by high saving rates, robust manufacturing sectors, high levels of education, more advantageous demographic structures, a peaceful environment and more equal income distribution. China is quite similar to those successful economies in all of these aspects except for its rising inequality. Therefore, China still has great potential for growth, but some deliberate policies on income distribution are needed, especially in increasing the education levels of rural youth and providing adequate training to migrant workers.

Some commentators argue that China is unable to innovate because most of its industries are built on low-cost advantage, with technology copied from advanced countries. More importantly, China's protection of intellectual property rights (IPR) is insufficient. All these observations are probably true. But learning from others is a natural process of catching up for low-income economies. And such experience is not limited to China alone. The same thing happened in Japan and the four Asian 'Tigers' several decades earlier. In an interesting article, Charles Morris (2012) describes in detail how the Americans stole textile technology from the United Kingdom in the nineteenth century.

But it is wrong to extrapolate from the above observation that there is no innovation in China. Innovation has been happening every day. In the 1980s and the 1990s, millions of farmers in the Pearl River Delta and the Yangtze River Delta became self-trained entrepreneurs. China had already created some internationally competitive companies, such as Huawei and Alibaba. Today, many young and not-so-young people think about starting their own businesses or creating their own products.

Data suggest that China is already experiencing a science and technology take-off, which is happening at a much earlier development stage compared with international experiences. In 1996, research and development (R & D) expenditure accounted for 0.6 per cent of GDP. In 2006, it more than doubled to 1.4 per cent. This was still lower than Japan's 3 per cent, Korea's 3 per cent, Singapore's 2.2 per cent and the United States' 2.6 per cent. However, it was already significantly ahead of many developing countries (Figure 4.4).

Jian Gao and Gary Jefferson (2007) examine cross-country behaviour of R & D expenditure. They find that, on average, a country's R & D started to take off (or cross the level of 1 per cent of GDP) when its purchasing power parity (PPP) measured income per capita at $8,000 in 1999 prices. When this happened in China, its PPP-measured per capita income was $3,600. They offer three potential explanations for this somewhat unusual phenomenon. The first is the relatively low illiteracy rate. At 16.5 per cent, China's adult illiteracy rate in 1999 was similar to that of Brazil (15.1 per cent) and Turkey (15.4 per cent) with substantially higher incomes, and well below that of India (43.5 per cent). The second is market size. And the third is proximity to dynamic economies. Arguably, China's greatest asset is its close physical and cultural proximity to Hong Kong and Taiwan and, to a lesser but still significant degree, to Korea, Japan and South East Asia.

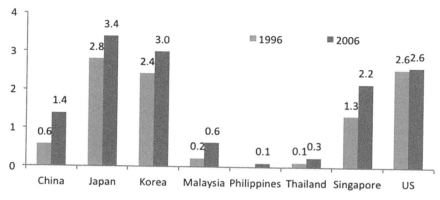

Figure 4.4 R & D intensity of China and selected countries, 1996 and 2006 (per cent)
Source: World Bank.

China is already one of the three largest R & D spenders in the world, alongside the United States and Japan. Even if measured by resident patent filing per R & D expenditure, China is still among the top group (Figure 4.5). China is the only middle-income country in that top group. This is probably even more important evidence of the early take-off of China's science and technology. Admittedly, most of the Chinese patents are concentrated at the bottom of the technological ladder.

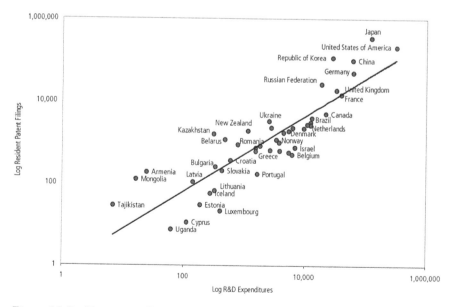

Figure 4.5 Resident patent filings per R & D expenditure, 2003–7
Source: Compiled by Rio Tinto.

This is consistent with the country's level of economic development. It would not be fair to compare China's innovation capability with that of advanced economies. However, going forward, it remains to be tested whether China can rely on innovation to continuously improve the quality of the economy.

To further foster the country's capability in innovation and upgrading, China will need to make a lot more effort in at least the following three areas, in addition to transitioning to a market economy by further reforming the SOEs and removing factor market distortions. The first is to develop a stronger education and research base and to improve the human capital of workers. The second is to liberalize the financial system and provide more flexible and effective financial support to technological and business innovation. And the third is to devise an institutional environment that is conducive both to freer exchange of ideas and to better protection of human and property rights.

China needs stronger education and research capability to support technological innovation. In general, the government should reallocate its spending from infrastructure projects to research and education, since the single most important contributor to innovation is human capital. China's illiteracy rate is relatively low compared with countries at a similar stage of development. During the past 10 years, however, there has been a strong disincentive to undertake higher education, especially for rural kids. The labour market exhibits a special pattern, with a surplus of college graduates and a shortage of migrant workers, because China's two largest industries – labour-intensive manufacturing and construction – employ mainly unskilled workers. The country has a migrant worker force of more than 300 million, whose average education level is junior high school. It is critical to devise some training schemes for these migrant workers to improve their human capital.

Also, the formal education system needs significant reform. The current compulsory education policy covers only nine years of schooling and should be extended to at least 12 years. More importantly, rural kids do not enjoy the same benefits as those in urban areas. Inequality in education hinders social mobility. As a result, the proportion of rural kids among university students has dropped drastically during the past three decades. To some extent, basic education is more important than higher education. The quality of Chinese universities is improving and their research funding has also increased significantly, but they still suffer from too much administrative control. The Ministry of Education appoints top university managers and sets all sorts of criteria for academic performance. All this runs against the spirit of innovation.

In short, China needs a stronger research and education base. This includes strengthening the basic education system, training for migrant workers and basic research. The government should increase its spending in these areas but, at the same time, should refrain from heavy intervention in management of research and education institutions, particularly administrative controls of personnel and allocations of research grants.

Second, China needs more liberalized and richer financial intermediation to facilitate industrial upgrading. China's current financial system was developed after economic reforms began. Today, the financial system is already one of the largest in the world, whether measured by the number of financial institutions or by the size of financial assets. The top five Chinese banks have regularly been ranked among the 10 largest in the world. However, the government still maintains heavy intervention in the financial system, including the regulation of interest rates, guidance on credit allocation, intervention in foreign exchange markets and controls on cross-border capital flows. The financial system is dominated by the banking sector, while direct finance through capital markets is relatively underdeveloped. As the authorities depress deposit and lending rates in the formal banking sector, there is excess demand for credit. The authorities, in turn, have to ration credit and often allocate funds in favour of SOEs or other large enterprises.

Such a financial system does not support technological innovation and industrial upgrading. The essence of innovation is uncertainty: one success in innovation is often built on a large number of failures. Therefore, innovation requires special channels of financial intermediation that can identify, price and take risks, such as venture capital and private equity. Banks are not suitable for such tasks, although they are quite effective in supporting manufacturing investment and production.

The government already has plans to liberalize the interest rate, lifting the upper ceiling of the deposit rate during 2015, and to develop multilayer capital markets, including the money market, government bond market, corporate bond market and stock market. It takes professional investors to identify promising projects and take risks. Without these, innovation cannot flourish. One important reform that is not yet on the government's agenda is ownership reform. In a recent study, we find that financial reforms in most areas have distinctive costs and benefits. However, two particular reform measures – financial regulation and ownership reform – can both accelerate growth and reduce risk (Figure 4.6). Ownership reform is important as without hard budget constraints for both lenders and borrowers, financial liberalization could lead to disaster.

And, third, China also needs a set of legal and political policies that ensure order and protect rights. Protection of IPR is a basic requirement. This is an area where substantial improvement is necessary. International experience suggests that a developing country's IPR protection improves significantly when indigenous IPR become a dominant phenomenon. China is probably reaching that turning point. Also, China is negotiating with the United States a bilateral investment treaty, in which protection of IPR is an important subject for negotiation.

So far, innovation takes place mainly in areas where government regulation is light or even absent – for instance, online shopping and internet finance. Innovation activities are quite rare in monopoly industries, especially those dominated by SOEs. Therefore, the government needs to liberalize or at least lower the entry barriers to many sectors.

One of the most contentious institutional issues is whether it is necessary for China to transition to a Western-style political system in order to avoid the middle-income trap. For instance, Acemoglu and Robinson propose that Chinese growth has occurred under extractive political institutions and, therefore, will likely run out of steam (Acemoglu and Robinson, 2012). We do think that some important

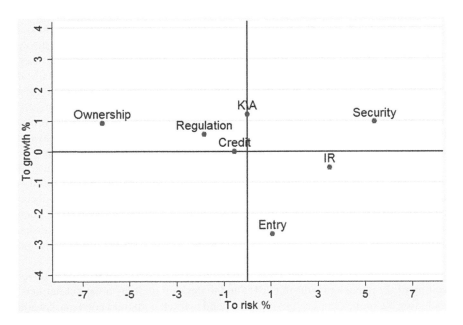

Figure 4.6 Growth and risk effects of individual reform measures
Source: Huang and Ji (2015).

steps of political reform are possible, although transition to a Western-style democracy is unlikely to happen in the foreseeable future. It is true that political measures are necessary to eradicate many social and economic problems, such as corruption, disparity and monopolies. But we believe that Acemoglu and Robinson's assertion may be too simplistic. First, experiences in East Asia suggest that there is probably more than one form of political institution that can support long-run growth. This is particularly so if the economy is still in a technological catch-up mode. Second, although institutions are very important, economic policies under the same institutions can still make a huge difference in terms of economic growth, as illustrated by the comparison of Jamaica and Barbados (Henry and Miller, 2009). And third, as well as politics determining economic institutions and, therefore, growth, economic activities can influence politics.

The last point is the reason we are optimistic that positive changes may take place. This is already evidenced by the introduction of grassroots democracy in the countryside more than 10 years ago. A number of municipal governments in the coastal regions scrapped plans to construct polluting industrial projects after protests by local residents. Social media, such as Weibo, is already an important informal channel of dialogue between the public and the government and has played a critical role in the purging of some corrupt senior officials.

Our overall assessment is that it is possible for China to rise to high-income status some time in the coming decade, although the country needs to undertake a lot of changes, especially in areas of research and education, finance, and legal and political institutions. Positive changes are already happening across the country. China is leading the world in the internet economy and in some manufacturing industries. Shenzhen has clearly become a national centre for innovation, with Hangzhou and Beijing quickly catching up. But more reforms are needed to turn this trickle of innovation and upgrading into a nationwide wave.

One controversial issue is the role of industrial policy, which to a large extent depends on its definition. In this study, we do not regard support for broader research and education, or the provision of finance for innovation and upgrading, as industry policy. Here, industry policy refers to narrowly defined measures of government support for specific industries and even particular companies, using financing and subsidy policy instruments. Experiences of East Asian economies, including Japan and Korea, confirm that industrial policies do not have a positive effect on economic growth. If specific measures are needed to support an 'infant industry', they should be designed to meet two requirements. One, industrial policy should not hinder competition – therefore, the practice of 'picking the winner' should be avoided. And two, there should be an exit plan for the industrial policy to avoid perpetuation.

Towards a high-income economy

The middle-income trap is probably the biggest challenge facing the Chinese economy today. In this chapter, we address this issue by asking three questions. First, how should we understand the current growth slowdown? Second, how can China's growth model be transformed? And third, how can China foster its innovation and upgrading capability?

We think there are currently two economic cycles at work, leading to slower growth. The first is a shorter-term, typical macroeconomic cycle. Following recent aggressive monetary and fiscal policy expansion, the macroeconomic cycle may bottom out during the second or third quarter of 2015. But this bottoming out will likely be temporary and short-lived. The longer-term industrial transition still pushes the growth trend lower until new leading industries are well established to take the economy to the next level. At the moment, some new industries are already being formed, such as online shopping, express delivery, large machinery equipment, heavy vehicles, and so on. But these are not yet ready to replace the previous leading industries – mainly the labour-intensive manufacturing export sector and the heavy industry investment goods producers.

Continuation of rapid economic growth requires transformation of the current growth model, which is often characterized by strong growth performance and serious structural imbalances. The current growth model, however, has its roots in China's transition strategy, which may be summarized by two dual-track approaches: the first between SOEs and non-SOEs, and the second between product and factor markets. Continuous protection of SOEs ensured social and economic stability during the early stage of reform but also caused social, financial and fiscal consequences. The need to protect SOEs also gave rise to the second dual-track approach – that is, distortions to the factor markets. Factor market distortions, such as financial repression and resource price setting, act like subsidies to producers, investors and exporters, but like taxes on households. These explain why economic growth has been extraordinarily rapid. At the same time, however, structural imbalances grew. Therefore, transformation of the growth model requires completion of the transition to a market economy, especially abandoning factor market distortions. This, again, requires successful reform of SOEs.

The good news is that China's growth model is already changing, evidenced by a narrowing current account surplus, rising shares of consumption and services in the economy, improving income distribution, and so on. But so far, this has been mainly triggered by changes in the labour market, the so-called Lewis turning point. Liberalization of financial markets, the land system and energy policy is critical for this transformation to continue.

Transformation of the growth model is only the first step towards sustainability of economic growth. A more important step is to promote technological innovation and industrial upgrading. China might have been able to achieve rapid economic growth by exploiting its low cost base in the past, but now costs are rising rapidly. Therefore, the only way to sustain economic growth is for the economy to continuously move up the technological ladder to stay competitive.

Compared with most countries at a similar stage of development, China's innovation and upgrading capability is already quite high. Its share of R & D in GDP exceeded the 1 per cent benchmark at a much lower income level than the average of the developing world. It is already one of the leading owners of patents globally, although most of the patents are at the lower end of the technological scale.

But China still needs to make significant efforts to foster its innovation capability, at least in the following three areas. The first is to strengthen the research and education base, including training of more than 300 million migrant workers. The second is to reform the financial system, including liberalizing the interest rate and developing new channels of financial intermediation, in order to provide better financial services to innovation activities. And the third is to construct new legal and political institutions that are conducive to technological innovation. This includes protection of IPR and liberalization of entry barriers to many sectors. We are not certain whether China will move to a Western-style democracy any time soon, but certain political changes are necessary to ensure free flows of information, maintain order and resolve social conflict.

In summary, we believe that with necessary reforms, China will be able to rise to high-income status and become the largest economy in the world, although it does need to overcome very high hurdles on the way.

Notes

1　The author would like to thank David Dollar, Peter Drysdale, Ross Garnaut, Justin Yifu Lin, Vo Tri Thanh and other participants of the 37th PAFTAD conference for valuable comments.

2   According to a report compiled by wallstreetcn.com, China's first-quarter GDP growth in 2015 was estimated to be 4.9 per cent by Capital Economics, 4.6 per cent by Citibank, 4 per cent by the Conference Board and 3.8 per cent by Lombard Street (http://wall streetcn.com/node/218370).

References

Acemoglu, D and Robinson, JA 2012. *Why Nations Fail: The Origins of Power, Prosperity and Poverty*. New York: Crown.

Cai, F and Lu, Y 2013. The end of China's demographic dividend: The perspective of potential GDP growth. In R Garnaut, F Cai and L Song (eds), *China: A New Model for Growth and Development*. Canberra and Beijing: ANU E Press and Social Science Academy Press China.

Feng, Y and Yao, Y 2014. The middle-income trap and China's growth prospects. In R Garnaut, F Cai and L Song (eds), *Deepening Reform for China's Long-Term Growth and Development*. Canberra and Beijing: ANU E Press and Social Science Academy Press China.

Gao, J and Jefferson, GH 2007. Science and technology takeoff in China? Sources of rising R&D intensity. *Asia Pacific Business Review*, 13(3), Special Issue: Global R&D in China, 357–72.

Henry, PB and Miller, C 2009. Institutions versus policies: A tale of two islands. *American Economic Review*, 99(2), 261–67.

Huang, Y 2010. Dissecting the China puzzle: Asymmetric liberalization and cost distortion. *Asia Economic Policy Review*, 5(2), 281–95.

Huang, Y and Cai, F (eds) 2010. Special issue: Debating the Lewis turning point in China. *China Economic Journal*, 3(2).

Huang, Y and Ji, Y 2015. How will financial liberalization change the Chinese economy? Lessons from middle-income countries. Presented at The Indispensable Relationship: China–US Economic Interdependence, American Committee for Asian Economic Studies.

Huang, Y and Tao, K 2010. Factor market distortion and the current account surplus in China. *Asian Economic Papers*, 9(3), 1–36.

Huang, Y and Wang, B 2010. Cost distortions and structural imbalances in China. *China and World Economy*, 18(4), 1–17.

Huang, Y, Chang, J and Yang, L 2011. *China: Beyond the miracle – China's next transition*. September. Hong Kong: Barclays.

Lin, J 2012. *The Quest for Prosperity: How Developing Economies Can Take Off*. Princeton, NJ: Princeton University Press.

Lin, J, Cai, F and Li, Z 1995. *The China Miracle: Development Strategy and Economic Reform*. Hong Kong: The Chinese University of Hong Kong Press.

Lin, JY and Zhang, F 2015. Sustaining growth of the People's Republic of China. *Asian Development Review*, 1(32), 31–48.

Morris, C 2012. We were pirates, too: Why America was the China of the 19th century. *Foreign Policy*.

Naughton, B 1994. Chinese institutional innovation and privatization from below. *American Economic Review*, 84(2), 266–70.

Naughton, B 1995. *Growing Out of the Plan: Chinese Economic Reform, 1978–1993*. Cambridge: Cambridge University Press.

Perkins, DH 2015. Understanding the slowing growth rate of the People's Republic of China. *Asian Development Review*, 1(32), 1–30.

Pritchett, L and Summers, LH 2014. *Asiaphoria meets regression to the mean*. NBER Working Paper No. 20573. Cambridge, MA: National Bureau of Economic Research.

Sachs, JD and Woo, WT 2000. Understanding China's economic performance. *Journal of Policy Reform*, 4(1), 1–50.

World Bank 2012. *China 2030: Building a Modern, Harmonious, and Creative Society*. Washington, DC: The World Bank.

Wu, H 2014. *China's growth and productivity performance debate revisited: Accounting for China's growth sources with a new data set*. Economics Program Working Paper Series No. 14(1). New York: The Conference Board.

Zhuang, J, Vandenberg, P and Huang, Y 2012. *Growing Beyond the Low-Cost Advantage: How the People's Republic of China Can Avoid the Middle-Income Trap*. Manila and Beijing: Asian Development Bank and National School of Development, Peking University.

5 Is Indonesia trapped in the middle?

Haryo Aswicahyono and Hal Hill[1]

Introduction

Few countries have experienced such dramatic changes in economic fortunes and political governance as Indonesia. The world's fourth most populous nation and the tenth largest economy – in purchasing power parity (PPP) terms – it experienced more or less continuous economic decline for at least half a century before the mid-1960s (van der Eng, 2002). By then it was one of the world's poorest countries, characterized in the leading development economics text of the time as 'a chronic economic dropout' (Higgins, 1968), and one with little prospect of development in the leading socio-economic survey of the period (Myrdal, 1968). Then, in a remarkable turnaround, from 1966, the country achieved rapid economic development for the next three decades, such that it was classified as one of the 'East Asian miracle economies' in the World Bank's (1993) major comparative study. Indonesia's per capita GDP more than quadrupled over this period.

However, shortly after it had graduated to the middle-income group of developing economies, and when rapid, East Asian-style economic development seemed assured, the country experienced another major discontinuity. In 1998, during the Asian Financial Crisis (AFC), its economy contracted sharply – by more than 13 per cent. This translated into one of the largest growth collapses in modern economic history: from peak to trough (that is, the average annual growth of about 7 per cent during the preceding decades) of about 20 percentage points. This collapse was accompanied by, and triggered, a major political crisis, with the sudden end of the 32-year rule of President Soeharto in May 1998. As in the mid-1960s, the country's prospects were again regarded as exceptionally gloomy. The economy appeared to be in freefall. The value of the currency was at one point just 10 per cent of that pre-crisis. The modern banking system had collapsed. The country's territorial integrity was in doubt, with 'Yugoslav'-type scenarios considered likely. Compounding these problems, there was no clear process – or historical precedent – for an orderly transfer of political authority.

Yet as in the mid-1960s, the doomsayers were incorrect. The economy recovered surprisingly quickly, and returned to a moderately strong growth trajectory of 5–6 per cent from 2000. The political transformation was just as remarkable. From three decades of authoritarian, military-based, centralized rule, in some respects centred on just one figure, Indonesia quickly emerged as South East Asia's most vibrant democracy – a status it retains a decade and a half after the transition, according to comparative benchmarks. The country also undertook a 'big bang' decentralization in 2001, with the result that much administrative, financial and political authority has been devolved to subnational governments. In sum, this was one of the most comprehensive and rapid reconstructions of a country's political institutions and processes in recent times, with only a brief loss of economic momentum.

This chapter examines Indonesian economic development in the context of the widely discussed middle-income trap literature outlined by Kharas and Gill (in this volume). This literature (see also Eichengreen *et al.*, 2013; Felipe *et al.*, 2014; Perkins, 2013) draws attention to the presence of per capita GDP thresholds beyond which there is an empirical regularity of growth slowdowns. One estimate puts this threshold at about $15,000 (in 2005 PPP dollars). Other authors raise the possibility of a multimodal threshold, with a lower one of about $11,000. Extending this analysis to explain the causes of the growth slowdown, it is argued that a variety of factors are relevant, including the quantity and quality of education and the share of high-tech products in exports. An alternative approach has been to investigate abrupt slowdowns, defined as large, sudden and sustained deviations from the growth path predicted by the basic conditional convergence framework. Aiyar *et al.* (2013) examine these cases, finding that institutions, demography, infrastructure, the macroeconomic environment, output structure and trade structure are all potentially associated with such outcomes. Theories have also been proposed that allow for multiple equilibriums and convergence to higher and lower per capita incomes (see, for example, Agenor and Canuto, 2012; Eeckhout and Jovanovic, 2012). In addition, there is a country literature exploring growth slowdowns. The most widely discussed East Asian experience relates to Malaysia, where a range of economic and political economy factors is identified as contributing to this country's slow growth since the AFC. Much of this literature focuses on Malaysia's long-running affirmative action policies, and the politicization of them, embedded on almost six decades of continuous, virtually single-party political rule (see Hill *et al.*, 2012).

Returning to the Indonesian case, with its record of economic dynamism and political transformation, the notion of a 'trap' therefore hardly appears relevant. If Indonesia can maintain the development momentum of the past decade and a half, per capita incomes will double approximately every two decades, and the country will be on course to graduate to the high-income group within half a century. If it were to regain the momentum of the Soeharto era, this graduation process would occur more quickly still. Moreover, while the democratic transition is in some respects still incomplete, the prospect of violent and economically disruptive regime change – a prospect that by definition authoritarian regimes have to worry about – has receded given the existence of functional democratic institutions.

Although the notion of a 'trap' is therefore not analytically helpful, Indonesia's growth rates remain below those of East Asia's most dynamic economies, as represented by China for the past three decades and the Asian newly industrializing economies earlier. In spite of the progress, the economic policies of recent and current administrations have struggled to achieve faster economic growth. After surveying Indonesian economic development in the next section, the focus of this chapter in the section after that is therefore on the factors that are holding back the country's growth dynamism. These obstacles to faster growth are not amenable to quantitative explanation, and so we develop an analytical narrative that identifies the principal factors. A concluding section summarizes our main arguments.

Indonesian economic development: an overview[2]

Indonesia experienced sustained and rapid economic development for the first time in its history from 1967. Under Soeharto, who took power in early 1966, and guided by a group of gifted economic policymakers, the country rejoined the global economic community, restored macroeconomic stability, adopted a welcoming attitude towards the private sector, including foreign investment, and began to rebuild dilapidated physical infrastructure. Development was further boosted by large foreign aid inflows, the accelerating green revolution in agriculture and, in the 1970s, high energy prices.

The economy responded surprisingly quickly to the new regime (Figure 5.1).[3] Over the period 1967–96 – that is, a year after Soeharto's accession to power and the year before the AFC – annual economic growth averaged an impressive 7.4 per cent, translating into per capita growth of slightly more than 5 per cent. There were distinct episodes in this development record, with very strong growth during the 1970s and again from the late 1980s, alongside much slower growth in the early and mid-1980s. The growth variability is explained by the interplay of a range of exogenous and domestic factors. Indonesia enjoyed large windfall revenue gains during the 1970s, and much – but certainly by no means all – of this revenue was invested in productivity-enhancing activities, particularly rural infrastructure. As energy prices began to fall rapidly in the early 1980s, Indonesia looked precarious, with the energy sector contributing two-thirds of fiscal revenue and three-quarters of merchandise exports. However, unlike most other developing country commodity exporters outside the Middle East, Indonesia managed to avoid the 1980s debt crisis through adroit macroeconomic management and comprehensive microeconomic reform. As a result, new economic drivers emerged, particularly export-oriented labour-intensive manufactures, such that strong growth was restored by 1987.

This growth was maintained until 1997 when, as noted, Indonesia experienced a deep economic and political crisis. Although the AFC originated in Thailand, and it also severely affected Korea and Malaysia, Indonesia was the most adversely affected because the economic crisis triggered regime collapse, with no immediately apparent institutionalized succession scenarios. In the event, the democratic transition proceeded much more smoothly than most observers had dared to hope, and by 2000 economic recovery was under way. By 2004, per capita income (and associated social indicators such as poverty incidence) had recovered to pre-crisis

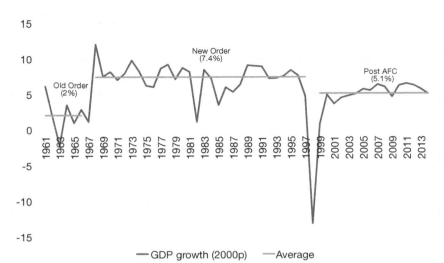

Figure 5.1 Indonesian GDP growth, 1961–2014

Sources: GDP growth 1961–2000, WDI Online; GDP growth 2001–14, BPS Online (ID 1202).

levels. By any reasonable yardstick, Indonesia's twin transitions – from economic crisis to growth, and from authoritarian to democratic rule – were impressive.[4] The country also navigated the 2008–9 Global Financial Crisis (GFC) with little difficulty, owing to good policy (including reforms introduced in the wake of the AFC) and some good fortune (Basri and Hill, 2011). Nevertheless, as Figure 5.1 shows, economic growth during the democratic era has lagged that achieved during the Soeharto period by a little more than 2 percentage points. (Population growth during the two periods was similar.) Part of the explanation for the slower growth was the complicated post-crisis recovery trajectory in the early 2000s, as firms and the financial sector restored balance sheets, and also the short-lived slowdown during the GFC. However, as Figure 5.1 also shows, even at its peak, growth since 2000 has not matched the average for the earlier period. For several years in this recent period, moreover, Indonesia again enjoyed exceptionally favourable terms of trade, driven by China's demand for raw materials. The data therefore portray a story not of a 'trap' but rather one of slowing growth. It is to this issue that we return in the next section.

Five dimensions of Indonesia's economic performance warrant attention. First, the growth of total factor productivity (TFP) portrays a broadly similar story to that of the national accounts. There is a substantial literature on TFP in Indonesia.[5] Some of the detailed estimates are dated, and we therefore draw on the three major sets of cross-country international estimates, by the Conference Board, the Asian Productivity Organization and the Groningen/Penn World Tables. The results vary depending on estimation methodologies, data sources and assumptions. Figure 5.2 summarizes the results for the three series, which show broadly similar trends.

There is considerable year-to-year volatility, reflecting Indonesia's growth volatility and also its variable input growth, especially investment. Moreover, consistent with the empirical regularity known as 'Verdoon's Law', the fluctuations in TFP growth are generally similar to those in GDP growth. In particular, there was a sharp reduction in 1998, similar in magnitude to that of the economic contraction. Abstracting from these outlier cases, for most of the period TFP growth is positive, and generally in the range of 1–4 per cent per annum. A fitted trend line, excluding the outlier years, does indicate a declining TFP growth rate since the early 1990s, suggesting that the secular decline in underlying growth discussed above may have had its origins before the AFC. It also needs to be emphasized that Indonesia's TFP has been lagging global benchmarks over the past decade, and also its middle-income Association of South East Asian Nations (ASEAN) neighbours, with the exception of the Philippines.

Second, Figure 5.3 places Indonesia's growth trajectory in comparative perspective. The country began rapid growth at about the same level of per capita income as China and India, but a good deal lower than the Philippines and Thailand. Twenty years into this growth – that is, by the late 1980s – it had overtaken the Philippines and had a per capita income significantly higher than that of both China and India. However, the combined effects of the AFC and China's accelerating growth meant it slipped behind China in the early 2000s, and now has a per capita income of a little more than half the latter. Although India has grown faster for periods of the past decade, Indonesia's per capita income remains substantially above that of both it and the Philippines.

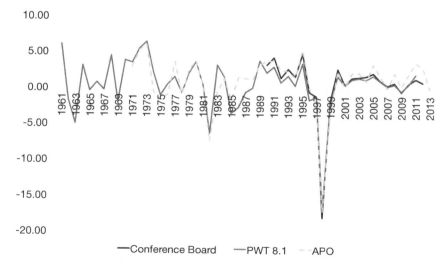

Figure 5.2 Estimates of Indonesian total factor productivity growth, 1961–2012

Sources: Gini 1970–95, Mishra (2009); Gini 1996–2013, BPS Online (ID 1493); Poverty 1970–2013, BPS Online (ID 1494).

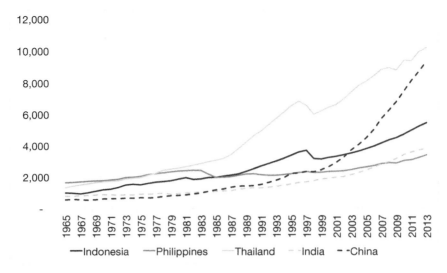

Figure 5.3 Per capita GDP, Indonesia and comparators, 1965–2013
Source: The Conference Board's Total Economy Database.

Third, Indonesian economic growth may also be viewed with reference to that of the frontiers, the latter proxied by the United States. Relative to the United States, over the period 1965–2013, Indonesia's per capita GDP approximately doubled, and is now about 17 per cent of the US figure. As with the other countries in the comparison, excluding the Philippines, this is a clear case of 'catch-up', albeit at a much slower pace than China. This confirms the estimates of long-run economic growth presented by Perkins (2013: Table 1.1). Over the half century 1961–2010, Indonesia's real per capita GDP (in PPP terms) rose 5.7 times, compared with China's 12.4, Thailand's 8.2 and the Philippines' 2.1.[6]

Fourth, in any assessment of the country's economic performance and political economy, it is important to keep in mind Indonesia's geography. It is the world's largest archipelagic state, featuring exceptional diversity in its economy, human settlement and ecology. Java–Bali, with 7 per cent of the land area, generates about 60 per cent of total GDP. Greater Jakarta constitutes about one-quarter of the economy. Most modern manufacturing and service activities are located on these islands, which also serve as the major gateways to Indonesia's international commercial engagements. The very large spatial differences in productivity are illustrated by the fact that, among the country's 34 provinces, the per capita income of the richest is approximately 15 times that of the poorest. At the subnational level of administration, in the districts and municipalities (*kabupaten* and *kotamadya*) – now numbering more than 500, and to which the major decentralization of 2001 was directed – the richest regions have a per capita income more than 50 times that of the poorest. We return to this issue below.[7]

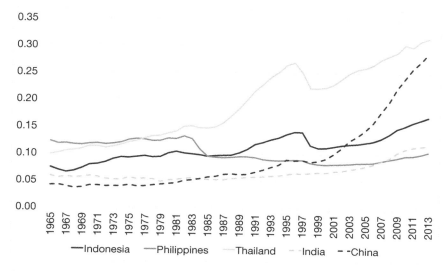

Figure 5.4 Per capita GDP relative to the frontiers, Indonesia and comparators, 1965–2013
Source: The Conference Board's Total Economy Database.

A fifth dimension concerns social progress. Economic growth has resulted in a rapid decline in poverty incidence.[8] Headcount poverty incidence has declined from about 55 per cent in the mid-1960s to less than 15 per cent currently (Figure 5.5). The most rapid decline occurred during the Soeharto era, when growth was faster, inequality was stable and most of the growth was labour-intensive in nature (especially in rice and manufacturing). Poverty incidence rose during the AFC but, as with per capita income, it had returned to pre-crisis levels by 2004. Over the past decade, the rate of decline has been slower, owing to slower economic growth and a significant increase in inequality as measured by the Gini ratio. This increased inequality – one of the sharpest in the developing world over this period – is a subject of much debate. The poor record of formal sector labour absorption since the late 1990s, together with a probable weakened commitment to 'egalitarian' tax and spending programmes, is likely to have been a key factor in the increase. Since the AFC, the Indonesian government has begun to develop targeted social safety net programmes, with some success, although the expenditures remain very modest and they evidently have very little impact on post-tax and transfer inequality.

Finally, the drivers of Indonesian economic growth have changed over this period. This is to be expected. In the 1960s, Indonesia was an overwhelmingly agrarian economy, with more than half its economy and three-quarters of its labour force in agriculture. This sector now contributes slightly more than 10 per cent of GDP. This is a conventional story of rapid economic growth resulting in significant structural change. Services have grown consistently quickly in both periods,

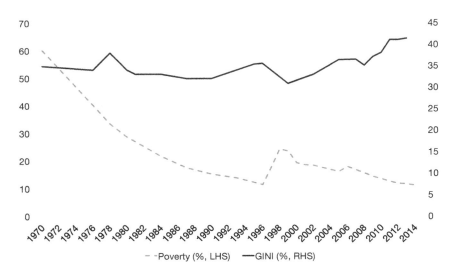

Figure 5.5 Poverty and inequality in Indonesia, 1970–2014

Sources: GINI 1970–1995, Economic Inequality in Indonesia: Trends, Causes, and Policy Response; GINI 1996–2013, BPS' Gini Ratio Menurut Provinsi Tahun 1996, 1999, 2002, 2005, 2007-2013; Poverty 1970–2013, BPS' Jumlah Penduduk Miskin, Persentase Penduduk Miskin dan Garis Kemiskinan, 1970-2013.

driven by liberalization, the information technology and transport revolutions, the consumption patterns of a rising middle class and, for much of the period since 2005, an appreciating real exchange rate. But one contentious feature of the sectoral growth story is the industrial slowdown. Manufacturing growth exceeded 10 per cent in almost every year over the period 1967–96, but since 2000 it has grown at about half this rate (Figure 5.6).

This has prompted a vigorous debate about alleged deindustrialization, which in some quarters is also (mistakenly) attributed to a variant of the middle-income trap. Two points need to be made with reference to the country's spurious deindustrialization debate. First, it overlooks the fact that, relative to the country's per capita income, Indonesia's share of manufacturing value added in GDP is actually larger than that predicted by a standard cross-country regression equation. Figure 5.7 plots manufacturing value-added shares and per capita GDP at constant 2005 prices for Indonesia and 40 countries, both developed and developing, for the period 1960–2012.[9] It shows that its share is consistently higher over time than countries with similar per capita incomes. The same exercise is undertaken for employment shares over this period, as reported in Figure 5.8. In fact, Indonesia is 'below average' with respect to employment shares. Of course, these findings have no normative implications, in the sense that there is no necessary 'desirable' share for manufacturing. But they serve as a corrective to simplistic assertions that Indonesia's manufacturing share is 'too low'.

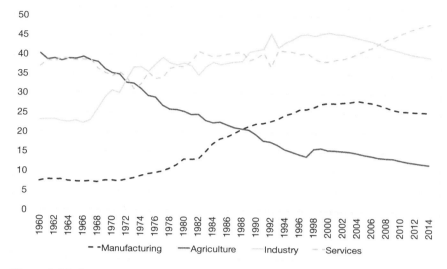

Figure 5.6 Indonesia's sectoral share, 1961–2014
Source: WDI Online.

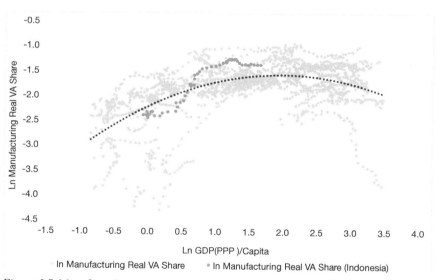

Figure 5.7 Manufacturing value-added shares, Indonesia compared
Sources: Value-added share, GGDC 10-Sector Database; GDP per capita, the Conference Board's Total Economy Database.

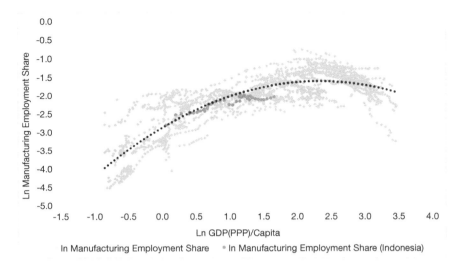

Figure 5.8 Manufacturing employment shares, Indonesia compared

Sources: Value-added share, GGDC 10-Sector Database; GDP per capita, the Conference Board's Total Economy Database.

In fact, what the comparative data highlight is another, less discussed issue – namely, that Indonesian manufacturing is relatively more capital intensive than its comparators. That is, its output share is above average and its employment share is below average. Here, too, the results carry no normative implications. Indonesian industry may be more capital intensive for a range of reasons, including its sectoral mix and institutional settings. But the data are at least suggestive that labour market regulations are pushing the manufacturing sector towards premature capital intensity at the cost of weak labour absorption. We also discuss this issue below.

Second, in any case, it is not necessary to employ middle-income trap theories to understand the reasons for the industrial slowdown since the AFC. At least three sets of factors are at work (for more discussion, see Aswicahyono *et al.*, 2010). First, Indonesia has experienced historically high terms of trade for most of the period since the early 2000s. Thus, the familiar Dutch Disease factors have been at work, resulting in a larger natural resource sector (measured at current prices), and also a real exchange rate appreciation and hence a squeeze on non-commodity tradable sectors such as manufacturing. Second, key elements of the Indonesian policy regime have hindered the competitiveness of the hitherto dynamic manufacturing export sector. Mandated minimum wages have risen significantly, while the efficiency of internationally oriented logistics and infrastructure has declined. We discuss these factors in the next section. Third, the scale effects of the rise of China as the major supplier of a wide range of manufactures have been such as to lower the global supply price of these goods, thus depressing returns for labour-intensive manufacturers such as Indonesia.

So far so good, but why not better?

Indonesia's record of long-term growth is superior to that of most developing countries. The explanations for this record are beyond the scope of this chapter, but they are well documented and are consistent with the general literature on the determinants of economic growth (see, for example, Hill, 2000; Temple, 2003) – that is, macroeconomic management has been reasonably good; Indonesia is moderately open to international trade and investment; it has been politically stable for most of the past half-century; poverty and social indicators have improved significantly; and there have been positive neighbourhood effects. However, the purpose of this chapter is to explore why the country has not grown faster still, at rates comparable with those at the East Asian frontiers, and why growth appears to be somewhat slower in the democratic era than that of the Soeharto era. Democracy in principle might be expected to be growth supporting, even if the empirical evidence is mixed.[10] It needs to be emphasized at the outset that these questions are not amenable to precise quantification. We organize our arguments around four growth-inhibiting factors, and by implication highlight some of the reforms needed to achieve faster growth.

First, however, it is important to keep in mind Indonesia's political economy context, and especially the fundamental transformation in its institutions that occurred in the transition from Soeharto-era authoritarianism to the highly pluralistic and occasionally volatile democracy that has emerged since 1999.[11] At least seven key political parameters have changed, and these together have far-reaching implications for economic policymaking. First, there is a weakened presidency. Although deriving legitimacy from a popular, directly elected mandate, the President has to contend with many more checks and balances than were present during the Soeharto era, when Soeharto was himself the key political institution. Second, and central to the first proposition, the President invariably presides over a rainbow coalition of parties both in Cabinet and in the Parliament (DPR). The coalition members have little personal or institutional allegiance to the President, and their support on key policy issues cannot be assumed. Third, the bureaucracy remains a powerful yet largely unreformed institution, but one that is now subject to significantly greater community accountability, especially through the Corruption Eradication Commission (Komisi Pemberantasan Korupsi, KPK), which we discuss below. One result of this new institutional configuration is reluctance in certain sections of the bureaucracy to take key spending decisions, especially on major infrastructure projects. Fourth, the DPR, which served as a rubber stamp for Soeharto, is an assertive and sometimes unpredictable institution, in which key government policies and bills may be rejected or substantially modified. Fifth, the judiciary – also suppressed under Soeharto – has become an important yet also often unpredictable actor, with a propensity to overturn government bills and regulations. Sixth, governments now have to contend with a highly active and noisy civil society that, whether through social media or street demonstrations, can challenge and shape policies. Finally, much of the public sector administrative and financial resources have been devolved to the country's subnational tiers of government, posing in turn complex inter-jurisdictional and coordination challenges on issues as diverse as health, education and infrastructure (see below).

Ambivalence towards globalization

Indonesian public opinion has always been somewhat reluctant to embrace liberalism and globalization. And yet it is frequently observed that, with its 17,000 islands, 'Indonesia was made by God for free trade'. The pendulum has swung from the global disengagement of the early 1960s, when the country joined the 'Peking–Pyongyang–Hanoi–Phnom Penh–Jakarta' axis of newly emerging forces, through to a very open regime from the late 1960s, growing state intervention during the 1970s oil boom, and then major deregulation (incidentally never referred to as 'liberalization' in government pronouncements) from the mid-1980s. It might have been expected that these reforms would have been reversed over the past two decades, given the deep unpopularity of the International Monetary Fund (IMF) rescue package in 1997–8, the perceived lack of support from the international donor community more generally, and the shock of the GFC of 2008–9.

Nevertheless, the economy has remained reasonably open during this period, at least in relation to comparators. Average tariffs are moderate at about 6 per cent, and continue to trend down slightly. Non-tariff barriers remain a challenge for economic reformers, but have generally been contained to some agricultural products (including a prohibition on rice imports for several years) and heavy industry. Total exports and imports are equivalent to about 55 per cent of GDP – the lowest in ASEAN apart from (probably) Myanmar, but this in part reflects the country's size. The country remains somewhat open to foreign investment, with the stock of realized foreign direct investment equivalent to about 14 per cent of GDP – the lowest among the major ASEAN economies, alongside the Philippines. The country's economic freedom ranking, at 131st, is the lowest among the ASEAN-5 but above that of Vietnam (which is 145th).

Basri and Hill (2004) refer to this outcome as a case of being 'precariously open'. There are persistently pro- and anti-reform currents, and in large measure they balance each other out. The former include the continuing – though perhaps waning – influence of a partly insulated technocracy in the Cabinet, able to resist special pleading pressures. Reformers can also point to past successes, especially in the 1980s, which built up coalitions in support of reform. They are also able to point to the general rule of thumb in Indonesia that once tariffs are much above 25 per cent, especially for high value-to-weight products, smugglers are in business. At the margin also, the ASEAN Economic Community (AEC), taking effect from December 2015, will constrain some trade policy excess.

However, the country's rising economic nationalism in recent years has intensified protectionist pressures (for a recent survey, see Patunru and Rahardja, 2015). This policy stance, combined with declining commodity prices, has resulted in indifferent export performance in recent years. In response, much of the official rhetoric continues to emphasize a variety of unproductive strategies. One example has been discussion about the impact of the AEC, and the proposed Regional Comprehensive Economic Partnership among 16 Asian-Pacific economies (that is, ASEAN plus six). Outgoing Industry Minister Mohamad S. Hidayat reflected the continuing priorities of his department, arguing that the government should issue 'bolder and more protectionist regulations, including more fiscal incentives and non-tariff barriers'. Moreover, he said, 'basic industry is most important, as it prevents massive imports'.[12]

Meanwhile, Indonesia continues to underperform in the crucial area of connecting to global production networks (GPNs). These vertically integrated, many-country, cross-border production and buying operations are now the major form of intra-East Asian trade. Within ASEAN alone, they account for almost 50 per cent of trade within the region (Athukorala, 2010). Although concentrated principally in the electronics and automotive industries, they are an organizational structure that is relevant to any products that comprise discrete production processes with diverse factor intensities. Most of this trade is intra-firm in nature, and thus it is dominated by multinational enterprises (MNEs). Indonesia is a relatively minor participant in these networks, and is thus missing out on major commercial opportunities and employment creation. Although it is the largest economy in South East Asia, in 2010–11, for example, it accounted for 0.5 per cent of global 'network trade' – much lower than its South East Asian neighbours, Malaysia (2.6 per cent), the Philippines (1.2 per cent) and Thailand (1.6 per cent).

The reasons for this underperformance are both well known (Soejachmoen, 2012) and amenable to policy intervention. Participation in the GPNs requires open trade and investment policies, since the parts and components frequently cross international boundaries, and much of the production occurs within MNEs. They also require highly efficient logistics infrastructure, including port movements, customs procedures and port-to-factory transport. Competitive labour inputs have to be available, across the range from unskilled to managerial staff. In these three key areas, Indonesia lags, as is demonstrated by some of the comparative indicators presented below. Yet they are all amenable to relatively straightforward policy reforms, of the sort that Indonesia undertook for a period in the 1980s, and that even slower reformers such as the Philippines have initiated. The absence of reform does not mean that Indonesia is excluded from these industries. For example, its automotive industry is now one of the largest in South East Asia. However, its industries will be primarily domestic market oriented, and Indonesia will forgo the opportunity to emerge as a major international hub the way that Singapore and Thailand have in the electronics and automotive industries, respectively.

Compounding these problems is Indonesia's decision not to participate in the negotiations concerning a second round of the International Technology Agreement (ITA II). The ITA governs the trade in electronic components. Recognizing the reality of GPNs, and that final electronics products include components produced in many countries, there is free trade for these products among signatories to the ITA. Originally, the ITA focused mainly on components. However, the distinction between components and final goods is now increasingly blurred. Therefore, under ITA II, it is proposed to extend the coverage to electronics products. Several major electronics producers, among them Singapore, Malaysia and Japan, have already signed the accord. However, Indonesia has decided not to participate in the negotiations, presumably owing to concerns that its already protected electronics goods industries will come under further import pressure.

Meanwhile, much public policy discussion focuses on the need to 'revitalize' manufacturing through selective industrial promotion initiatives, particularly in 'high-tech' activities. There is a strong case for greater government expenditure in support of knowledge-based activities. But developing a bold new research and development (R & D) strategy is very much a second-order priority for the foreseeable future when the country ranks second-lowest in the recent Programme for International Student Assessment (PISA) education results (see next section), when it is substantially excluded from the dynamic East Asian and global production hubs by its inadequate infrastructure and ambivalence to foreign investment, when widespread corruption stymies many of the government's major spending programmes, when the labour market is unable to function as the transmitter of prosperity and when property rights are uncertain owing to unexpected judicial outcomes. In any case, the government currently spends only about 0.1 per cent of GDP on R & D and 0.3 per cent on higher education. (Private sector spending on the latter is about three times this figure, but on the former it is negligible.) Until the recent major reform of energy subsidies, the government was spending about 10 times more on these than it was on R & D and higher education. Even after the reforms, subsidies expenditure remains significantly higher.

Education and the labour market

Indonesia has achieved impressive gains in education since the 1970s in overcoming the colonial-era backlog, with major expansions in enrolments at all levels. The country is now close to achieving universal literacy for its school-age population, and there is a strong commitment to education funding, through a law that mandates that 20 per cent of the government's budget shall be allocated to the sector, net of transfers and subsidies. However, the country lags in terms of the high post-primary dropout rates, and also according to most comparative 'quality' indicators, such as international examination performance. For example, according to the latest round of PISA rankings, computed by the Organization for Economic Cooperation and Development, Indonesia ranked 65th out of 66 countries. Admittedly, many of the countries in this survey are high-income, and the survey was selective in several developing countries. Figure 5.9 summarizes Indonesia's education indicators in comparative perspective. While, as noted, the quantitative expansion – here proxied by the Barro–Lee years of schooling –

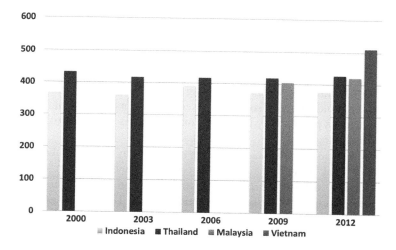

Figure 5.9 Education indicators

Source: PISA: Mean performance on the mathematics scale, WDI Online.

has increased significantly, on practically every quality indicator, from the two major international comparison exercises, Trends in International Mathematics and Science Study and PISA, Indonesia falls behind its neighbours, with little sign of relative improvement.

Education indicators typically adjust slowly, as broader societal and family factors are influential determinants. It may be the case that this lagging performance reflects the country's historical underinvestment in education. However, recent survey research indicates that the problems are deep-seated, and will not necessarily be overcome by the higher funding allocations. For example, although teacher salaries have increased in recent years, teacher absenteeism and poor-quality instructional techniques persist. Examination processes and results are frequently corrupted.[13]

Indonesia also faces major challenges in higher education, which will become more pressing as the country progresses through the ranks of the middle-income group. This sector is growing extremely rapidly, with about five million tertiary students enrolled currently – up from 2,000 at the time of independence in 1945.[14] Historically within the university sector, state universities, which were run as extensions of the civil service, dominated the system. However, the government spends only about 0.3 per cent of GDP on higher education – just one-quarter of the total national expenditure – and thus it has had to recognize the reality that most of the growth will be in the private sector, either through a de facto 'privatized' state university system or through private institutions. The government remains ambivalent about deregulating and internationalizing the system, preferring to maintain the historically tight regulations over state institutions, and providing little of the requisite regulatory framework that would enable a more effective private system to develop. Examples include underinvestment in arm's-length information flows, trusted accreditation procedures, support for staff upgrading, and international collaborative networks. As a result, the quality of tertiary institutions is highly variable, with small pockets of excellence alongside large areas of rudimentary quality. Funding support mechanisms, particularly for able but needy students, are also largely absent. Thus, none of the country's tertiary institutions ranks prominently in international comparisons, including also those just for developing Asia.

These educational challenges are compounded by related labour market problems of weak formal sector employment growth and skill mismatches. Here a brief recourse to history is useful.[15] Over the period 1966–96, formal sector employment and modern sector wages grew strongly. This was an environment, like much of East Asia over this period, of strong, labour-intensive economic growth, combined with repression of labour rights. The AFC resulted in a sharp fall in formal sector employment and real wages. Since the labour market was flexible, much of the impact was on the latter (which was one reason poverty did not increase as much as was feared). The sudden democratic transition unleashed powerful 'pro-labour' sentiments, which resulted in labour's freedom to get organized, press for minimum real wages and demand punitive severance pay provisions. The first of these changes was of course welcome, but the last two, combined with slower growth, resulted in anaemic formal sector employment growth for much of the period since 2000, especially in the manufacturing sector, which had been the source of much of the dynamic employment growth (Aswicahyono *et al.*, 2010).[16] Combined with the strong real exchange rate over much of this period, the result was that Indonesia lost competitiveness in international markets for labour-intensive manufactures.

Trends in unit labour costs (ULCs) illustrate these outcomes. The first series (Figure 5.10) shows labour productivity, average wages and ULCs for Indonesian manufacturing, as estimated from the national accounts (for value added), and wages and employment from the national labour force survey (SAKERNAS). The results show average wage growth quickly outstripping labour productivity over the period 2000–12, resulting in ULCs more than doubling. The sharpest increase in ULCs occurred in the early 2000s, and again in the period 2010–12, when nominal wages rose quickly, while productivity increased very slowly, especially in the later years. The next figure (Figure 5.10) provides an alternative set of estimates, derived from the annual industrial survey of manufacturing firms employing at least 20 workers (Statistik Industri, SI). Although the results for the wage and productivity series differ somewhat, and the SI data are more volatile, the ULC series is broadly similar and these data therefore corroborate the first set of estimates. Both series, moreover, predate the large nominal wage increases that occurred in 2013 in the run-up to the 2014 parliamentary and presidential elections – increases that occurred just as the country's terms of trade continued to deteriorate.[17]

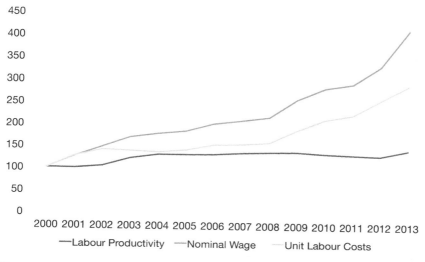

Figure 5.10 Wages and unit labour costs in Indonesia

Sources: GDP atas dasar harga konstan 2000, Badan Pusat Statistik; Employment and Wage, SAKERNAS.

Infrastructure

Indonesia's infrastructure performance has been studied intensively, and it receives high priority in official policy statements through the formulation of master plans and logistics blueprints to reduce transport costs and increase their reliability. President Joko Widodo's maritime vision, released in May 2015, was just one of many such pronouncements over the decades. The problem is that inter-island transport costs are very high in this, the world's largest, archipelagic state. High transport costs push up the general cost structure, particularly for more remote regions, and thus there are large inter-regional price differences. For example, Sandee *et al.* (2014) present comparative data demonstrating that Indonesian logistics costs are considerably higher – sometimes by a very large margin – than its more efficient neighbours. The authors draw attention to the problems at the country's major port, Tanjung Priok, where throughput doubled over the period 2007–13, but there has been no expansion in facilities: 'for more than 10 years no substantial investments have been made to improve productivity' (Sandee *et al.*, 2014). For comparative purposes, Figure 5.11 reports the results from the annual World Bank Logistics Performance Index, confirming the fact that, again, Indonesia lags its ASEAN neighbours except the Philippines.

The problems derive from both limited infrastructure investment and regulatory barriers. The underinvestment in infrastructure since the late 1990s has contributed to the low quality and quantity of roads, ports and railways. As a percentage of GDP, Indonesia's infrastructure expenditure is about half that of both the Soeharto

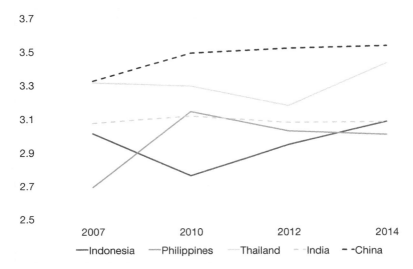

Figure 5.11 Logistics indicators, Indonesia and neighbours
Source: World Bank's Logistic Performance Index.

era and high-growth East Asian economies. Regulatory constraints on competition and efficient service provision compound the problems. The contrast with the successful deregulation in air transport and the lack of reform in shipping is striking. In fact, the 2008 Shipping Law introduced cabotage principles that limit the movement of cargo between Indonesian ports to Indonesian-flagged vessels. The various master plans and blueprints lay out a strategy to improve connectivity. The question is whether they will be able to address crucial bottlenecks, such as the lack of coordination between local and central governments, the continued domination of state enterprise providers and regulators, and the uncertain commercial environment for potential private sector providers.

With regard to funding, the government's development expenditures were severely curtailed in the wake of the AFC, and its fiscal space continues to be highly constrained. At about 14 per cent of GDP, the government's tax effort is rather weak. On the revenue side, more than 30 per cent of allocations pass directly to local governments, while until recently subsidies absorbed about 20 per cent – a figure that is now likely to fall but in all likelihood will continue to exceed 10 per cent. Personnel, overheads and debt service – all relatively inflexible items – together absorb more than 30 per cent of the total, while all levels of government are required to meet the 20 per cent education target.

Moreover, strong post-AFC aversion to foreign borrowings has meant that successive Indonesian governments have not availed themselves of much of the long-term concessional finance potentially available. Decentralization to inexperienced local governments introduced additional problems of coordination and assignment of responsibility. Land acquisition has emerged as a serious constraint in newly democratic local communities intent on redressing past grievances. Private sector infrastructure suppliers are hesitant to invest because of resistance to setting prices at levels that would make such investments economic. The bitter experience of many foreign infrastructure providers during the AFC has deterred investors (Wells and Ahmad, 2007). There is also considerable resistance to infrastructure deregulation, principally from bureaucrats and state-owned utility providers who would lose their rents in a more deregulated market.

Building institutions

From a longer-term perspective, Indonesia is in the early stages of establishing a democratic consensus around the institutions needed for a prosperous, equitable and internationally oriented economy. Institutions are complex mechanisms for establishing accepted 'rules of the game', the more so in a young, highly fluid democracy such as Indonesia. Generalizations are at best hazardous, and we therefore briefly survey various aspects of institutional development in the country during the democratic era.[18]

Macroeconomic policy

A legacy of the disastrous macroeconomic policymaking under President Sukarno (1945–65), particularly the hyperinflation episode of the mid-1960s, is that macroeconomic management since then has been reasonably effective. Apart from a brief period of very high inflation in 1998 – the result of fiscal expansions in support of an open-ended bank recapitalization programme being monetized – inflation has been moderate, although consistently higher than Indonesia's low-inflation neighbours. Again with the exception of the AFC period, fiscal policy has been prudent. Importantly, effective macroeconomic policymaking has been maintained during the transition from authoritarian to democratic rule. During the Soeharto era, the government operated what it called a 'balanced budget rule', under which its spending was constrained to the total of domestic revenue and foreign aid. The central bank, Bank Indonesia (BI), operated essentially as an adjunct to the Ministry of Finance, with a fixed but adjustable exchange rate setting designed to ensure international competitiveness.

As part of the controversial letter of intent with the IMF, BI was granted full operational autonomy in 1999, and over time it instituted a conventional regime of inflation targeting and a floating exchange rate. There is now broad political support for the notion of an independent central bank, and BI's performance has improved over time. The major fiscal policy challenge in the wake of the AFC was to control government debt, which had ballooned dramatically to about 100 per cent of GDP in 1999. An overriding priority was to quickly exit the loathed IMF programme, which was implemented in 2003 with the enactment of a fiscal law. This was essentially modelled on the Maastricht principles of deficits not exceeding 3 per cent of GDP and public debt of less than 60 per cent of GDP.

Unlike what has happened in the European Union, Indonesia has stayed well within these limits. Combined with modest sales from the nationalized distressed assets, public debt has fallen sharply since 1999, and is now about 25 per cent of GDP. This is an impressive fiscal consolidation. Challenges remain, but overall macroeconomic policy, and the institutions that underpin it, must be counted as a major success, illustrated most recently in the country's effective response to the GFC.[19]

The legal system

The legal system is in transition from being a subservient arm of the executive, as it was in the Soeharto era, to a powerful and independent institution designed to protect citizens and property rights. This is a long-term process that will take decades rather than years to accomplish. But in the institutional vacuum that was created with the collapse of the Soeharto regime, the judiciary is now expected to resolve highly complex issues, ranging from deep-seated commercial disputes, especially those involving landownership, to a wide range of civil liberties. In this new environment, the quality of judicial appointments is highly variable. Bribery and the 'purchase' of court decisions are evidently quite common. Commercial cases have unpredictable results, with a tendency to favour domestic over foreign firms, and debtors over creditors (Butt, 2009). These outcomes are not surprising. Building up a high-quality judiciary is a complex, lengthy and expensive process.

One significant achievement in building effective legal infrastructure has been the Corruption Eradication Commission (KPK). The KPK is the most respected institution in the country, according to various opinion surveys, and is generally regarded as the most effective organization of its type in ASEAN. Established in 2002, it has the authority to investigate and prosecute cases of more than IDR1 billion (about US$70,000 at the time of writing), and involving members of law enforcement agencies and other state officials, as well as parties linked to them. Its powers are extensive, including being able to tap telephones, ban overseas travel, freeze bank accounts and obtain information from financial institutions. It does not require presidential authority to begin investigations, and it has the authority to appoint prosecutors. It also has the power to take over investigations from the police and the Attorney General's office. Most assessments of its operations are positive.[20] One indicator of the KPK's success is the increased hostility towards it from within the Parliament and bureaucracy in recent years. However, public opinion has so far acted as a safeguard in preventing attempts to weaken its authority.

Bureaucratic reform

Nevertheless, on most comparative rankings of corruption, Indonesia continues to score poorly. One explanation is that the KPK is by definition addressing the symptoms of corruption, not its fundamental causes. This is illustrated in the case of the bureaucracy, where there has yet to be any significant reform during the democratic era. Its remuneration structures remain highly complex and opaque, and also uncompetitive at senior levels. There is a weak link between performance and reward. There is little inter-agency mobility, let alone external recruitment. The opportunities for training and other types of long-term professional development are limited (see McLeod, 2005). Moreover, state-owned enterprise (SOE) reform has proceeded very slowly. There is powerful resistance to divesting SOEs, even though it is well known that they are highly politicized and inefficient. One hopeful exception to these generalizations is the small number of agencies that are given greater staffing autonomy in exchange for clear performance mandates. BI is the most important of these agencies, and as noted above, it is evolving into a competent, professional organization.

Local-level governance

Indonesia was a highly centralized state under Soeharto, with little scope for local authority and autonomy. Then, in a dramatic initiative, in May 1999 the government announced a 'big bang' decentralization, to take effect from 1 January 2001. The scheme was radical in its intent, with major revenue and administrative authority being passed down to the sub-provincial levels of government, the *kotamadya* (municipalities) and *kabupaten*. The fear of territorial disintegration, involving Timor, Papua, Aceh, Maluku and other outlying regions, was a key motivation for the hasty action. The reforms were accompanied by democratization, with direct elections for local leaders as well as for the assemblies. As a result, Indonesia now has elections for its 530 or so (and counting) provincial and sub-provincial authorities. In 2014 the government extended this subnational architecture by introducing direct grants to the country's 73,000 villages. This decentralization has more or less 'worked', in the sense that the nation's territorial integrity has been preserved, and the functions of government have been maintained. But major challenges remain, in the proliferation of sub-provincial jurisdictions, in coordinating these many local governments, in the highly variable quality of local governance and in the tendency for these local governments to spend on administrative enlargement at the expense of much-needed infrastructure and other local services.[21]

Conclusions

We have argued that Indonesia is not in any sense 'trapped', as it continues to achieve moderately strong economic growth. Looking forward, if it maintains its currently unspectacular but steady growth trajectory, it can expect to lose its comparative advantage in labour- and resource-intensive activities, and to graduate into the ranks of the upper middle-income group of countries, and eventually the high-income club. However, it has not grown as fast as some of its neighbours, and the growth rate over the past decade and a half is slower than that of the three decades of Soeharto rule.

These outcomes – both the moderate success and a growth performance falling short of East Asian frontiers – can be explained through recourse to conventional economic and political economy factors. That is, its growth can be explained by reasonably good macroeconomic management, moderately open trade and investment policies, political stability for most of the past half-century, broad-based social progress and positive neighbourhood effects. But we have also highlighted four sets of factors that are constraining growth: continuing ambivalence towards globalization, low education achievements and poor labour market performance, major underinvestment in physical infrastructure, and the need to develop a set of high-quality institutions that will deliver much better governance at national and local levels. How future governments are able to address these four sets of factors will significantly influence the speed at which Indonesia is able to graduate from middle- to high-income status.

Notes

1 We thank Francis Hutchinson, our two discussants, Siwage Dharma Negara and Archanun Kohpaiboon, and other participants at the June conference for many useful comments on an earlier draft.
2 This chapter draws on some of the authors' recent and ongoing research, in particular Aswicahyono and Hill (2014a, 2014b). The Indonesian economy is monitored regularly in the 'Survey of recent developments' published since 1965 in the *Bulletin of Indonesian Economic Studies*.
3 See Hill (2000) for more details of the events discussed in this paragraph.
4 See Pritchett (2011) for an analysis of the Indonesian record in comparative perspective. The closest comparator nation is arguably the Philippines. The latter's economic-political crisis of 1985–6 was very similar in both its origins and its severity, but it took 20 years (1983–2003) to recover to pre-crisis levels of per capita income. See Balisacan and Hill (2003).
5 See Aswicahyono and Hill (2014a), on which this paragraph draws.
6 The frontier growth rates in this East Asian sample were Korea and Taiwan, which achieved increases in GDP per capita of 15.6 and 16.8, respectively, over this period.
7 See the papers in Hill (2014) for a wide-ranging examination of regional issues in Indonesia.
8 Manning and Sudarno (2011) provide a comprehensive analysis of Indonesian living standards, on which this paragraph draws. Wai-Poi (forthcoming) provides a comprehensive review of trends in poverty and inequality since the 1980s.
9 The employment and real value-added shares are from the Groningen manufacturing datasets. See: www.rug.nl/research/ggdc/data/10-sector-database (GDP per capita is in millions of 1990 US dollars, converted at Geary Khamis PPPs).
10 For a comprehensive recent survey arguing that the link is a positive one, see Acemoglu *et al.* (2015).
11 See Crouch (2010) for an authoritative assessment.
12 *Jakarta Post*, 20 August 2014.
13 See Suryadarma and Jones (2013) for a detailed analysis of Indonesia's education challenges.
14 This paragraph draws on Hill and Thee (2012).
15 See Manning (2014), on which this paragraph draws.
16 Manning (2014) concludes that formal sector employment growth did begin to increase from about 2009, as the commodity boom intensified. It is probable that this increase

has been short-lived, as commodity prices have fallen since 2012 and given the large formal sector minimum wage increases in 2013.

17 Indonesia was not alone in this labour market populism. Similar outcomes, for similar reasons, occurred in the Philippines after the overthrow of the Marcos regime in the mid-1980s. Minimum wages have also increased significantly in Thailand in recent years. See Aswicahyono and Hill (2014a) for ULC estimates for Indonesia compared with its neighbours.

18 Some of our thinking on these issues is developed in more detail in Aswicahyono *et al.* (2009).

19 Until recently, Indonesia's macro policymakers have also had responsibility for supervision of the financial sector. Here too they have achieved much, rehabilitating it after the collapse of 1997–8, navigating the GFC and developing new modalities to cope with global financial volatility. The sector needs to be deepened and strengthened, and its financial safety-net provisions remain precarious, but the overall record to date is an impressive one. For a recent authoritative review, see Grenville (2015).

20 See, for example, the conclusions of Crouch (2010: 228–9): 'The KPK . . . soon began a series of prosecutions that, although limited in number, obtained significant high-profile convictions . . . The convictions obtained by the KPK brought about a dramatic change in the atmosphere and provided a deterrent that had been largely absent in the past.'

21 See the chapters in Hill (2014), particularly by Blane Lewis, for detailed discussion of these issues.

References

Acemoglu, D, Naidu, S, Restrepo, P and Robinson, JA 2015. Democracy does cause growth. Unpublished paper. MIT, Cambridge, MA.

Agenor, P and Canuto, O 2012. *Middle-income growth traps.* Policy Research Working Paper No. 6210. Washington, DC: The World Bank.

Aiyar, S, Duval, R, Puy, D, Wu, Y and Zhang, L 2013. *Growth slowdowns and the middle-income trap.* Working Paper No. 13/71. Washington, DC: International Monetary Fund.

Aswicahyono, H and Hill, H 2014a. Does Indonesia have a 'competitiveness' problem? Unpublished paper.

Aswicahyono, H and Hill, H 2014b. Survey of recent developments. *Bulletin of Indonesian Economic Studies*, 50(3), 1–28.

Aswicahyono, H, Bird, K and Hill, H 2009. Making economic policy in weak, democratic, post-crisis states: An Indonesian case study. *World Development*, 37(2), 354–70.

Aswicahyono, H, Hill, H and Narjoko, D 2010. Industrialisation after a deep economic crisis: Indonesia. *Journal of Development Studies*, 46(6), 1,084–108.

Athukorala, PC (ed.) 2010. *The Rise of Asia: Trade and Investment in Global Perspective.* London: Routledge.

Balisacan, A and Hill, H (eds) 2003. *The Philippine Economy: Development, Policies, and Challenges.* New York: Oxford University Press.

Basri, MC and Hill, H 2004. Ideas, interests and oil prices: The political economy of trade reform during Soeharto's Indonesia. *The World Economy*, 27(5), 633–56.

Basri, MC and Hill, H 2011. Indonesian growth dynamics. *Asian Economic Policy Review*, 6(1), 90–107.

Biro Pusat Statistik (BPS Online). *Growth rate of gross domestic product at constant 2000 prices (per cent).* Available online at: www.bps.go.id/linkTabelStatis/view/id/1202.

Biro Pusat Statistik (BPS Online). *Gini Ratio by Province 1996, 1999, 2002, 2005, 2007–13.* Available online at: www.bps.go.id/linkTabelStatis/view/id/1493.

Biro Pusat Statistik (BPS Online). *Number of Poor People, Percentage of Poor People and Poverty Line.* Available online at: www.bps.go.id/linkTabelStatis/view/id/1494.

Butt, S 2009. 'Unlawfulness' and corruption under Indonesian law. *Bulletin of Indonesian Economic Studies*, 45(2), 179–98.

Crouch, H 2010. *Political Reform in Indonesia after Soeharto.* Singapore: Institute of South East Asian Studies.

Eeckhout, J and Jovanovic, B 2012. Occupational choice and development. *Journal of Economic Theory*, 147(2), 657–83.

Eichengreen, B, Park, D and Shin, K 2013. *Growth slowdowns redux: New evidence on the middle-income trap.* NBER Working Paper No. 18673. Cambridge, MA: National Bureau of Economic Research.

Felipe, J, Kumar, U and Galope, R 2014. *Middle-income transitions: Trap or myth?* Economics Working Paper Series No. 421. Manila: Asian Development Bank.

Grenville, S 2015. Deepening the Indonesian financial sector. The Third Hadi Soesastro Lecture, Centre for Strategic and International Studies, Jakarta, June.

Higgins, B 1968. *Economic Development.* 2nd edn. New York: WW Norton.

Hill, H 2000. *The Indonesian Economy.* 2nd edn. Cambridge: Cambridge University Press.

Hill, H (ed.) 2014. *Regional Dynamics in a Decentralized Indonesia.* Singapore: Institute of South East Asian Studies.

Hill, H and Thee, KW 2012. Indonesian universities in transition: Catching up and opening up. *Bulletin of Indonesian Economic Studies*, 48(2), 229–51.

Hill, H, Yean, TS and Zin, RHM 2012. Malaysia: A success story stuck in the middle? *The World Economy*, 35(12), 1,687–711.

Lewis, B 2014. Twelve years of fiscal decentralization: A balance sheet. In H Hill (ed.), *Regional Dynamics in a Decentralized Indonesia.* Singapore: Institute of South East Asian Studies, 135–55.

McLeod, R 2005. The struggle to regain effective government under democracy in Indonesia. *Bulletin of Indonesian Economic Studies*, 41(3), 367–86.

Manning, C 2014. Labour market regulation and employment during the Yudhoyono years in Indonesia. In PC Athukorala, AA Patunru and BP Resosudarmo (eds), *Trade, Development and Political Economy in East Asia.* Singapore: Institute of South East Asian Studies, 153–72.

Manning, C and Sudarno, S (eds) 2011. *Employment, Living Standards and Poverty in Contemporary Indonesia.* Singapore: Institute of Southeast Asian Studies.

Mishra, SC 2009. *Economic Inequality in Indonesia: Trends, Causes, and Policy Response.* Strategic Asia. Available online at:

Myrdal, G 1968. *Asian Drama.* New York: Twentieth Century Fund.

Patunru, AA and Rahardja, S 2015. *Trade Protectionism in Indonesia: Bad Times and Bad Policy.* Sydney: Lowy Institute.

Perkins, DH 2013. *East Asian Development: Foundations and Strategies.* Cambridge, MA: Harvard University Press.

Pritchett, L 2011. How good are good transitions for growth and poverty? Indonesia since Suharto, for instance? In C Manning and S Sudarno (eds), *Employment, Living Standards and Poverty in Contemporary Indonesia.* Singapore: Institute of South East Asian Studies, 23–46.

Sandee, H, Nurridzki, N and Dipo, MAP 2014. Challenges of implementing logistics reform in Indonesia. In H Hill (ed.), *Regional Dynamics in a Decentralized Indonesia.* Singapore: Institute of South East Asian Studies, 386–408.

Soejachmoen, M 2012. Why is Indonesia left behind in global production networks? Unpublished doctoral dissertation. The Australian National University, Canberra.

Suryadarma, D and Jones, GW (eds) 2013. *Education in Indonesia*. Singapore: Institute of South East Asian Studies.

Temple, J 2003. Growing into trouble: Indonesia after 1966. In D Rodrik (ed.), *In Search of Prosperity: Analytical Narratives on Economic Growth*. Princeton, NJ: Princeton University Press, 152–83.

van der Eng, P 2002. Indonesia's growth performance in the twentieth century. In A Maddison, DS Prasada Rao and WF Shepherd (eds), *The Asian Economies in the Twentieth Century*. Cheltenham, UK: Edward Elgar, 143–79.

Wai-Poi, M Forthcoming. Inequality in Indonesia: Why is it rising and what can be done? Unpublished paper, Jakarta.

Wells, LT and Ahmed, R 2007. *Making Foreign Investment Safe: Property Rights and National Sovereignty*. New York: Oxford University Press.

World Bank 1993. *The East Asian Miracle: Economic Growth and Public Policy*. Washington, DC: The World Bank.

World Development Indicators Online (WDI Online). Available online at: http://data.worldbank.org/data-catalog/world-development-indicators (accessed 13 July, 2015).

6 India

Escaping low-income traps and averting middle-income ones

Shekhar Shah and Rajesh Chadha[1]

What you imagine, you create.

– The Buddha

We are working day and night to create conditions for faster and inclusive growth. We want a quantum jump in all this. There is no time for incremental changes.

– Narendra Modi, Seoul, Korea, 19 May 2015

Introduction

When a country the size of India's is also one of the fastest-growing economies in the world and has entered middle-income status, it is enticing to imagine it attaining high-income status soon. And certainly, there is no dearth of reasons why we should not be hopeful about India realizing its vast potential.

India's economic growth in the 2000s before the Global Financial Crisis (GFC) was spectacular, reducing poverty substantially. India's saving rate remains one of the highest in the world. For much of the past 15 years, 'India Inc.' has been a destination of choice for foreign portfolio investment and foreign direct investment (FDI). India's large population is the youngest in the world, promising a demographic dividend that will be in the same league as China's. India's middle class is large, growing rapidly and hungry to consume.

Since May 2014, the new Bharatiya Janata Party (BJP)-led government of Prime Minister Narendra Modi has promised to refocus on growth and productive jobs. After more than a year in power, the new government has talked more about the vision for India's future, and perhaps also tried to do more to attain it, than other recent governments.

Seen from the outside, the notion of India as an upper middle-income country is alluring. India is part of the Asian Century narrative – the idea that economic and strategic power is shifting to Asia. Adding to the allure are developments such as India's G20 membership, its economy becoming the third-largest in the world in purchasing power parity (PPP) terms, and the increasing influence of the Indian diaspora. And as China rebalances away from investment to consumption, and its economic growth slows, it is natural to think about the world's second most populous economy growing rapidly to fill the void.

But India is equally, or perhaps more likely, to remain a lower middle-income country for the next decade and a half. India has the world's largest concentration of poor people, with more than 723 million (59 per cent) in 2011 living on less than $2 PPP a day and 288 million (24 per cent) on less than $1.25 PPP a day. India also remains a country of many different realities. Its bigger states are larger than most countries, some firmly in middle-income territory (for example, Delhi, Haryana, Maharashtra, Tamil Nadu and Gujarat), while some would be among the poorest in the world (Bihar, Uttar Pradesh, Manipur, Assam and Jharkhand). Bihar's per capita income is about one-third of the national average, while Delhi's is two and a half times bigger.

This suggests that even as India deals with its poorest states and low-income traps, it may start bumping up against a middle-income trap in its richer states. While it deals with how to finance badly needed basic infrastructure, provide an attractive investment climate and generate employment for its large informal and unskilled labour force, it may also have to worry about the productivity and innovation capacity of its industrial economy. As it deals with problems that its competitors dealt with decades ago, it must start thinking about how it will compete in the changing global manufacturing and commerce landscape shaped by global supply chains and disruptive technologies not yet invented. India may have to deal with low- and middle-income traps at the same time. This chapter explores the dual challenges India faces.

The Modi government appears to be focused on regaining the growth momentum India generated in the mid-2000s. If successful, India will rise rapidly through the lower middle-income range and in a decade or two will approach the income levels of China today. By then, however, India will also be well into its demographic transition, close to becoming the world's largest population. It will have to satisfy the rising expectations of one of the youngest labour forces in the world to earn its demographic dividend and avoid domestic social unrest.

This raises the question: can India become rich before it becomes old? It is important and timely to ask this question now because in a very real sense the expectations for India perhaps exceed the country's expectations of itself. This gap will have far-reaching consequences if it is not closed, not just giving rise to a greater gulf between India's potential and its achievements, but also making it that much harder for India to catch up with the rest of a rapidly rising Asia. Seen from the Asian perspective, whether or not India is caught in a middle-income trap will also shape the future of the so-called Asian Century.

This chapter is organized as follows. The next section provides a comparison of the growth trajectories of India and several East Asian comparators. The section that follows that one focuses on India's persistent low-income traps and the pathways it is pursuing to escape them. The section after that turns to how India might prepare to enter upper middle-income terrain and build an economy that innovates and has high productivity. India's idiosyncratic service sector-led growth pattern offers opportunities and challenges for dealing with possible middle-income traps. The next section explores several initiatives, such as Make in India, which the Indian government has launched in the past year. These initiatives bring together many of the challenges that India faces in escaping its low-income traps and averting middle-income ones. The final section concludes with suggestions for an institutional mechanism within government to ensure that at least some policymakers' sights remain sharply focused on averting middle-income traps, even as the majority of policymakers remain preoccupied with escaping India's many low-income ones.

The journey through middle income: India's comparators

The term 'middle-income trap' has come to refer to a panoply of ills that seem to afflict countries that grow relatively rapidly through middle-income territory but thereafter experience persistent slow growth for a long period and fail to transform themselves into high-income economies.[2] Gill and Kharas (2007: 5), the originators of the term, used it to describe economies that were being 'squeezed between the low-wage poor-country competitors that dominate mature industries and the rich-country innovators that dominate in industries undergoing rapid technological change'. In a recent update, Gill and Kharas (2015) talk about at least three broad definitions of the middle-income trap: the structural definition they pioneered and that we use here; an empirical one (Aiyar *et al.*, 2013; Eichengreen *et al.*, 2013; Spence, 2011); and a benchmarked definition based on lack of convergence to a benchmarked country, typically the United States (Agenor and Canuto, 2012; Gill and Kharas, 2015).

According to the World Bank's World Development Indicators, there are currently 50 countries in the lower middle-income (LMI) group and 55 in the upper middle-income (UMI) group (World Bank, 2015). The 50 LMI countries have a 2013 gross national income (GNI) per capita ranging from $1,046 to $4,125, and the 55 UMI countries range from $4,126 to $12,745. India, at a GNI per capita of $1,570, became an LMI country in 2007. Some of the other Asian LMIs are Indonesia, the Philippines, Sri Lanka and Vietnam (Table 6.1).

Countries spend a lot of time in the middle-income range. Felipe *et al.* (2012) show that of the 52 countries that attained middle-income status between 1950 and 2010, only eight of 38 LMI countries and only six of the 14 UMI countries managed to move to the high-income category. As of 2010, Sri Lanka had been a middle-income country for 24 years, the Philippines for 34 years, and Malaysia for 15 years. The recent World Bank China study (2013) shows of the 101 countries that had reached middle-income status in 1960, only 13 graduated to high-income status by 2008. Based on best-case scenarios, the Organization for Economic Cooperation and Development (OECD) estimates that Malaysia will become a high-income country by 2020, China and Thailand by about 2030, Indonesia just after 2040, the Philippines by 2050 and Vietnam and India by 2060 (OECD, 2013).

How does India's growth trajectory compare with its East Asian neighbours? In 1950, India's per capita GDP in 1999 PPP terms was $619, compared with China's $448, $817 for Indonesia and Thailand, $854 for South Korea, $1,070 for the Philippines, and $1,559 for Malaysia. South Korea – with its strong

Table 6.1 Lower and upper middle-income economies, 2013 (105 countries)

Countries	GNI per capita, Atlas method (current US$)	GNI per capita, PPP (current international $)
Lower middle-income countries		
Indonesia	3,580	9,270
Philippines	3,270	7,840
Sri Lanka	3,170	9,470
Vietnam	1,740	5,070
India	1,570	5,350
Pakistan	1,360	4,840
Bangladesh	1,010	3,190
Upper middle-income countries		
Brazil	11,690	14,750
Turkey	10,970	18,570
Malaysia	10,430	22,530
Mexico	9,940	16,020
China	6,560	11,850
Thailand	5,340	13,430

Source: World Bank (2015).

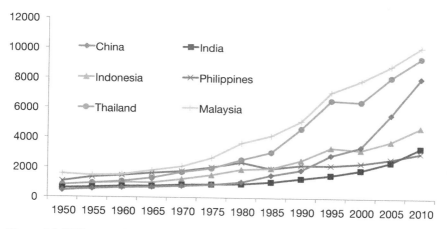

Figure 6.1 GDP per capita, selected countries (US$)
Source: The Maddison Project (2010).

manufacturing prowess based on large investments in human and physical capital, particularly infrastructure, efficient allocation of resources and modern managerial practices – had reached a per capita GDP of $21,701 by 2010. Malaysia, Thailand and China also did well, but the Philippines, with the second-highest per capita income in 1950, was left behind, and had the lowest per capita GDP by 2010 (Figure 6.1).

Unfortunately, India's GDP growth also did not do well from the 1960s through the 1980s, and only started picking up steam in the early 1980s (Figure 6.2).

In thinking about how India might progress as an LMI, the comparison with China is inevitable. China in 2013 was the world's second-largest economy, at $8.9 trillion GNI, while India, at $2 trillion GNI, was in tenth position. In 2013 PPP dollars, China ranked second globally, at $16.1 trillion, and India ranked third, at $6.7 trillion. The 2010 per capita GNIs of India and China were $1,570 and $6,560, respectively. China entered the LMI group in 1999; India made its entry in 2007. In 11 years, China became a UMI country (Figure 6.3). For the sake of comparison, if the Indian economy had started growing at 10 per cent a year in 2014 and continued at that rate, reaching China's current GNI per capita would take more than 16 years. Also on this basis, India would take at least 25 years to

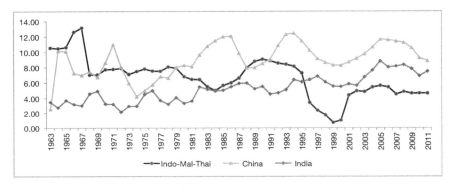

Figure 6.2 GDP growth, selected Asian countries (five-year moving average, per cent)
Source: World Bank (2015).

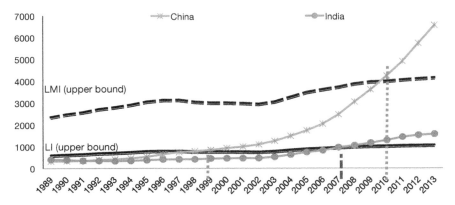

Figure 6.3 Trends in GNI per capita (Atlas method, current US$)
Notes: LI = lower income; LMI = lower middle income.
Source: World Bank (2015).

touch the current floor value of the high-income countries at $12,746 – that is, by 2040. More realistically, as suggested by the OECD (2013), this will not happen until about 2060.

Each of these early developers in Asia, much like countries elsewhere, lost GDP and employment shares in agriculture, expanded the share of industry and later expanded service sector shares. India, too, lost agricultural share in GDP, but, remarkably, saw no expansion of the shares of industry, with massive expansion instead in the output and employment shares of its service sector (Figures 6.4 and 6.5). India's unusual pattern of sectoral growth sets it apart from almost all

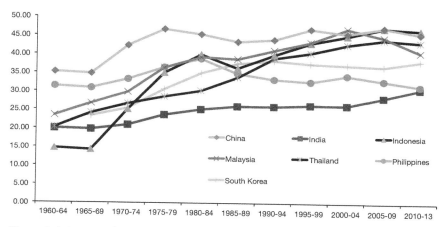

Figure 6.4 Average share of industry in GDP (per cent)
Source: World Bank (2015).

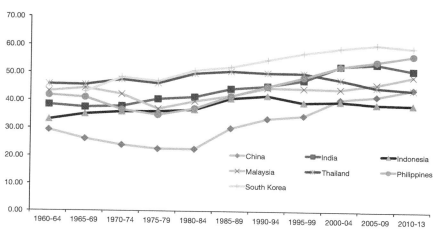

Figure 6.5 Average share of services in GDP (per cent)
Source: World Bank (2015).

countries in Asia and elsewhere. This has important implications for a country that will have a larger population than China by 2028, since output and employment growth in industry have traditionally led the way for producing the unskilled or semi-skilled jobs that an economy needs as its agricultural sector shrinks.

Recent work by Pritchett and Summers (2014) suggests that India and China should not depend on predictions of continual growth. They find that the most striking and robust aspect of the evidence of economic growth is regression to the mean – that 'abnormally rapid growth is rarely persistent' (Pritchett and Summers, 2014: 2) and 'China's super-rapid growth has already lasted three times longer than a typical episode and is the longest ever recorded' (2014: 58). They ask 'Why will growth slow?' and their answer is '[m]ainly because that is what rapid growth does' (2014: 19). They show that the growth process is marked by sharp discontinuities and large growth accelerations or decelerations. They argue that neither China nor India has the quality institutions associated with the steady if somewhat slower growth in the current high-productivity countries, which makes discontinuities more likely for both China and India.

Escaping low-income traps: pathways and challenges for India

The Indian economy saw a GDP growth rate of about 3.6 per cent per annum during the first three decades of its planned growth (1951–80), and thereafter a jump to 5.4 per cent in the 1980s. This more rapid growth in the 1990s continued at 5.7 per cent per annum, and then rose further to 6.1 per cent during 2001–2 to 2004–5. It then had a second growth spurt, touching an unprecedented average growth rate of 9.5 per cent during 2005–6 to 2007–8. Growth after the GFC in 2008–9 to 2011–12 declined to 7.7 per cent, and declined further, to 4.5 per cent, in 2012–13 and 2013–14. Saving and gross fixed capital formation dropped to about 31 and 30 per cent of GDP, respectively, in 2013–14 (Figure 6.6). Returning the economy to 8 or 9 per cent growth is an often-stated goal of the new government, and pushing it upwards to 9–10 per cent growth is often cited as India's medium-term challenge.

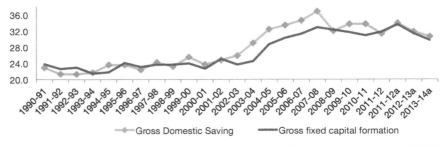

Figure 6.6 Gross domestic savings and gross fixed capital formation (percentage of GDP at market price)

Source: Government of India (2015b).

For readers less familiar with the course of economic policymaking in India, there is fortunately a large literature available, including contributions by two current policymakers, Arvind Panagariya (2008) and Arvind Subramanian (2008). Panagariya (2014) lists five goals for the new government – covering poverty, jobs, literacy, healthcare, electricity, roads, water and sanitation – and explains why they are achievable.

India began its major economic reforms and moved towards globalization in 1991 with the liberalization of product markets, and also reforming fiscal, monetary and trade policies. This paid handsome dividends. The total factor productivity (TFP) of the economy during the 2000s increased substantially: TFP growth was higher during 2000–8 than 1980–99, with the exception of labour's contribution (Table 6.2). Attention was supposed to turn soon after 1991 to liberalizing factor markets in labour, land, infrastructure and capital, but domestic coalition politics had taken over by the mid-1990s, and these factor markets remained largely unreformed through the 1990s and 2000s. Only in the past year with the Modi government has there been discussion about and serious movement on factor market reforms.

A major challenge in returning to faster job-creating growth will be the extent to which the government can improve the investment climate, particularly to boost investments in low- or semi-skilled, labour-intensive organized manufacturing, and improve the functioning of factor markets and access to high-quality infrastructure such as power, where generation had kept pace with GDP growth between 1994–5 and 2001–2, but slipped behind in the 2000s.

Dealing with labour reforms, land acquisition and India's comparative advantage

India's share of manufacturing in value added has remained stagnant, but that of services has increased dramatically, unlike almost any other middle-income or advanced country. India's failure to reform factor markets in labour and land is often blamed for the organized manufacturing sector's growth remaining so sluggish in such a labour-abundant country, and for so much of India's labour force remaining informal. A resulting challenge for India will be the dilemma of conforming to its comparative advantage in its most abundant factor of production, labour.

Table 6.2 Total factor productivity, growth rates per annum (contribution of factors)

	Total GVA growth rate	*Labour contribution*	*Capital contribution*	*Total factor productivity growth*
1980–1999	5.24	1.62	2.51	1.11
2000–2008	7.56	1.41	3.89	2.26
1980–2008	5.82	1.53	2.89	1.40

Source: Reserve Bank of India (2014).

Labour reforms

Indian workers and firms have two distinctive features: both are largely informal, and firms remain small. The roughly 400 million informal employees who make up 93 per cent of the Indian labour force form possibly the world's largest informal workforce. They strongly reflect the country's burdensome, archaic labour regulations, which have become increasingly restrictive and have produced a highly complicated regulatory regime. There are more than 40 national and 100 state labour laws that overlap, and there are differences across states in regulations governing workers and employers.

A big challenge will be to bring greater numbers of informal workers into the formal workforce so as to raise their productivity and wages. Unfortunately, labour regulation has gone the other way, driving people into the informal sector rather than away from it. Firms are forced to remain small and informal to avoid regulatory difficulties. Workers end up with low-paid, uncertain livelihoods and limited social security. In 1976, under India's Industrial Disputes Act, firms employing more than 300 people needed government permission to lay off or retrench workers or close. In 1982, this was made more restrictive and applied also to smaller firms employing more than 100 workers, adding to the difficulty of hiring new or seasonal workers and letting go of inefficient workers. Firms that want to grow prefer to have contract labour and use capital-intensive technology. As a result, organized manufacturing as a sector has remained small and does not create enough stable skilled or semi-skilled jobs.

There are a variety of studies that support the observation that labour laws are hurting productive and remunerative job creation. States with pro-worker legislation have experienced weaker industrial growth (Besley and Burgess, 2004) and have benefited less from investment delicensing (Aghion *et al.*, 2008). Investment delicensing has been weaker in labour-intensive industries than in capital-intensive ones (Gupta *et al.*, 2009). Labour-demand elasticities in industry are higher in states with flexible labour laws (Hasan *et al.*, 2007). Hasan and Jandoc (2012) find that a majority of firms are clustered in very small enterprises but provide employment to a large share of the workforce. In states with labour-intensive industries, those with more flexible labour regulations tend to have a greater share of employment in larger-sized firms.

Under the Modi government, labour reforms are being discussed again, but with the focus shifting to the states. According to the Indian Constitution, both the union and the states can pass labour laws. In the past, reform measures proposed at the union level have not budged because of vested interests. State governments have also been reluctant to take the initiative, with Gujarat the first to do so. With the Chief Minister of Gujarat now the Prime Minister, several states, starting with Rajasthan and Madhya Pradesh, are taking the lead on amending their labour laws, with formal approval from the President. More states are expected to take this route, driven by competition for investments and growth. The central government will need to watch the fairness and balancing of interests in this process. As state laws change, the process will likely gather momentum as comfort levels with this approach increase.

Land acquisition

Public infrastructure and industry, particularly manufacturing, need land. Although land is a state responsibility in the Constitution, acquisition and requisitioning of property are on the concurrent list, so both Parliament and state legislatures can make laws covering the acquisition of privately held land for public purposes and private entities. The Land Acquisition Act of 1894, originally designed to serve the British, governed land acquisition until 2013. It did not provide for rehabilitation of the owner, provided only for cash compensation without accounting for rising future land values, and used an expansive definition of public purpose. Despite amendments, the 1894 Act did not provide a cohesive law that addressed fair compensation and rehabilitation.

In response, the previous United Progressive Alliance government enacted the 2013 Land Acquisition, Rehabilitation and Resettlement Act. The Act provided for compensation at rates four times higher than previously; a mandatory obligation to rehabilitate and resettle landowners; involvement of locally elected bodies; safeguards against the displacement of tribal people; a strict consent clause for acquisition by private entities; the requirement for a Social Impact Assessment; the establishment of other dispute-resolution bodies; and return of unutilized land after five years.

The passage of the Act was followed by strong industry criticism that it was tilted against industry and infrastructure, with a complex and impractical process of acquisition that would stall most transactions, hurting both sellers and buyers (PRS Legislative Research, 2015). Most projects faced landowners holding out for higher prices. As land records remain unreliable in India, the new Act led to a spike in litigation, adding to land prices and increasing project costs. Neither farmer nor the entrepreneur seemed to be benefiting.

The Modi government tried to pass a new Bill in Parliament in late 2014, but failed. In December 2014, the President promulgated a land acquisition ordinance to temporarily replace the Act. After another major attempt to pass the Bill, the government allowed the ordinance to lapse in August 2014. It issued orders to align some 13 previous Acts, not mentioned in the 2013 Act, which would now use the compensation, rehabilitation and resettlement provisions of the 2013 Act. It also gave a free hand to state governments to acquire land under their own laws.

As with labour reforms, the central government now clearly expects the states to come up with their own norms for land acquisition. This is already happening in states ruled by the BJP, with Rajasthan leading the way.

India's comparative advantage and 'premature deindustrialization'

The Economic Survey 2014–15 (Government of India, 2015b) suggests two disturbing findings about the source of dynamism in the Indian economy. Unskilled labour is India's most abundant factor of production, and therefore the most likely to gain from productivity growth and contribute to greater equity if it is used extensively in the country's most dynamic sector. The presumption is that manufacturing would, at least initially, deploy relatively unskilled labour most intensively. Unfortunately, as the Economic Survey and Kochar *et al.* (2006) show, registered manufacturing is itself a sector that is relatively intensive in *skilled labour* in India. This implies registered manufacturing will not be aligned to India's comparative advantage, unless it develops very differently from the past or it absorbs more and more of the informal sector, which currently employs the bulk of Indian labour.

The second disturbing finding in the Economic Survey relates to registered manufacturing itself.[3] As part of its idiosyncratic pattern of growth, India's share of output and employment in registered manufacturing has not only not rapidly expanded, but indeed may have stopped expanding before the country and many states have fully industrialized. The Economic Survey finds that with the exception of Gujarat and Himachal Pradesh, registered manufacturing as a share of value added has been declining in most states, and has been doing so for a long time. Most states have also not been experiencing secular growth in employment shares in registered manufacturing over time.

Rodrik (2013) has noted that formal manufacturing tends to be technologically the most dynamic, exhibiting unconditional convergence (faster productivity growth in lower productivity areas). Deindustrialization removes the main channel through which rapid growth and formal job creation have taken place in most countries. Rodrik notes the subtle political consequences of a large organized labour force providing discipline and coordination, which make it easier to strike bargains between the elites and non-elites, triggering greater democratic consolidation; a large informal labour force makes that difficult.

The growth drivers for India are unlikely to be as neatly sequenced as they were for its Asian neighbours, and will therefore also be different for its richer states compared with its poorer states. Given the sheer size of India's informal sector, Indian policymakers need to take the formal and informal manufacturing sectors and the formal and informal service sectors into account when looking for the sources of productive, job-creating growth.

One old and two new challenges

As the Modi government strives to pursue these reforms and promote rapid job-creating growth, three things stand out as being different for India compared with its East Asian neighbours: first, the political economy of India as a very large democracy with a high incidence of poverty; second, concerns about environmental pollution and climate change; and third, the international trading system.

The scale of populist policies in India

As the world's largest democracy with regular elections that also has a high incidence of poverty, India has faced a peculiar political economy problem.[4] In order to be elected and stay in office, politicians have often tried to ensure that poor people, who are in the majority, see immediate consumption benefits in public programmes in order to obtain their votes. The size of the country and its low average income levels have meant that the have-nots have typically outnumbered the haves, and it takes a long time to rebalance the two in ways in which the majority of voters favour investment in physical and human capital, which will have a growth pay-off only over a much longer horizon, ahead of consumption handouts.

In such a setting, in the guise of providing for the poor, politicians have tended to pursue patronage politics rather than growth politics. This is seen in: the large numbers of subsidies for food, fertilizer, kerosene, water, electricity and train travel; reluctance to deal with issues such as labour market reforms or land acquisition; procurement of food grains for subsidized public distribution from agro-climatic regions in which such food should not be grown because of its adverse impact on soil quality and the water table; and championing of cereal food security when dealing with child malnutrition requires other solutions. Populist programmes have taken precedence over systematic and efficient investments in human and physical capital that can lay the foundations for faster economic growth and universal job and opportunity creation based on the country's comparative advantage in low-cost, unskilled labour.

A disorderly international trading environment and domestic compulsions

India's share of world trade continues to be small, at 1.7 per cent of global merchandise exports in 2013. The government's 2015–20 Foreign Trade Policy, released in April 2015, seeks to raise that to 3.5 per cent by 2020. The East Asian economies grew largely under a benign and disciplined international trade regime marked by multilateralism. But with the establishment of the World Trade Organization in 1995, trade relations started getting muddled, with less and less transparency in trading regimes and the discipline and predictability of multilateralism giving way to the unchartered territory of regionalism.

India has been a strong advocate of multilateralism, but it has also increasingly turned to regional and bilateral trade agreements to enhance market access. India currently has 11 free-trade agreements (FTAs) and five limited-scope preferential trade agreements, and is negotiating some 17 other agreements. India is negotiating the Regional Comprehensive Economic Partnership with the Association of South East Asian Nations Plus 10 (ASEAN-10) and their six FTA partners. India's long-standing but on-and-off interest in joining the Asia-Pacific Economic Cooperation (APEC) forum may now be seeing some traction, with the APEC 2015 Summit likely to discuss India's membership and the Indian government proposing talks with industry about compliance with international standards.

The size of the Indian domestic market and its rising purchasing power lead Indian policymakers, unlike their East Asian neighbours, to believe that India cannot and should not rely only on export-led growth, but must seek to cater to both domestic and foreign demand for low- and high-value products and services. To that end, while India continues to liberalize and facilitate trade, Indian trade policy remains driven by domestic supply considerations, has relatively short-term objectives (such as smoothing commodity price fluctuations) and requires constant fine-tuning. This makes the trade regime less predictable and raises costs. While trade facilitation continues, the import regime remains complex, with its licensing and permit system and multiple exemptions and rates.

In contrast, India seems to be doing better on measures for attracting FDI, including gradually increasing the numbers of sectors in which FDI is permitted; raising foreign ownership limits in sectors such as defence, insurance and railways; allowing 100 per cent FDI in most sectors; and improving its low ranking on the World Bank's Ease of Doing Business Index. The introduction of a goods and services tax (GST) will help Indian exporters and FDI investors by simplifying and harmonizing India's indirect tax regime and unifying the Indian market.

Climate change constraints

In seeking to grow much more rapidly, India faces a set of constraints and costs, but also opportunities, related to the environment. These constraints and costs were largely not present when the Asian high-income countries, including the four Asian 'Tigers', experienced their rapid growth from the 1960s to the 1980s. These economies, including South Korea, did not have the compulsion to establish low-emission, high-cost technologies that India must now do. Even though India has not set binding emission reduction targets, it has committed to a 20–5 per cent reduction in its GDP emission intensity by 2020 from its 2005 emission levels. India has also moved from a carbon subsidy to a carbon tax regime, with an increase in excise duties for diesel and petrol in its 2015 Budget. The challenge for India will be to both reduce emissions and exploit growth opportunities emerging from green technologies and the increasing global demand for green goods and services.

Averting middle-income traps

India faces myriad challenges as it seeks to regain the growth momentum of the mid-2000s, and then increase and maintain that momentum as it climbs the middle-income ladder. If India is to succeed, its poorest and middle-income regions must escape low-income traps through growth based on increasing inputs and technology absorption, and its most productive states and cities must contribute through growth based on productivity and technological innovation. This is a tall order. Can India leapfrog and increase its chances of rapid growth to move more rapidly from low middle-income to UMI status? And thereafter, can the Indian economy avoid a sharp and persistent slowdown? How can India avoid getting old before it gets rich?

Recent cross-country work on the middle-income trap (Agenor and Canuto, 2012; Aiyar *et al.*, 2013; Eichengreen *et al.*, 2012, 2013) suggests that countries slow when there is a persistent decline in productivity growth as measured by TFP. Much of this empirical analysis suggests that moving to higher-income status will require – in addition to improving infrastructure – easing stringent product and labour market regulations, deepening trade integration and shifting to a development model that fosters innovation, where governments will have a role to play in raising research and development (R & D) spending and tertiary education attainment (Eichengreen *et al.*, 2013).

This section looks at two elements associated with rapid-growth economies: first, their ability to innovate and protect innovation and creativity; and second, their ability to be inclusive, particularly in ensuring that women participate fully in the workforce. Finally, this section ends with a discussion of the policy dilemmas India faces in its idiosyncratic development pattern so far, resulting in a large and low-productivity services sector, and a small formal manufacturing sector that is relatively skill intensive.

Supporting innovation: R & D, patents, designs and IP protection

India's ready supply of information and communication technology (ICT) human resources and the resulting establishment of major ICT R & D facilities in India by almost all the large global ICT players show how, with well-trained human resources, India could aspire to become one of the top R & D destinations in the world.

The world's gross expenditure on R & D in PPP terms was estimated to be $1.62 trillion in 2014. China was the second-highest R & D investor after the United States, followed by Japan (Table 6.3). Singapore, South Korea and Japan are the most R & D-oriented countries of Asia; South Korea spends about 4 per cent of its GDP on R & D. India spends about 0.8 per cent of its GDP on R & D – less than half that of China. A large portion of R & D expenditure in India comes from the central government, with much less spent by the domestic private sector.

Table 6.3 Expenditure on R & D by various countries

	2012		2013		2014	
	GERD PPP, US$ bl.	R&D as % GDP	GERD PPP, US$ bl.	R&D as % GDP	GERD PPP, US$ bl.	R&D as % GDP
Americas (21)	485	2.5	489	2.4	504	2.5
US	447	2.8	450	2.8	465	2.8
Asia (20)	561	1.8	596	1.9	633	1.9
China	232	1.8	258	1.9	284	2.0
Japan	160	3.4	163	3.4	165	3.4
India	41	0.9	42	0.9	44	0.9
Europe (34)	350	1.9	349	1.9	351	1.8
Germany	92	2.8	92	2.8	92	2.9
Rest of world (36)	81	0.9	83	0.9	87	0.9
Global total	1,517	1.8	1,559	1.8	1,618	1.8

Notes: GERD = gross expenditures on R & D; PPP = purchasing power parity.
Source: Battelle & R&D Magazine (2013).

India does have about 870 global R & D hubs belonging to multinational companies, particularly in ICT. Many more are expected to enter. Multinational corporations (MNCs) want to locate R & D in India for three reasons: the large burgeoning market for virtually all types of products and favourable demographics; access to young science and engineering talent with working fluency in English; and the opportunity to reduce R & D costs.

Patents and designs are an indicator of R & D outcomes. India's pace in patents granted has been picking up slowly since the 1980s, but remains well behind China's performance (Table 6.4). More than 50 per cent of patents registered in India during 1999–2013 were in pharmaceuticals, organic fine chemistry and computer technology. The share of patents registered in digital communication (3.3 per cent) and information technology (IT) methods of management (2.5 per cent) – two ICT sectors that have driven growth – was surprisingly low (Table 6.5). A major portion of patents granted goes to foreign rather than domestic companies; domestic firms receive only about one-fifth of patents granted (Table 6.6).

India faces several challenges for it to become a global R & D hub. It needs an efficient judicial system and a strengthened intellectual property rights (IPR) regime. It needs to encourage the R & D participation of the domestic private sector, ensuring funding for small- and medium-sized enterprises, particularly start-ups; help channel government investment towards application-oriented R & D; and solve industry-specific problems essential for an industry-friendly R & D ecosystem.

In order to more effectively protect IPR, India has finally started discussing a national IPR policy. The Department of Industrial Policy and Promotion released the first draft of its National IPR Policy in December 2014 (Government of India, 2014). The draft makes clear India's willingness to bend the intellectual property (IP) system to its own needs, but it also shows signs of a major change towards more international goals of enforcement and the promotion of strong IPR.

The National IPR Policy has raised concerns about both its content and its development process, including the absence of serious prior consultation. Thambisetty (2014) summarizes the questions posed – from whether the government should even be in the business of promoting IP (rather than simply facilitating it) and what the design of a patent office that is fit for purpose should be, to what the appropriate sources of comparative law might be and the dangers of detaching IP laws from constitutional or generalist reasoning by creating specialized IP tribunals for the certainty that such tribunals promise.

It would make a lot of sense for the Indian IPR policy process to take global best practice into account and adapt it to India's needs to make full use of the latecomer's advantage. Thambisetty suggests, for example, looking at the international Commission on Intellectual Property Rights (CIPR, 2002) to ensure that India's IPR policy is not developed and does not operate in a vacuum. News reports at the end of July 2015 suggest that the final draft of the National IPR Policy has been circulated for inter-ministerial consultation and is likely to be considered by the Cabinet.

Table 6.4 Average annual patents granted by country

Year	India	China	Indonesia*	Malaysia	Philippines	Thailand	Brazil	Mexico	China, Hong Kong SAR	Singapore	South Korea	Japan	United States of America
1980s	1,882	770	—	454	1,095	67	5,027	2,153	1,001	516	2,962	56,841	73,702
1990s	1,586	5,382	349	1,113	778	468	2,444	3,838	1,843	3,349	25,083	118,827	117,553
2001–6	3,132	39,193	—	2,691	1,279	886	3,279	7,119	3,692	6,646	61,212	125,332	163,410
2007–13	8,214	146,008	1,811	3,189	1,416	941	2,805	10,519	5,213	5,853	95,474	221,163	208,216

Note: *Averages have been calculated based on the data available.

Source: WIPO (2015).

Table 6.5 Patent applications in India ranked by technology fields, 1999–2013

Field of technology	Share (%)
Pharmaceuticals	20.40
Organic fine chemistry	18.61
Computer technology	14.31
Biotechnology	5.05
Basic materials chemistry	3.83
Digital communication	3.34
IT methods for management	2.48
Medical technology	2.25
Chemical engineering	2.18
Materials, metallurgy	2.11
Others	25.44

Source: WIPO (2015).

Table 6.6 Patents granted, India (2001–13)

Year	Shares (%)		Total no.
	Resident	Non-resident	
2001	34.2	65.8	1,549
2002	40.2	59.8	1,540
2003	40.3	59.7	1,526
2004	36.7	63.3	2,317
2005	32.3	67.7	4,320
2006	25.3	74.7	7,539
2007	20.8	79.2	15,261
2008	15.8	84.2	16,061
2009	28.0	72.0	6,168
2010	16.9	83.1	7,138
2011	15.0	85.0	5,168
2012	16.7	83.3	4,328
2013	17.6	82.4	3,377

Source: WIPO (2015).

Increasing female labour force participation

India stands out in international comparisons for its extremely low female participation rate. India's 2012 female participation rate of 33 per cent is well below the international average, of 50 per cent, and the East Asian average, of 63 per cent. India's female workforce participation rate is the second-lowest among all the economies of the G20 and Brazil, Russia, India and China. Not only has the rate been low but, paradoxically, it has also been declining, particularly since 2004–5, and particularly for rural women, even though employment opportunities, incomes and education levels for women have been rising (Das *et al.*, 2015).

Female employees in India remain concentrated in entry- or middle-level positions and are scarce in senior management or board positions. Not surprisingly, the World Economic Forum's Corporate Gender Gap Report 2010 (Zahidi and Ibarra, 2010) found that India has the lowest percentage of women corporate employees. Various studies have highlighted how low female labour force participation or weak entrepreneurial activity drags down economic growth, and that empowering women has significant economic benefits in addition to promoting gender equality (Duflo, 2012; World Bank, 2012).

For India to enjoy its full demographic dividend, more women must come into the organized labour force. A number of recent studies show that a concerted effort in this area could have a multiplier effect on GDP growth. Estimates by Booz & Company/PwC (2012) suggest that India could see a 27 per cent jump in GDP if it matches female to male employment rates (Figure 6.7).

What explains the fall in female participation? Previous research has focused on the role of educational attainment for urban women: the highly educated may choose not to work if they are also well off. A number of studies (Goldin, 1995; Mammen and Paxson, 2000) suggest that women could be withdrawing from the labour market as a result of rising household incomes. Klasen and Pieters (2013) found that the decline in urban female labour force participation between 1987 and 2009 was caused, on the supply side, by rising household incomes, the husband's education level and the social stigma against educated women seeking menial work. On the demand side, they found that employment in sectors appropriate for educated women grew more slowly than the supply of educated workers, leading to many women withdrawing from the labour force.

The 2011 Census suggests that almost 66 per cent of Indian women are now literate – up from just 54 per cent in 2001. Rural female literacy has seen the biggest jump, from 46 to 59 per cent, which is nearly double the gain for urban women.

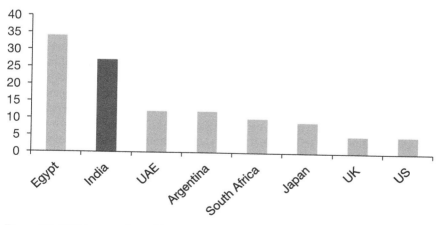

Figure 6.7 GDP impact of matching female to male employment rates (percentage of GDP)
Source: Booz & Company/PwC (2012).

Women's average share in the university science classroom rose from 30 per cent in the mid-1980s to 43 per cent in 2011–12 (Table 6.7). The jump is especially striking in engineering, agriculture, law and commerce. So, India is clearly undergoing a massive transformation in women's educational attainment; the policy challenge is to create conditions in which educational attainment does not lead to withdrawal from the labour force.

How should policy be made to address the gender gap in labour force participation and address concerns about the triple goals of education, employability and employment of women? First, more effective public social spending is needed in education that emphasizes learning outcomes and ensures that gender gaps in access are minimized. Second, structural, supply-side reforms discussed in this chapter, including in labour markets, and improvements in infrastructure, can spur job creation and allow more women to enter the labour force. Increasing labour market flexibility can lead to more formal sector jobs, and help informal sector workers move to the formal sector, allowing more women, many of whom work in the informal sector, to move into the formal sector.

Promoting growth drivers: manufacturing or services?

The East Asian economies started their growth process relying on relatively low-skilled manufacturing to generate increasing output and employment shares consistent with their most abundant resource of unskilled and low-skilled labour. Their services sectors expanded much later in this more traditional growth process. In contrast, India's idiosyncratic pattern of output growth – from agriculture to services, bypassing low-skilled manufacturing – has resulted in a manufacturing sector whose output and employment shares have hardly changed in 30 years. Instead, the services sector has grown dramatically, going from about 35 per cent to more than 50 per cent of GDP. At the same time, the share of services in employment has registered much more modest changes, though some service subsectors have increased their employment shares faster than registered manufacturing.

Looking ahead to the next two decades, India's idiosyncratic growth path will pose a dilemma for policymakers. Should policymakers focus on facilitating the growth of low-skilled manufacturing, and hope that it will generate badly needed employment for India's demographic transition, while also starting to increase the share of manufacturing in output? Or should policymakers focus instead on a service-led growth strategy that can yield skill-intensive patterns of growth, and that will better position India to deal with the issues around possible middle-income traps? As a matter of strategy, which should dominate policy thinking today?

The dilemma facing India is nicely articulated by the government's Economic Survey 2014–15, following Amirapu and Subramaniam (2015): which should be India's transformational sector – manufacturing or services? The sectors that are highly productive and dynamic – registered manufacturing and highly skilled ICT services – and hence likely to be transformational all use relatively scarce skilled and semi-skilled labour rather than abundant unskilled labour. And the sectors that

Table 6.7 Enrolment of women in higher education by discipline, 1985–6 to 2011–12 (percentage share of women in total enrolment)

	Science and technology disciplines					Other disciplines					Total
	Science	Engineering	Medicine	Agriculture	Veterinary science	Arts	Commerce	Law	Education	Others	
1985–6	31	7	31	6	6	39	20	9	47	35	30
2005–6	40	23	47	17	22	46	37	22	51	38	41
2011–12	44	29	49	26	25	48	40	29	59	38	43

Source: Adapted from Government of India (2013: Table 23).

Table 6.8 India, services versus manufacturing scorecard

Desirable feature of sector growth	Registered manufacturing	Trade, hotels and restaurants	Transport, storage and communications	Financial services and insurance	Real estate, business services, etc.	Construction
High productivity	Yes	No	Not really	Yes	Yes	No
Unconditional domestic convergence	Yes	Yes	Yes	Yes	Yes	Yes
Unconditional international convergence	Yes, but not for India	No	No	Yes	Yes	Yes
Converging sector absorbs resources	No	Somewhat	Somewhat	No	Somewhat	Yes
Skill profile matches underlying endowments	Not really	Somewhat	Somewhat	No	No	Yes
Tradable and/or replicable	Yes	No	Somewhat	Yes	Somewhat	No

Sources: Government of India (2015b); Amirapu and Subramanian (2015).

use low-skilled labour, such as informal manufacturing and services, do not have much transformational potential.

Like manufacturing, services are also diverse, with high-productivity subsectors such as telecommunications and software development, and low-productivity ones such as security guards and restaurant waiters. A meaningful analysis of the growth and transformational potential of services must distinguish between a software engineer and a waiter.

Amirapu and Subramanian (2015) prepare a manufacturing versus services scorecard, assessing their transformational potential along five dimensions (Table 6.8). The scorecard makes it obvious that India does not have a choice: it will have to both rapidly promote manufacturing and continue to support services sector growth. Firing on all cylinders means that the goal of manufacturing policy has to be to expand registered manufacturing, bringing more informal manufacturing into its ambit, and to make it more unskilled-labour intensive and globally competitive, so that India's many unskilled workers can benefit. The goal of skills policy should be to transform as much unskilled labour as possible into semi-skilled and skilled labour, so they can be employed not only in formal manufacturing, but also in high-productivity, globally competitive services that are dynamic and transformational. National programmes such as the recently launched Make in India and Skill India are needed.

New government initiatives

The Modi government has put in place a number of new initiatives designed to revive growth and dynamism in the economy. We look at some of these to ascertain the contribution they are likely to make to overcoming structural problems and addressing both low- and middle-income traps. We also look at some possibilities that have emerged recently to address India's political problem of populist policies, as discussed earlier.

The Make in India and Skill India programmes

The Make in India programme includes major initiatives to improve the efficiency of producing in India by facilitating investment, building best-in-class infrastructure, linking to skill building, improving the ease of doing business, making access to finance easier, fostering innovation and protecting IP.

The initiative focuses on 25 sectors for job creation and skill enhancement, including automobiles, chemicals, IT, pharmaceuticals, textiles, ports, aviation, leather, tourism and hospitality, wellness, railways, automotive components, design manufacturing, renewable energy, mining, biotechnology and electronics. Make in India hopes to attract capital and technology in these areas, and it aims at setting high-quality standards and minimizing adverse environmental impacts. To attract investment, the government has now allowed 49 per cent FDI in defence (previously 26 per cent) and 100 per cent in railway infrastructure (previously none was allowed). In defence, multiple Indian companies can hold the 51 per cent Indian stake, making partnerships easier.

Although these broad goals are unexceptional, there is a tendency to interpret Make in India as focusing only on manufacturing and seeking to replicate the East Asian success with export-led growth. Indeed, several specific goals of Make in India relate to this: increasing manufacturing sector growth to 12–14 per cent per annum over the medium term; increasing the share of manufacturing in GDP from 16 per cent to 25 per cent by 2022; creating 100 million additional manufacturing jobs by 2022; increasing domestic value addition and technological depth in manufacturing; and enhancing the global competitiveness of Indian manufacturing.

Rajan (2014) cautions against export euphoria and the industrial policy equivalent of picking winners, preferring to be agnostic about choosing between manufactures, agricultural commodities, mining products or services – as long as India makes all these more efficiently. There are others in government, particularly in the Ministries of Finance and Industry, who appear to think differently. While Rajan does not advocate export pessimism, he notes that India should not pursue an export strategy that subsidizes exporters with cheap inputs and an undervalued exchange rate, because this is not likely to work in current global circumstances. Rajan also cautions against picking a single sector, such as manufacturing. Instead of subsidizing inputs to specific industries because they are deemed important or labour intensive – a strategy that Rajan feels has not paid off for India over the decades – he urges the Make in India programme to determine the public goods each sector needs and for the government to then provide them.

Rajan also urges the idea of Make in India for India – that is, also producing for the large Indian domestic market, particularly in view of uncertain demand conditions in the developed world. But he also cautions against doing this behind tariff or non-tariff walls, as India did in the heyday of import substitution. Introducing a GST would help greatly in integrating India's large domestic market and would assist the Make in India campaign in producing goods and services that are internationally competitive for the large Indian domestic market.

The Skill India programme complements Make in India in important ways. The newly formed Ministry of Skill Development and Entrepreneurship has just put out for comment the Draft National Policy for Skill Development and Entrepreneurship 2015 (Government of India, 2015a). The policy notes that '[t]he country presently faces a dual challenge of a severe paucity of highly-trained, quality labor, as well as non-employability of large sections of the educated workforce that possess little or no job skills' (Government of India, 2015a: 3).

The labour force in the industrialized world will decline by about 4 per cent in the next 20 years but will increase by 32 per cent in India. India has one of the youngest populations in the world today. More than 62 per cent of the population is in the 15–59 years working-age group, and more than 54 per cent is below 25 years of age. India's demographics mean that one million youths will join India's labour force every month for the next 20 years. To reap this demographic dividend, which is expected to last for the next 25 years, India needs to equip its workforce with employable skills and knowledge. If they are not adequately skilled, the dividend will be hard to realize.

A skills-gap study conducted by the National Skill Development Corporation in 2014 shows that 119 million new entrants to the workforce over the next seven years will need to be skilled. In addition, 307 million existing farm and non-farm sector workers will need to be skilled, upskilled or reskilled. This is a gigantic task: India's current annual skilling capacity, including training for the farm sector, is estimated at seven million. One of the biggest challenges of skill development in India is that 93 per cent of the workforce is in the informal sector. It is difficult to track those workers in the unorganized sector who receive informal training. On the other hand, the rate of job creation in the informal sector is estimated to be twice that in the formal sector.

A recent positive development has been the passage of crucial amendments to the Indian Apprentices Act of 1961. The new Act seeks to make apprenticeships more responsive to the needs of youth and industry. It views an apprenticeship as a classroom rather than a job, and shifts the regulatory burden from control (employers are no longer under the penal threat of jail for being non-compliant, which prevented most employers from offering apprenticeships) to incentives (employers may come together and provide training through a shared, joint facility). A new public–private partnership programme called the National Employability through Apprentice Program (NETAP) will assist the government in reaching out to 20,000 new employers and appointing more than 500,000 apprentices over the next three years. NETAP's ambition is to be the world's largest apprenticeship programme by 2020.

The 100 Smart Cities and Digital India programmes

As the experience of East Asia has shown, cities will be vital to overcome low-income traps and to avert middle-income ones. According to the McKinsey Global Institute (2010), India's urban population is expected to climb from some 340 million in 2008 to almost 590 million in 2030. This pace of urbanization is unprecedented: it took nearly 40 years for India's urban population to rise by 230 million by 2008; it will take only half that time to add the next 250 million. Five states – Tamil Nadu, Gujarat, Maharashtra, Karnataka and Punjab – will be more than 50 per cent urbanized. Nearly 70 cities will have populations of more than one million. Cities will be vital to realize India's demographic dividend. If this growth is handled well, cities could generate 70 per cent of the net new jobs created to 2030, produce about 70 per cent of Indian GDP (from 46 per cent in 1990), and drive a near fourfold increase in per capita incomes across the nation. Cities could potentially add 1 to 1.5 per cent to annual GDP growth.

In response to the urbanization challenge, the new government has launched the 100 Smart Cities programme, which will initially fund 20 cities chosen through a City Challenge Competition to the tune of some $16 million a year for five years. Cities will be chosen on the basis of their implementation and financing capacity. This will be expanded to 100 cities by 2017. The overall budget for 100 Smart Cities is about \$15.8 billion. There will be a special focus on adequate and clean water supply, sanitation and solid waste management, efficient transportation, affordable housing for the poor, power supply, robust IT connectivity, e-governance, safety and security of citizens, and health and education. States and private entities will need to fund the 100 Smart Cities programme with matching funds.

Simultaneously, the government plans to spend as much as \$1.2 billion in the next three to five years to provide internet connections to all citizens through an initiative called Digital India, which is designed to transform India into a digitally empowered society and a knowledge economy. Digital India will act as an umbrella to integrate and synchronize all digital initiatives, including the national broadband plan and the domestic manufacturing policy. Digital India's vision is to make available digital infrastructure as a utility to every citizen, provide digital governance and services on demand and empower citizens digitally. However, many questions remain about Digital India's vision being overly government-centric, rather than focusing on the wider potential of IT in India's economy and its implementation priorities (Singh, 2015).

Railways as an engine of growth

The new government proposed a massive \$138 billion, five-year public investment push on India's railway network in the 2015–16 Railway Budget announced in February 2015. It plans to invest roughly \$16 billion in 2015–16 – about two and a half times the investment in 2011–12. Previous railway budgets have been gravy trains, with many populist projects, such as new trains to favoured constituencies with little commercial viability. No new train was introduced in the 2015–16 Budget.

It has been known for decades that Indian railways require massive capacity expansion for both freight and passenger traffic (NCAER, 2001). The lack of investment has resulted in congestion, strained capacity, poor services and weak financial health for India's railways. India's fastest passenger trains are capable of doing 130 km/h, yet their average speed does not exceed 70 km/h. India's growth in revenue-earning freight traffic has actually been declining in recent years. India had some 62,000 rail kilometers in 1990 compared with China's 58,000 km. In 2010, India had 63,800 km and China had 90,000 km. Compared with India, China's railway system annually invests about 11 times as much in per capita terms.

The new government is hoping that the new public investment in railways – sensibly financed and well executed – will help it break out of the vicious cycle of chronic underinvestment leading to congestion and underutilization, poor service delivery, falling passenger and freight traffic, poor financials and low investment. If it does, the gains to the economy could be large. Indian railways are already the fourth-largest employer in the world, and even a modest gain in the average productivity of railway personnel would be very welcome.

Using fiscal resources for targeted public investment makes sense, particularly if it crowds in private investment. The Economic Survey 2014–15 shows that rail investments can have large pay-offs, can crowd in private investment and will not jeopardize India's public debt. The Economic Survey estimates that the backward linkages multiplier (based on rail demand from other sectors) is about 3.3 – increasing railway output by $1 would increase output in the economy by $3.30 – and the forward linkages multiplier (railways as an input) is 2.5, suggesting a large overall multiplier of more than five for railway investments.

These multipliers suggest that railway investment will assist in India escaping its low-income problems of poor infrastructure. Could it also help avert middle-income traps, spurring innovation and higher productivity? Possibly, yes. For example, railway investments could link with green and digital technologies and programmes such as Digital India. India's 8,000 railway stations cover almost the entire country and are linked by fiber or last-mile wireless. They offer a ready-made, countrywide digital platform, which if combined with enhanced bandwidth and free wireless access on platforms and structured approaches to learning, could transform stations (even in rural areas) and small and medium cities into incubators, and learning and skilling centres. Digital display signage could be an excellent vehicle for providing information and a railways technology portal could foster research for rail and other solutions, and help crowdsource innovations and ideas.

Ways out of India's problem of the politics of a large, poor country

Several recent developments hold the promise of being able to deal more effectively with the problem of patronage politics and the focus by politicians on consumption rather than on investment in human and physical capital and the creation of jobs and entrepreneurship opportunities for poor people.

Decentralization, the 14th Finance Commission and NITI Aayog

The 14th Finance Commission's recommendations for the sharing of the net tax revenue between the union and the states have broken dramatically from previous commissions, increasing the states' share substantially from 32 to 42 per cent. This will not only give states considerably more fiscal autonomy, but also, to avoid fiscal stress, it is more than likely that the central government will have to reduce its discretionary transfers tied to specific, centrally sponsored schemes in which states have little discretion. The institutional counterpart to this is the demise of the Planning Commission and its rebirth as the National Institution for Transforming India (NITI Aayog), with its emphasis on cooperative federalism.

Giving greater autonomy to the states will bring local politicians closer to the citizens they are supposed to serve, increasing their accountability. More block grants and untied resources in the hands of local politicians will remove the ability of distant national politicians and bureaucrats to use blunt, poorly targeted, one-size-fits-all transfers to garner votes.

Aadhaar, direct cash transfers and safety nets

India has had huge success with its biometric identification (ID) system, Aadhaar, now the world's largest such ID system. As of early September 2015, more than

910 million of India's population of 1.2 billion had been issued with an Aadhaar number. Another of the new government's plans is to have all households possess a bank account (more than 156 million new accounts had been opened by mid-May 2015). When a person's ID is connected with his or her bank account, Aadhaar will enable direct cash transfers to intended beneficiaries and a move away from in-kind or general price subsidies. The government is already successfully doing this for cooking gas for some 97.5 million households.

This new approach has the potential to change the politics of patronage. The estimated direct fiscal cost of the most prominent price subsidies offered by the central and state governments is 4.2 per cent of GDP. The commodities that are subsidized form a very long list, including rice, wheat, pulses, sugar, kerosene, cooking gas, naphtha, water, electricity, diesel, fertilizer, iron ore and railway transport. These subsidies are regressive, distort markets, lead to corruption and suffer from massive leakages (Government of India, 2015b).

The triangulation between Aadhaar, universal bank accounts and mobile phones and other delivery platforms is also making possible new ways of delivering social protection using the insurance route. These new forms of protecting the poor are likely to fundamentally alter the problem of political patronage that has been at the root of the political economy of subsidies.

The possibility of converting price subsidies and social protection payments into electronic transfer payments based on a person's unique ID for the first time offers India a way of rationalizing the politics of providing for and protecting the poor.

Conclusions

India became a middle-income country in 2007. In PPP terms, it became the third-largest economy after the United States and China in 2013. By 2028, it will have the world's largest population. It already has one of the world's youngest populations. During its last growth spurt in the mid-2000s, India's GDP managed to grow at an average of 9.5 per cent per year. That India remains a land of opportunities has never been lost on anyone.

Yet India is also a land of missed opportunities. Had India pushed ahead with the market-friendly reforms that it launched in 1991, rather than getting lost in coalition politics and corruption, things today might look different. Stretching one's imagination even further, had India built on its mixed public–private economy starting in the 1950s and 1960s, and allowed the free flow of entrepreneurship, technology, factor mobility and production, with some luck it might even have joined the famed Asian 'Tigers' to its East.

The world that India faces today is far more complex. It requires India to deal with the old problems of literacy, child malnutrition, water and sanitation, access to electricity, and one of the world's largest informal workforces, which India's early leaders thought they could easily solve within a decade or so of the country's independence. And it also requires Indian policymakers to think about policies and programmes that will allow Indian companies to compete with countries that are already at per capita incomes four times that of India. They must also think about how these workers and firms will earn, save and accumulate wealth that in 40 years will be able to pay for one of the world's largest populations of senior citizens. Indian policymakers will need to ensure that India gets rich before it gets old.

So it seems while India tries to escape from its low-income traps, it must also prepare to avert the middle-income ones that seem to catch countries unaware just as they emerge from their low-income status. Fortunately, India has the latecomer's advantage of knowing what works and what does not, and why. It also has the ability to offer returns on investment in physical and human capital that are hard to come by elsewhere, and it has the human talent and entrepreneurship to adapt all this knowledge to its own needs. What is missing is a deeper appreciation that time is not on India's side, and that India must operate at both ends of the development effort, and not become so mired in the problems of today as to forget those of tomorrow.

The Modi government in many ways understands this double-sided problem better than governments before it. But, like its predecessors, it also runs the risk of becoming submerged in the pressing issues that confront it every day. What is needed is a small but empowered group of policymakers, researchers and, perhaps, even some younger politicians (who have a stake in the future) located at the apex of government who are charged with doing nothing but thinking about the future and how what the government and the economy are doing today will shape that future. This group's job would be to continuously vet the time consistency of today's policymaking and implementation, pointing out actions today – however expedient they may sound – that will hinder the future. Just as importantly, their job would be to point out ideas and programmes that no one is even thinking of, but should be.

There are many examples of such groups worldwide. In the end, they are all concerned about the future productivity of the country. India is at a juncture in time and the quest for its destiny when such a group might make a difference to whether the country keeps its 'tryst with destiny' that its founding fathers had felt was so reachable, and yet has remained so elusive.

Notes

1   Director-General, National Council of Applied Economic Research (NCAER): sshah@ncaer.org; and Senior Research Counselor, NCAER: rchadha@ncaer.org. Shah is grateful for comments at an April 2015 Roundtable organized by the East Asia Bureau of Economic Research at The Australian National University, where he first discussed these ideas (Shah, 2015). At NCAER, our thanks go to Akansha Dubey and Premila Nazareth for their valuable inputs. Research assistance from Jahnavi Prabhakar, Roopali Aggarwal and Praveen Sachdeva is gratefully acknowledged.

2   Based on the World Bank Atlas method, the World Development Indicators (World Bank, 2015) define low income as 2013 GNI per capita of $1,045 or below; middle income as between $1,045 and $12,746; and high income as $12,746 or more. Lower and upper middle-income economies are separated at a 2013 GNI per capita of $4,124.

3   Units registered under the Factories Act (and a Tobacco Workers' Act) employing 10 or more workers and using power, or 20 or more workers but not using power. Registered units account for about two-thirds of the share of manufacturing in GDP.
4   Garrett (2004), one of the first to comment on slow growth in middle-income countries, also noted that such countries (referring to those in Latin America and Eastern Europe) may find it difficult to escape this trap because '[t]he transition to democracy has not itself proved the necessary catalyst. Instead, it has raised popular expectations that politicians find increasingly difficult to satisfy.'

References

Agenor, P and Canuto, O 2012. *Middle-income growth traps*. Policy Research Working Paper No. 6210. Washington, DC: The World Bank.

Aghion, P, Burgess, R, Redding, SJ and Zilibotti, F 2008. The unequal effects of liberalization: Evidence from dismantling the license Raj in India. *American Economic Review*, 98(4), 1397–412.

Aiyar, S, Duval, R, Puy, D, Wu, Y and Zhang, L 2013. *Growth slowdowns and the middle-income trap*. IMF Working Paper No. 13/71. Washington, DC: International Monetary Fund.

Amirapu, A and Subramanian, A 2015. Manufacturing or services? An Indian illustration of a development dilemma. CGD Working Paper No. 409. Washington, DC: Center for Global Development. Available online at: www.cgdev.org/publication/manufacturing-or-services-indian-illustration-developmentdilemma-working-paper-409.

Battelle and R&D Magazine 2013. *2014 R&D Magazine/Battelle Global R&D Funding Forecast*. December 2013. Available online at: www.rdmag.com/sites/rdmag.com/files/gff-2014–5_7%20875x10_0.pdf (accessed 31 August 2015).

Besley, T and Burgess, R 2004. Can regulation hinder economic performance? Evidence from India. *Quarterly Journal of Economics*, 119(1), 91–134.

Booz & Company/PwC 2012. *Empowering the Third Billion: Women and the World of Work in 2012*. New York: Strategy&. Available online at: www.strategyand.pwc.com/global/home/what-we-think/reports-white-papers/article-display/empowering-third-billion-women-world (accessed 31 July 2015).

Commission on Intellectual Property Rights (CIPR) 2002. *Integrating Intellectual Property Rights and Development Policy*. London: Commission on Intellectual Property Rights. Available online at: www.iprcommission.org/papers/pdfs/final_report/CIPRfullfinal.pdf (accessed 31 July 2015).

Das, S, Chandra, SJ, Kochhar, K and Kumar N 2015. *Women workers in India: Why so few among so many?* IMF Working Papers No. 15/55. Washington, DC: International Monetary Fund.

Duflo, E 2012. Women, empowerment and economic development. *Journal of Economic Literature*, 50(4), 1051–79.

Eichengreen, B, Park, D and Shin, K 2012. When fast-growing economies slow down: International evidence and implications for China. *Asian Economic Papers*, 11(1), 42–87.

Eichengreen, B, Park, D and Shin, K 2013. *Growth slowdown redux: New evidence on the middle-income trap*. NBER Working Paper No. 18673. Cambridge, MA: National Bureau of Economic Research.

Felipe, J, Abdon, A and Kumar, U 2012. *Tracking the middle-income trap: What is it, who is in it, and why?* Working Paper No. 715. New York: Levy Economics Institute of Bard College.

Garrett, G 2004. Globalization's missing middle. *Foreign Affairs*, 83(6), 84–96. Available online at: http://yaleglobal.yale.edu/content/globalizations-missing-middle (accessed 31 July 2015).

Gill, I and Kharas, H 2007. *An East Asian Renaissance: Ideas for Economic Growth*. Washington, DC: The World Bank.

Gill, I and Kharas, H 2015. The middle income trap turns ten. Paper prepared for the 37th PAFTAD Conference, Institute of South East Asian Studies, Singapore, 3–5 June.

Goldin, C 1995. The U-shaped female labor force function in economic development and economic history. In TP Schultz (ed.), *Investment in Women's Human Capital and Economic Development*. Chicago: University of Chicago Press, 61–90.

Government of India 2013. *National Science and Technology Management Information System*. September 2013. New Delhi: Ministry of Science and Technology, Government of India. Available online at: www.nstmis-dst.org/SnT-Indicators2011–12.aspx.

Government of India 2014. *National IPR Policy*. New Delhi: IPR Think Tank, Ministry of Industrial Policy and Promotion, Government of India.

Government of India 2015a. *Draft National Policy for Skill Development and Entrepreneurship 2015*. New Delhi: Ministry of Skill Development and Entrepreneurship, Government of India.

Government of India 2015b. *Economic Survey 2014–15*. New Delhi: Ministry of Finance, Government of India.

Gupta, P, Hasan, R and Kumar, U 2009. Big reforms but small payoffs: Explaining the weak record of growth in Indian manufacturing. *India Policy Forum*, 5, 59–123.

Hasan, R and Jandoc, KRL 2012. *Labor regulations and firm size distribution in Indian manufacturing*. ISERP Working Paper No. 2012–3. New York: School of International and Public Affairs, Columbia University.

Hasan, R, Mitra, D and Ramaswamy, KV 2007. Trade reforms, labor regulations, and labor-demand elasticities: Empirical evidence from India. *Review of Economics and Statistics*, 89 (3), 466–81.

Klasen, S and Pieters, J 2013. *What explains the stagnation of female labor force participation in urban India?* IZA Discussion Paper No. 7597. Bonn: Institute for the Study of Labor. Available online at: http://ftp.iza.org/dp7597.pdf (accessed 31 July 2015).

Kochar, K, Kumar, U, Rajan, R, Subramanian, A and Tokatlidis, I 2006. *India's pattern of development: What happened, what follows?* IMF Working Paper No. 6/22. Washington, DC: International Monetary Fund.

McKinsey Global Institute 2010. *India's Urban Awakening: Building Inclusive Cities, Sustaining Economic Growth*. Sydney: McKinsey & Company.

The Maddison Project 2010. *Maddison Project Data*. Groningen: University of Groningen. Available online at: www.ggdc.net/maddison/maddison-project/home.htm (accessed 31 July 2015).

Mammen, K and Paxson, C 2000. Women's work and economic development. *Journal of Economic Perspectives*, 14(4), 141–64.

National Council of Applied Economic Research (NCAER) 2001. *Indian Railways Report 2001: Policy Imperatives for Reinvention and Growth*. New Delhi: National Council of Applied Economic Research for the Expert Group on Indian Railways.

Organization for Economic Cooperation and Development (OECD) 2013. *Economic Outlook for Southeast Asia, China and India 2014: Beyond the Middle-Income Trap*. Paris: OECD Publishing.

Panagariya, A 2008. *India: The Emerging Giant*. Oxford: Oxford University Press.

Panagariya, A 2014. *A Reform Agenda for India's New Government, The Second NCAER C.D. Deshmukh Memorial Lecture, February 2014.* New Delhi: National Council of Applied Economic Research. Available online at: www.ncaer.org/event_details. php?EID=48.

Pritchett, L and Summers, LH 2014. *Asiaphoria meets regression to the mean.* NBER Working Paper No. 20573. Cambridge, MA: National Bureau of Economic Research.

PRS Legislative Research 2015. *All about the Land Acquisition Debate.* New Delhi: PRS Legislative Research. Available online at: www.prsindia.org/pages/land-acquisition-debate-139/ (accessed 31 July 2015).

Rajan, R 2014. *Make in India,* largely for India. Talk at the Bharat Ram Memorial Lecture, New Delhi, 2 December. Available online at: www.rbi.org.in/scripts/BS_SpeechesView. aspx?Id=930 (accessed 15 August 2015).

Reserve Bank of India 2014. *Estimates of Productivity Growth for the Indian Economy.* New Delhi: Reserve Bank of India. Available online at: https://rbi.org.in/Scripts/ PublicationReportDetails.aspx?ID=785#F (accessed 15 August 2015).

Rodrik, D 2013. Unconditional convergence in manufacturing. *Quarterly Journal of Economics,* 128(1), 165–204.

Shah, S 2015. Prosperity in Asia: The intergenerational dimension. Talk at EABER Public Forum, The Australian National University, Canberra, 17 April. Available online at: www.eaber.org/node/24815 (accessed 15 August 2015).

Singh, N 2015. Achieving Digital India. *Financial Express,* 27 August.

Spence, M 2011. *The Next Convergence: The Future of Economic Growth in a Multispeed World.* New York: Farrar, Straus & Giroux.

Subramanian, A 2008. *India's Turn: Understanding the Economic Transformation.* Oxford: Oxford University Press.

Thambisetty, S 2014. The 12 gifts of a national intellectual property policy. [Blog]. *India at LSE,* 24 December. Available online at: http://blogs.lse.ac.uk/indiaatlse/2014/12/24/ the-twelve-gifts-of-a-national-intellectual-property-policy/ (accessed 27 May 2015).

World Bank 2012. *World Development Report 2012. Gender Equality and Development.* Washington, DC: The World Bank.

World Bank 2015. *World Development Indicators.* Washington, DC: The World Bank. Available online at: http://data.worldbank.org/data-catalog/world-development-indicators.

World Intellectual Property Organization (WIPO) 2015. *Statistical Country Profiles, India.* March. Geneva: World Intellectual Property Organization.

Zahidi, S and Ibarra, H 2010. *The Corporate Gender Gap Report 2010.* Geneva: World Economic Forum. Available online at: www3.weforum.org/docs/WEF_GenderGap_ CorporateReport_2010.pdf.

Part IV
Determinants of growth

7 Institutional quality and growth traps

David Dollar[1]

> China will stay firm in its commitment to reform and opening-up. It will focus on structural reform, encourage mass entrepreneurship and innovation, increase supply of public goods and services . . . As long as we succeed in doing so, the Chinese economy will successfully overcome the 'middle-income trap' and move ahead along the path of sustainable and sound development.
>
> — Premier Li Keqiang, Davos Speech 2015

Introduction

The notion of a 'middle-income trap' has entered the lexicon of development. Leaders of countries that have grown well, such as China's Premier, Li Keqiang, worry that as they reach middle-income status there will be a sharp slowdown in the growth rate. What is generally meant by the middle-income trap is the notion that, after the easy sources of growth have been exploited (rural–urban migration, capital accumulation, export expansion from a low base), a country will fail to develop new sources of growth such as technological innovation and product differentiation, which are crucial for moving to high-income status (Gill and Kharas, in this volume). More generally, there is a risk for economies at every level of development that they will fall into a low-growth equilibrium. In this chapter, I use data on growth rates over the decades of the 1990s and 2000s to examine the phenomenon of low-growth traps, and in particular the relationship between growth and institutional quality. An appealing idea is that high-quality economic and political institutions will enable countries to adjust policies to changing circumstances and to maintain relatively high growth. One of the strongest empirical regularities about growth is 'convergence' – the tendency for economies to grow faster at low levels of development. Hence, 'relatively high growth' means doing well for one's income level, slowing gradually as per capita income rises, and avoiding large decelerations in the growth rate.

The next section takes an initial look at the data and highlights several stylized facts about growth and institutions in the 1990s and 2000s. Over these two decades, the group of countries that slowed significantly comprised high-income ones. Leaving aside high-income economies, developing economies saw an acceleration between the 1990s and the 2000s of about 3 percentage points, both for low-income and for middle-income economies. Hence there was no special tendency in this period for countries to slow in middle income. Nevertheless, there are always countries growing well and others doing poorly. One of the best predictors of which countries grew well over the whole 20-year period and which did not was the quality of economic institutions at the beginning of the period. I capture economic institutions by combing indices that measure property rights and the rule of law, anti-corruption efforts and the effectiveness of government. Another stylized fact is that the resulting measure of economic institutions is highly persistent, with little change over the period. One might think, then, that growth rates are persistent, but paradoxically they are not: growth rates in the 2000s have a slight, insignificant correlation with growth rates in the 1990s.

The next section looks in more detail at institutional quality relative to the level of development. Economic institutions tend to improve with per capita GDP. Countries that have good institutions relative to their income level grow faster, especially at low income. The fact that institutional quality measures are highly persistent, however, means that in most cases there is only slow progress, if any, in improving economic institutions. As countries grow successfully, their per capita GDP rises quickly, and a country that has good institutions at one level of development soon finds that it has poor ones at a higher level. Not constantly improving institutions is a kind of trap that countries can fall into at any income level.

The next section considers the relationship between political institutions and economic institutions. For the poorer half of countries in the world, there is little relationship between economic institutions and Freedom House's Civil Liberties Index. Authoritarian countries such as China and Vietnam have been able to develop good institutions for their income level and have grown well for some decades. For the richer half of countries in the world, however, there is a fairly tight link between political openness and good economic institutions. Authoritarian countries evidence very sharply diminishing marginal returns, suggesting that these countries can start an accumulation-driven growth process that takes them from low to middle income, but they lack the innovation capacity to continue growth from middle to high income. Thus, one kind of trap is not reforming political institutions as development proceeds. The last section of this chapter briefly concludes.

Stylized facts (and paradoxes) about institutions and growth in the 1990s and 2000s

In this section, I use data on the growth rates of 146 countries to illustrate some stylized facts about institutions and growth over the past two decades, some of which appear paradoxical. The two decades are interesting in that the 1990s was a difficult era for emerging economies, with crises in East Asia, Russia and Latin America. The 2000s, on the other hand, witnessed the Global Financial Crisis (GFC). Despite its name, the GFC was particularly hard on developed economies, whereas China and many other developing economies grew well throughout the decade. So, one can anticipate before going to the data that developing economies in general experienced growth accelerations between the 1990s and 2000s, whereas developed countries saw the opposite. The growth rates that I use are real per capita GDP growth rates from each country's national accounts, as reported in the Penn World Tables Version 8 (Feenstra *et al.*, 2013).

Figure 7.1 plots the change in average growth rate between the 1990s and the 2000s against the (log) per capita GDP in 2000. So, this figure is addressing whether slowdowns or accelerations were concentrated at any particular level of income in the year 2000. As anticipated, the growth rates of virtually all the rich countries slowed. Growth decelerations of at least 2 percentage points were experienced by Bahrain, Denmark, Ireland, Kuwait, Norway, Portugal, Qatar and South Korea. If we take out the richest one-third of countries (the top 48, to be exact), we are left with Figure 7.2. For these 98 developing countries, the average growth rate accelerated 2.9 percentage points in the 2000s, with no discernible difference between low-income and middle-income countries. The middle-income countries have more dispersion: some significant slowdowns and some impressive accelerations. Liberia, Bosnia/Herzegovina, Equatorial Guinea and Iraq experienced decelerations of at least 2 percentage points. In this period, there was no strong tendency for middle-income countries to slow.[2] Hence, the first stylized fact about these recent decades is that the growth rate of rich countries slowed, whereas growth rates both of low-income and of middle-income developing countries accelerated.

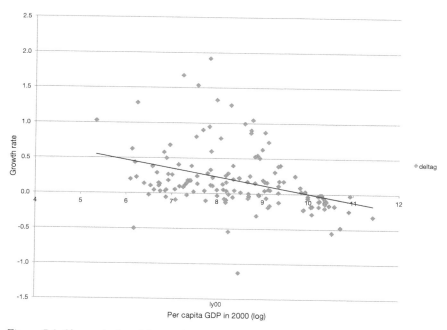

Figure 7.1 Change in decadal growth versus GDP per capita, 2000

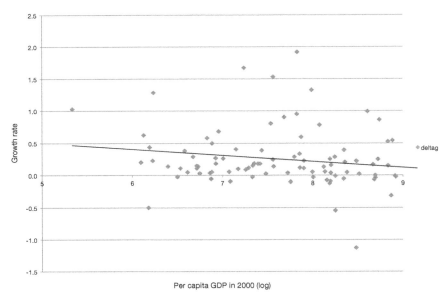

Figure 7.2 Change in decadal growth versus GDP per capita (without the rich countries)

The second stylized fact concerns the relationship between economic institutions and growth over the whole 20-year period. A popular and intuitive idea in the literature is that economic institutions are important determinants of economic growth (Acemoglu *et al.*, 2001; Knack and Keefer, 1997). Empirically, there are a number of options for measuring economic institutions. I choose to rely on three different indicators from the Worldwide Governance Indicators.

- **The Rule of Law Index** 'captures perceptions of the extent to which agents have confidence in and abide by the rules of society, and in particular the quality of contract enforcement, property rights, the police, and the courts, as well as the likelihood of crime and violence' (World Bank, 2015).
- **Control of corruption** 'captures perceptions of the extent to which public power is exercised for private gain, including both petty and grand forms of corruption, as well as "capture" of the state by elites and private interests' (World Bank, 2015).
- **Government effectiveness** 'captures perceptions of the quality of public services, the quality of the civil service and the degree of its independence from political pressures, the quality of policy formulation and implementation, and the credibility of the government's commitment to such policies' (World Bank, 2015).

The three measures capture different aspects of a good institutional environment for effective public action and for private market activity. Because the three are fairly highly correlated, there is little hope of separately identifying the impact of each. Therefore, I create a single index of 'Institutional Quality' by taking a simple average of the three, each of which is an index with a mean of zero and standard deviation of 1.0. Unfortunately, the earliest year of availability is only 1996, but this is nevertheless fairly close to the beginning of our period. The Institutional Quality Index in 1996 is highly correlated with growth rates over the 20-year period of 1990–2010. Figure 7.3, for example, shows a partial scatter plot of growth and institutional quality from a regression of the growth rate on (log) initial per capita GDP, Institutional Quality 1996 and natural resource rents as a share of GDP (Appendix 7.1). There is a large literature showing that the results of growth regressions are sensitive to the variables included and create scepticism about the prospect of carefully identifying the effect of one specific factor, such as economic institutions (Doppelhofer *et al.*, 2000; Levine and Renelt, 1992). The point here is that economic institutions are a fairly robust predictor of future economic growth, even if we cannot identify the specific quantitative effect.

The third stylized fact is that, not surprisingly, economic institutions are quite persistent. Such persistence is what one would expect given that institutions by definition are deep-seated features of constitutions, laws and norms. The cross-country correlation of the Institutional Quality Index 1996 and the index in 2010 is 0.92 (as illustrated in Figure 7.4).

Given that economic institutions are important for growth and are highly persistent, one would expect growth rates from decade to decade to be persistent as well. However, the paradoxical stylized fact is that growth rates from one decade to the next are in fact uncorrelated (Figure 7.5). This is the point of a recent paper

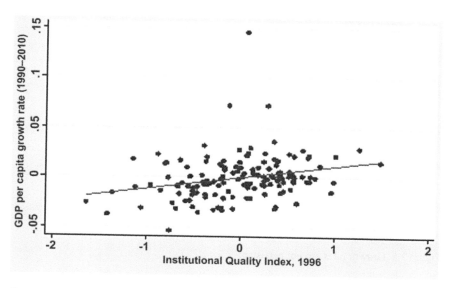

Figure 7.3 Countries with better institutional quality grow faster

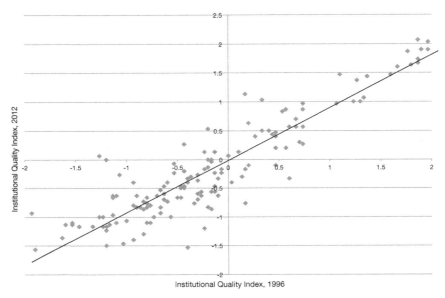

Figure 7.4 Institutional quality is highly persistent

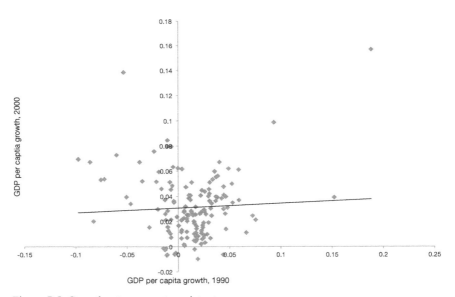

Figure 7.5 Growth rates are not persistent

by Pritchett and Summers (2013), which shows that one of the most powerful tendencies in growth dynamics is regression to the mean.

The conclusion from a first look at the data for 1990–2010 is that there is no particular tendency for middle-income countries to experience growth slowdowns. It happened that rich country growth rates slowed a lot in the 2000s, but that is not necessarily a general pattern that will always be repeated. What I take away from the data is that growth slowdowns and accelerations are possible at every level of development. How do we understand these slowdowns and accelerations? How can economic institutions play a role in the explanation, given that they tend to be persistent, whereas growth rates are not?

Economic institutions and level of development

One way to resolve the paradox of the persistence of institutions and non-persistence of growth rates is to focus on the quality of institutions relative to the level of development. In general, measures such as the Institutional Quality Index rise with per capita GDP, although in fact the fit is not that tight and there is a lot of dispersion (Figure 7.6). Most developing countries have below average institutional quality, but, as noted, there is large dispersion. Figure 7.6 illustrates institutional quality for 1996 (the first year available) and log per capita GDP in 1990. Ten Asian economies are identified; they fall into three groups. Of these countries, China, India and Vietnam were the poorest in 1990. By 1996 all three were well into their economic reform programmes. Compared with the planned-economy era, China and Vietnam had made initial steps to improve private property rights through the de-collectivization of agriculture, the introduction of foreign investment laws to partially open to foreign direct investment (FDI), and the opening of some sectors to a domestic private sector (on China's early reform, see Eckaus, 1997; and on Vietnam's, see Dollar and Ljunggren, 1997). China and Vietnam were each measured to be about half a standard deviation below the mean on the Institutional Quality 1996 Index. They did not have especially good economic institutions; however, they were far above the regression line, indicating that they had good institutions for their level of development. India was measured to be slightly better than China.

Think of these economies competing with other low-income countries in the early 1990s to attract FDI, generate exports and begin the growth process. They were very low-wage economies, befitting their low-income status. Among the countries with which they were competing, they proved to be attractive production locations and they have grown well in the past two decades.

A second group of Asian countries consists of Indonesia, the Philippines, Thailand and Malaysia. Of all the Asian countries identified, Indonesia had the weakest institutions in 1996. The Philippines and Thailand were well above the regression line in Figure 7.6, but as noted below, the quality of their institutions then deteriorated over the subsequent period. Malaysia, frankly, is something of a mystery. Of these countries, Indonesia, Thailand and Malaysia had growth through 1990–2010 that was above the world average of 2.2 per cent but was

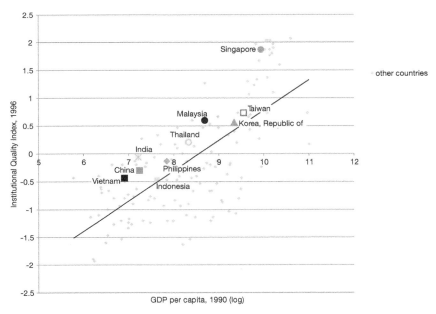

Figure 7.6 Institutional quality relative to development level is key

disappointing for East Asia. The Philippines, with growth of 1.7 per cent, did not reach the world average.

Figure 7.6 also identifies three higher-income Asian economies: South Korea, Taiwan and Singapore. Unfortunately, we do not have comparable data from an earlier period, but other information suggests that these Asian 'Tiger' economies were steadily improving their economic institutions, starting with initial reforms in the 1960s (Sakong and Koh, 2010; Tsiang, 1984). By 1996, South Korea and Taiwan were measured to have pretty good economic institutions – not quite at developed country levels, but again, above the regression line: good for their level of development. Singapore stands out as having among the best institutions in the whole data set: about 2 standard deviations above the mean. The three all grew well during the past 20 years, given that they were already at or near high income: South Korea at 4.8 per cent, Taiwan at 4.4 per cent and Singapore at 3.7 per cent. All of them grew faster than Indonesia, Thailand, the Philippines and Malaysia, even though, given their higher income, they would have been expected to grow more slowly because of convergence.

Economies that have good economic institutions for their level of development tend to grow faster in subsequent periods. A simple way to illustrate this is to separate the observations above the regression line in Figure 7.7, and those below; for each group, separately trace the quadratic relationship between growth (1990–2010) and initial per capita GDP (Figure 7.7).[3] Countries with relatively good economic institutions tend to grow faster, and the difference is particularly

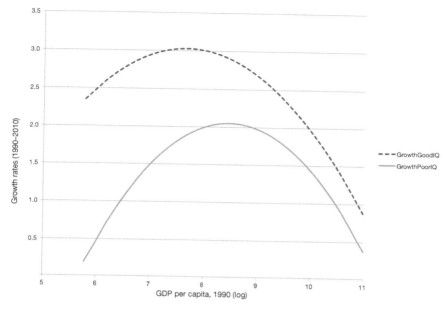

Figure 7.7 Growth trajectories for good and poor institutional quality

acute at low levels of development. A poor country that can manage to put reasonably good institutions in place has all of the convergence advantages: it can attract foreign investment, borrow technology from abroad and start the catch-up process. These economies, on average, grew at about 3 per cent at both low and middle income, whereas wealthy economies grew at about 1 per cent. Note that the evidence for convergence among economies with poor institutions is weaker. At low income, these economies do not grow any faster than developed ones; in middle income, they tend to grow somewhat faster, peaking at a growth rate of about 2 per cent.

Thinking about institutions relative to the level of development naturally leads to the question, are institutions keeping up? Is there regular institutional improvement as the economy develops? We know the general answer: institutions are persistent so, no, in most cases, there is not steady institutional improvement. Figure 7.8 shows the Institutional Quality Index and per capita GDP at the end of the 20-year period, 2010. For China, India and Vietnam, the institutional quality measure has barely changed from 1996; all three countries experienced stalls in their economic reform programmes starting in the early 2000s (Dollar, 2004; Naughton, 2014). But these countries' per capita GDPs have increased substantially because of their successful growth. This is especially true for China – growing at about 10 per cent per capita in both the 1990s and the 2000s. By 2010, China's institutional quality measure is well below the regression line; China now has poor economic institutions for its level of development. Vietnam is right on the

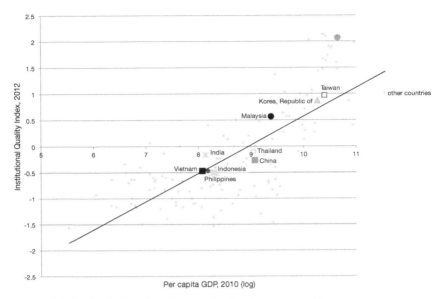

Figure 7.8 Are institutions keeping up with development level?

regression line; it has given up its previous advantage. India remains somewhat above the line and continues to grow well, but its institutions have not improved, so it will run into the same problem unless it can accelerate reform. Indonesia, the Philippines and Thailand have all fallen below the line, indicating a general problem of East Asian economies not keeping up with institutional reform.

Referring to Figure 7.7, imagine a developing economy shifting from the upper line to the lower line: it would experience a significant slowdown as its institutional quality lagged. As per capita GDP and wages rise, such an economy is competing with a new, higher-quality group of peers. Without continual institutional improvements, there will be a tendency for the growth rate to slow sharply. It is too early to be sure, but it appears that China and Vietnam have both been experiencing growth slowdowns in recent years that are consistent with this story.

Figure 7.8 also again identifies South Korea, Taiwan and Singapore. Their per capita incomes have risen, but the measure of institutional quality has also improved – from about 0.5 per cent in 1996 to 1 per cent in 2010 for South Korea and Taiwan, and from below 2 per cent to above 2 per cent for Singapore. Of the economies highlighted, these three had the best economic institutions in 1996 and yet they also had the biggest absolute increases in the Institutional Quality Index between 1996 and 2010 – although presumably increases are harder as one gets closer to the frontier.

To summarize among the Asian economies: the three poorest at the beginning of the period grew well through 2010, but their institutional quality has stagnated, raising questions about their future growth. Already China and Vietnam appear to be slowing quite sharply. The group in the middle either did not have relatively good institutions to begin with (Indonesia) or witnessed the largest declines in quality over the period (the Philippines and Thailand). Malaysia, admittedly, is a puzzle. The group as a whole grew okay, but not great. The biggest sustained improvement in economic institutions was achieved by South Korea, Taiwan and Singapore, and all have grown well among their cohort and reached high-income status.

Political and economic institutions

What about the relationship between political institutions and economic institutions? Acemoglu and Robinson's book *Why Nations Fail* (2012a) emphasizes the links from political institutions to economic institutions to outcomes. In their model, countries with democratic political institutions tend to develop inclusive economic institutions, which in turn leads to innovation and productivity growth and hence sustained improvements in living standards. An alternative view these days is the 'Beijing consensus' model: democratic countries seem incapable of making the difficult decisions and investments needed to sustain prosperity, whereas an authoritarian 'developmental' state is capable of operating more efficiently.[4] Huntington (1968) offers something of an intermediate argument: that premature increases in political participation – including early elections – could destabilize fragile political systems. This laid the groundwork for a development strategy that came to be called the 'authoritarian transition', whereby a modernizing dictatorship provides political order, rule of law and the conditions for successful economic and social development. Once these building blocks were in place, other aspects of modernity, such as democracy and civic participation, could be added. What does the evidence from the past 20 years suggest about this debate?

To measure political institutions, I use Freedom House's Civil Liberties Index. Freedom House also has a Political Rights Index, which focuses on democratic political institutions. I prefer the Civil Liberties Index, which measures aspects such as freedom of speech, the media, assembly and association. In practice, the two series are highly correlated and will not produce different empirical results. I prefer the Civil Liberties measure because I think of it as more closely connected to the environment for innovation and competition – that is, the economic institutions.

The Civil Liberties Index is available for a large group of countries starting in 1994. It ranges from 1 = completely free to 7 = completely unfree. Figure 7.9, which is based on the poorer half of countries in 1990, plots Institutional Quality 1996 against Civil Liberties 1994. Among the poorer half of countries in the world, there is little correlation between rule of law and political institutions (correlation coefficient = –0.33). I have already highlighted that authoritarian countries such as China and Vietnam had relatively good economic institutions among poor countries in 1996 (they are among the observations in the upper-right quadrant). Among the richer half of countries, on the other hand, there is fairly high correlation

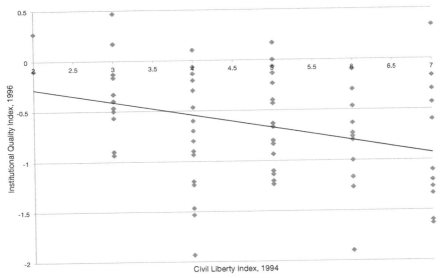

Figure 7.9 Correlation between rule of law and civil liberties (poor countries)

(= –0.67) between political freedom and institutional quality (Figure 7.10). It is striking that there is only one country rated 5, 6 or 7 on the civil liberties scale (that is, lacking freedoms) that was above 1.0 on the Institutional Quality Index: Singapore. In 1994, Freedom House rated Singapore 5 on civil liberties. As previously noted, it had among the best economic institutions in the world.

Do authoritarian or democratic countries tend to grow faster? I answer this question by focusing on political institutions relative to the level of development. Figure 7.11 shows the civil liberties measure in 1994 plotted against (log) per capita GDP in 1990. Observations below (above) the regression line are countries with relatively democratic (authoritarian) political institutions for their level of development. Then I look at the growth performance over the next 20 years for the two groups separately. It turns out that, in the period 1990–2010, at low levels of per capita income, authoritarian countries tended to grow faster than democratic ones, but the relationship switches at a per capita GDP of about $8,000 (Figure 7.12).[5] In 1990, $8,000 in purchasing power parity (PPP) terms was about 25 per cent of US per capita GDP. Given the important role of catch-up in growth at low-income levels, it may make more sense to understand the result as authoritarian economies grow well up to about the point where they reach 25 per cent of US productivity.

This is an interesting and plausible story. At low levels of per capita GDP, authoritarian governments can be effective. The economic priority at this stage is to establish basic law and order and an environment in which private investment, including foreign investment, can begin to operate. This is a catch-up stage in which

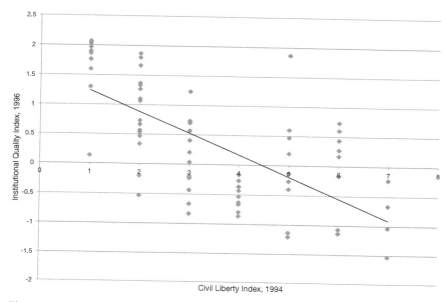

Figure 7.10 Correlation between rule of law and civil liberties (richer countries)

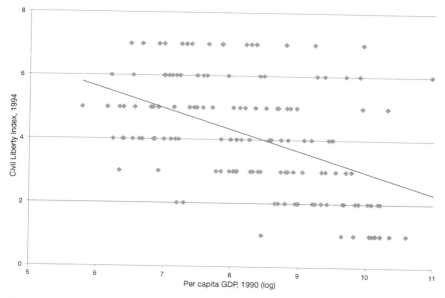

Figure 7.11 Civil liberties 1994 and per capita GDP 1990

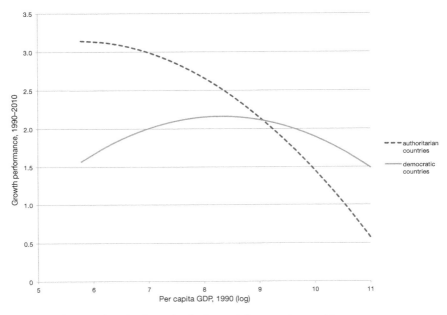

Figure 7.12 Growth paths for authoritarian and democratic countries

innovation is not yet that relevant. The growth path for authoritarian countries (the dotted line in Figure 7.12), however, suggests that there are sharply diminishing marginal returns. Authoritarian countries tend to rely on capital accumulation rather than innovation and productivity growth, so as diminishing returns set in, the growth rate drops sharply.[6] Past a per capita GDP level corresponding to about 25 per cent of US productivity, countries with good civil liberties tend to grow faster. This is consistent with the argument that such freedoms are necessary for an advanced, competitive economy in which innovation and productivity growth are able to offset diminishing returns to some extent so that countries can maintain a solid growth rate.

It is interesting that the 10 Asian economies highlighted in the previous section fit this pattern surprisingly well. Based on the civil liberties measure in 1994, China, Indonesia, Malaysia, Thailand, Singapore and Vietnam fall into the authoritarian group. Of these, China, Indonesia and Vietnam are in the poorer half of the data set and their average growth over the 20–year period was 6.4 per cent per year. Of the democratic countries, India and the Philippines were among the poorer half of countries: their average growth rate was 3.3 per cent – about half the rate of the authoritarian countries. Among the richer half of countries, however, the authoritarians (Malaysia, Singapore and Thailand) grew at 3.6 per cent, while democratic South Korea and Taiwan averaged 4.6 per cent growth. These groups thus evidence the sharply diminishing returns among authoritarian countries compared with smaller (or in this case, non-existent) diminishing returns among the democracies.[7]

These growth patterns suggest an optimal political evolution in which a country has relatively authoritarian institutions up to middle income, and then makes a democratic transition when the country reaches about 25 per cent of US productivity. Curiously, this is roughly the pattern followed by South Korea and Taiwan, two of the most economically successful developing economies. Figure 7.13 shows in red the average civil liberties measure for South Korea and Taiwan as their per capita incomes increased. They were measured to be authoritarian (index = 6) through the 1970s. Both countries had improved to 4 by 1987, at which point Taiwan was at 40 per cent of US per capita GDP and South Korea was at 31 per cent. After that their ratings continued to improve until they reached completely free status.

Figure 7.13 also includes Vietnam, a country that was rated to be authoritarian (index = 7) at the beginning of its economic reform. So far, Vietnam seems to be following in the footsteps of South Korea and Taiwan: it has liberalized somewhat in terms of political freedom and is now rated at 5 – slightly better than South Korea or Taiwan at the same stage of development. But Vietnam is now entering the development phase where this line of thinking implies that it needs further political liberalization over the next one to two decades if it is to continue to grow well. Greater freedom will be necessary to strengthen property rights and the rule of law and to improve government effectiveness so as to create an environment for innovation and productivity growth.

China, it should be noted, is not following the path of political liberalization as it transits through middle income. The civil liberties measure for China has remained at 6 for a long time, while its per capita GDP in PPP terms rose to

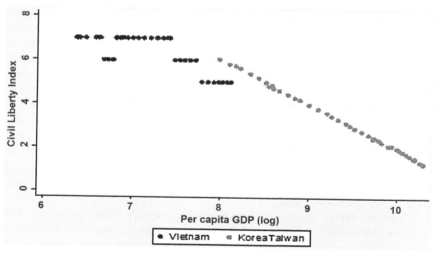

Figure 7.13 Correlation between civil liberties and GDP per capita (log scale)

22 per cent of the US level by 2011 (the most recent year in the Penn World Tables) and continued to rise further in subsequent years. The new leadership of Xi Jinping has made it clear that it wants to pursue economic reform without political reform.[8] Not only has there not been political reform, but also most observers feel that there has been recent backsliding in terms of freedom of ideas and debate. The recent historical evidence is that this path is likely to lead to sharply diminishing marginal returns to capital and a slowdown in growth. That appears to be happening: China's growth rate has slowed in a short time from above 11 per cent to about 7 per cent.

Acemoglu and Robinson (2012b) discussed how their findings applied to China:

> Our research on national economies throughout world history shows that long-term economic growth, while indeed based on technological innovation, only sustains itself in the presence of democratic political institutions that provide people with incentives to innovate. China may continue to grow in the near term, but the limited rights it affords its citizens places major restrictions on the country's longer-term possibilities for prosperity.
>
> The country still lacks an independent judiciary and an independent media. Entrepreneurs have been jailed for dubious reasons – not coincidentally when they went against businesses with stronger political backing. Many key economic decisions are still made by party elites who can change the CEOs of its largest companies on a whim.
>
> There will be limits on how much innovation such a system can generate, even if China keeps growing this decade. For all its changes, China still has what we term 'extractive' political institutions, those that direct resources away from the people and toward the state and a small number of its elites . . . By their nature, extractive states are against the kind of innovation that leads to widespread prosperity: this kind of change threatens the hold on political and economic power that elites in such states fight to maintain.

Perhaps China can avoid this pattern of authoritarian countries slowing sharply in middle income. However, until now no authoritarian country has reached 35 per cent of US PPP per capita GDP (Figure 7.14). We have omitted the oil states from Figure 7.14 because they are not really high-productivity economies; they just happen to sit on vast amounts of oil per capita. None of the countries rated 5, 6 or 7 on the Civil Liberties Index in 2011 had reached 35 per cent of US productivity. Singapore is something of an exception; by 2011 it was rated 4 and had reached US per capita income. One should be careful not to turn historical patterns into immutable economic laws. It is possible that China will be able to create an innovative society despite restrictions on the Internet and media, and what is taught in schools. But the historical evidence and China's recent economic performance are not encouraging.

A final important question is how countries improve their institutions. For economic institutions, there is a technocratic answer to this question. The things measured by the Institutional Quality Index used in this chapter would be improved by policies such as judicial reform and independence, systemic anti-corruption

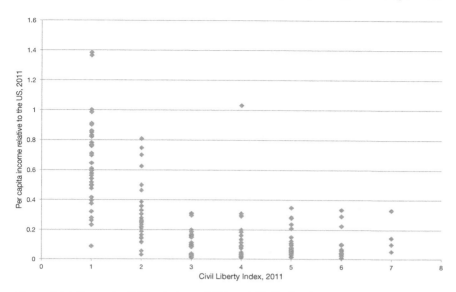

Figure 7.14 Per capita GDP relative to USA and Civil Liberties, 2011

measures (including asset and income disclosure for officials and their families) and civil service reform to professionalize the government. However, a deeper question is how societies can generate political coalitions in support of these technocratic reforms. Looking at the relatively small number of successful examples in modern times suggests two ideas. First, as emphasized by Pierson (2000), large consequences may result from relatively small or contingent events; particular courses of action, once introduced, can be almost impossible to reverse; and, consequently, political development is punctuated by critical moments or junctures that shape the basic contours of social life. In the cases of South Korea and Taiwan, for example, the deaths of Chiang Kai-shek and Park Chung-hee set in motion political changes that had broad effects. The critical moments are often exogenously created, but the important thing is to take advantage of them to promote political and economic reform (do not waste a good crisis). A second regularity is that successful cases often involve deep integration with more advanced polities and economies. In an earlier era, many of the success stories were Southern European countries that integrated with politically and economically more open Northern European economies. For South Korea and Taiwan, integration with the United States put pressure on them to carry out both economic and political reforms. Poorer societies integrating with richer ones will generally pay off with stronger institutions and convergence to the richer level of income. The Trans-Pacific Partnership is likely to provide opportunities to Malaysia, Vietnam and others willing to sign up to strengthen their economic and political institutions and lay a solid foundation for growth through to high income.

Conclusions

The recent evidence is that sharp slowdowns in growth can occur at every income level. Between the 1990s and the 2000s, growth slowdowns were most common for high-income countries – no doubt, a result of the fact that the locus of the GFC was in those countries. There were also examples of growth slowdowns at low income and at middle income. So, a first conclusion is that growth traps can occur at every level of development. One of the robust predictors of future economic growth is institutional quality, relative to the development level. This implies that countries, at every level of development, need to constantly improve the quality of institutions. In reality, there is often a tendency for institutions to stagnate. As per capita income increases, however, a set of institutions that were competitive at one stage become a drag on growth at a more developed stage. Countries that are successful over the long term react to temporary growth slowdowns with new reform plans.

Concerning political institutions such as freedom of the press, association and assembly, at low income there is little correlation between them, on the one hand, and economic institutions such as rule of law, on the other. But past an income level of about $8,000 PPP, there is a strong correlation between political institutions and economic ones. This suggests a particular type of growth trap for authoritarian developing countries: they can grow well based on capital accumulation up to a point, but then their lack of innovation becomes a serious impediment. Taiwan and South Korea managed the transition to political openness at the right moment and continued to grow well, but there are few historical examples of such smooth transitions.

Appendix 7.1 Dependent variables – growth rate of per capita GDP, 1990–2010

Specification #	(1)	(2)	(3)	(4)	(5)
Number of countries	146	76 Good institutions	70 Poor institutions	83 Demo.	63 Auth.
Included variables					
Log per capita GDP 1990	0.050 (2.35)	0.03 (1.21)	0.044 (1.29)	0.015 (0.95)	0.011 (0.23)
(Log per capita GDP 1990)^2	−0.003 (2.64)	−0.002 (1.33)	−0.003 (1.28)	−0.0009 (0.94)	−0.001 (0.34)
Institutional quality 1996	0.011 (3.48)	—	—	—	—
Natural resource rents/GDP	0.0003 (2.43)	—	—	—	—
R^2	0.10	0.06	0.024	0.011	0.035

Note: t-statistics in parentheses.

Notes

1   I would like to thank Wei Wang for excellent research assistance. I thank our discussants, Francis Hutchinson and Gilberto Llanto, as well as other participants at the PAFTAD Conference in Singapore, for useful comments that have been incorporated in this version.
2   Eichengreen *et al.* (2012, 2013) focus on a longer period and investigate growth slowdowns of 2 percentage points or more. They find a dispersion of incomes at which there is greater frequency of slowdowns with nodes at log 9.3 and log 9.6. Between the 1990s and the 2000s, 12 countries in the data set had slowdowns of 2 percentage points or more: one low income, three middle income and eight high income.
3   The regressions underpinning Figure 7.7 are in Table A7.1.
4   Ramo (2004) argues that China has created a superior development model with an authoritarian system and state capitalism. Williamson (2012) and Zhao (2010) acknowledge that the model has produced rapid growth for China up to a point, but argue that the model is unsustainable.
5   The regressions underpinning Figure 7.12 are in Appendix 7.1. While authoritarian countries grew faster than democratic ones at low levels of development, they also had more dispersion. In the 1990–2010 period, the authoritarian countries among the poorer half of the data set grew at an average rate of 3.1 per cent with a standard deviation of 3.7. The democratic countries grew at an average rate of 1.9 with a standard deviation of 1.6. One can think of authoritarianism in a poor country as a 'high risk, high reward' strategy. You might get Park Chung-hee or you might get Sese Seko Mobutu.
6   China has relied very heavily on capital accumulation to drive its growth, with an investment rate reaching nearly 50 per cent of GDP in recent years. But the marginal product of capital has dropped sharply in recent years, leading to a slowdown in growth (Dollar, 2013).
7   We use the beginning-period Freedom House ranking to determine authoritarian or democratic status. For almost all the countries, the rating would be the same if one used the end-of-period rating. The obvious exception is Indonesia, which after 1997 had a rapid political transformation that brought it to 3 on the Civil Liberties Index by 2011. If one categorizes Indonesia as a low-income democracy, that just strengthens the basic story because in that case the low-income authoritarians, China and Vietnam, grew at nearly 8 per cent, whereas the low-income democracies grew at 3.3 per cent. Indonesia is the only one of the highlighted countries that underwent a major political transformation in the period, and its growth rate accelerated from 2.9 per cent in the 1990s to 4 per cent in the 2000s. The other Asian economies averaged a minor slowdown of 0.2 percentage points between the decades.
8   The resolutions that came out of the important Third Plenum meeting in the fall of 2013 make clear that political reform is not on the agenda. See *Decision of the CCCPC on Some Major Issues Concerning Comprehensively Deepening the Reform* (www.china.org.cn/chinese/2014–01/17/content_31226494_3.htm).

References

Acemoglu, D and Robinson, JA 2012a. *Why Nations Fail: The Origins of Power, Prosperity and Poverty*. New York: Crown.

Acemoglu, D and Robinson, JA 2012b. Will China rule the world? *The Huffington Post*, 22 March. Available online at: www.huffingtonpost.com/daron-acemoglu/china-superpower_b_1369424.html.

Acemoglu, D, Johnson, S and James, AR 2001. The colonial origins of comparative development: An empirical investigation. *American Economic Review*, 91, 1,369–401.

Dollar, D 2004. Reform, growth, and poverty. In P Glewwe, N Agrawal and D Dollar (eds), *Economic Growth, Poverty, and Household Welfare in Vietnam*. Washington, DC: The World Bank.

Dollar, D 2013. *China's rebalancing: Lessons from East Asian economic history*. John L. Thornton Working Paper Series. Washington, DC: The Brookings Institution. Available online at: www.brookings.edu/~/media/research/files/papers/2013/10/02-china-economic-rebalancing-dollar/china-economic-rebalancing-dollar.pdf.

Dollar, D and Ljunggren, B 1997. Vietnam. In P. Desai (ed.), *Going Global: Transition from Plan to Market in the World Economy*. Cambridge, MA: MIT Press, 439–72.

Doppelhofer, G, Miller, RI and Sala-i-Martin, X 2000. *Determinants of long-term growth: A Bayesian averaging of classical estimates (BACE) approach*. NBER Working Paper No. 7750. Cambridge, MA: National Bureau of Economic Research.

Eckaus, RS 1997. China. In P Desai (ed.), *Going Global: Transition from Plan to Market in the World Economy*. Cambridge, MA: MIT Press, 415–38.

Eichengreen, B, Park, D and Shin K 2012. When fast-growing economies slow down: International evidence and implications for China. *Asian Economic Papers*, 11(1), 42–87.

Eichengreen, B, Park, D and Shin, K 2013. *Growth slowdowns redux: New evidence on the middle-income trap*. NBER Working Paper No. 18673. Cambridge, MA: National Bureau of Economic Research.

Feenstra, R, Inklaar, R and Timmer, M 2013. The Next Generation of the Penn World Table. Available online at: www.ggdc.net/pwt.

Freedom House 2015. *Freedom in the World*. Washington, DC: Freedom House. Available online at: https://freedomhouse.org.

Huntington, SP 1968. *Political Order in Changing Societies*. New Haven, CT: Yale University Press.

Knack, S and Keefer, P 1997. Does social capital have an economic payoff? A cross-country investigation. *Quarterly Journal of Economics*, 112(4), 1,251–88.

Levine, R and Renelt, D 1992. A sensitivity analysis of cross-country growth regressions. *American Economics Review*, 82(4), 942–63.

Naughton, B 2014. China's economy: Complacency, crisis & the challenge of reform. *Daedalus*, 143(2), 14–25.

Pierson, P 2000. Increasing returns, path dependence, and the study of politics. *American Political Science Review*, 94(2), 251–67.

Pritchett, L and Summers, L 2013. Asia-phoria meet regression to the mean. Proceedings of the Federal Reserve Bank of San Francisco, November, 1–35.

Ramo, JC 2004. *The Beijing Consensus*. London: The Foreign Policy Centre.

Sakong, I and Koh, YS 2010. *The Korean Economy: Six Decades of Growth and Development*. Seoul: Korea Development Institute.

Tsiang, SC 1984. Taiwan's economic miracle: Lessons in economic development. In A Harberger (ed.), *World Economic Growth*. San Francisco: Institute for Contemporary Studies, 301–25.

Williamson, J 2012. Is the 'Beijing consensus' now dominant? *Asia Policy*, 13(1), 1–16.

World Bank 2015. *Worldwide Governance Indicators*. Washington, DC: The World Bank. Available online at: www.govindicators.org.

Zhao, S 2010. The China model: Can it replace the Western model of modernization? *Journal of Contemporary China*, 19(65), 419–36.

8   Avoiding 'Tiger' traps

How human capital can propel countries beyond middle-income status in East Asia

Emmanuel Jimenez and
Elizabeth M. King

Introduction

The role of human capital in the growth narrative among the successful economies in East Asia and the Pacific – especially the so-called East Asian 'Tigers' – is well known and is a formula that other countries have tried to emulate.[1] Falling fertility rates opened a window of opportunity as these countries' demographic profiles changed: instead of a predominance of very young children, their population structure produced a large stock of potential workers who were entering the labour force with fewer dependents. The sheer number of these workers, trained and deployed well, relative to those who were not of working age, produced a demographic dividend. Some estimates showed that up to one-quarter to one-third of all of the Tigers' growth was due to this demographic phenomenon (Bloom *et al.*, 2000).

The dividend was not automatic. The demographic shift had to be accompanied by the right policies and institutions. Open economies, good governance and a favourable investment climate allowed countries to reallocate labour from agriculture to initially low-wage manufacturing, including assembly. At the same time, countries expanded primary education to ensure that workers had basic skills. As these enterprises succeeded, they moved up the value chain to higher-wage manufacturing, enabled by investments in secondary and tertiary education to meet the demands of higher-order skills.

Even within East Asia, not all countries shared this growth narrative. In 1960, South Korea and the Philippines had roughly the same GDP per capita (approximately $640 in US$ 1975) and population levels were similar (28 and 25 million, respectively). About 26 per cent of Philippine GDP was generated from agriculture, compared with 37 per cent in South Korea; manufacturing accounted for 28 per cent in the Philippines and about 20 per cent in South Korea. All primary school-age boys and about one-quarter of those of secondary school age enrolled in school in both countries, but the enrolment rate at tertiary level in the Philippines was more than double that of South Korea (13 per cent instead of 5 per cent). All in all, the two countries were statistically equivalent, with the Philippines slightly ahead (Lucas, 1993). Fifty years later, South Korea is a major world economy, while the Philippines has been unable to escape its lower middle-income status despite some recent growth.

There are many more countries like the Philippines than there are like South Korea. Their experiences have prompted some analysts (Kharas and Kohli, 2011) to warn of a potential 'trap' as countries reach middle-income status. As wages rise, countries that aspire to high-income status will have to compete with countries with much higher levels of productivity. Those that do not, will experience a slowdown and will be pressed from both ends: they will no longer be competitive with the bottom and are not yet able to compete with the top. Doing the latter has been a 'glass ceiling' through which relatively few countries have been able to break.

For many reasons some countries are able to join the ranks of higher-income countries while others remain 'stuck'. In this chapter, we consider the role of human capital, focusing on education, given its key role in the East Asian growth narrative. We make the following points.

- Using its human capital well is a critical ingredient in helping a country avoid the middle-income trap, however it is measured. Moreover, if a country fails to sustain growth during its demographic window of opportunity, the changing age structure of its human capital may actually lead into a potential trap.
- Countries that have succeeded in breaking through, which have been mostly in East Asia, have done so not only by expanding the opportunities for human capital accumulation as measured conventionally by years of schooling or amounts of money spent for education. They have also invested heavily in improving the quality of education and, in so doing, their youth developed the cognitive skills needed for the transition from basic agriculture to higher-productivity manufacturing and services. Beyond that, these countries have developed non-cognitive skills that have become increasingly important in today's workforce. In the future, the hurdle will become higher: given the evolving world of work, human capital must also foster creativity.
- There are reasonably clear and sensible hypotheses as to which policies and programmes countries need to develop cognitive and non-cognitive skills, many of which derive from the experience of the East Asian economies that successfully broke out of middle-income status – the so-called Tigers. But the specifics need to be tailored to the different country contexts. Unfortunately, the rigorous evidence base for specific policy and programmes is paltry for the emerging economies of East Asia and needs to be expanded as countries navigate their own way to high-income status.

The nature of a 'middle-income trap' and what it means for human capital

Who might be trapped?

There is no consensus on exactly which East Asian countries are 'trapped' in middle-income status. Some are easier to categorize than others. A country such as Japan has had high-income status for a while, even though in the past decade its growth has stagnated. Countries such as Cambodia and Laos have low-income status. They are growing rapidly now but are starting from such a low base that they are not yet in the middle. A country such as the Philippines has been on the verge of taking off but is arguably now further away than it was in the 1960s, and is decidedly 'trapped'. But what about countries such as China, Indonesia, Malaysia, Thailand and Vietnam?

The recent literature on the trap has provided several characterizations of what it means to be in a 'middle-income trap'. Aiyar *et al.* (2013) characterize the problem by comparing the evolution of GDP per capita over time. Brazil, Mexico and Peru reached a level of US$3,000 per capita about 50 or more years ago but have per capita income levels that are about 20–30 per cent of US levels today. On the other hand, Taiwan (China) and South Korea, two of the East Asian Tigers, took less time: they reached that level later but have progressed to about 60–70 per cent of US levels. Other countries in Asia are somewhere in between: Thailand and Malaysia have progressed at a slower pace than their Tiger counterparts but have already outperformed those in Latin America. China is on a faster trajectory, and Indonesia is on a slower one.

Some analysts have stressed the role of slowdowns in economic growth in describing the differentials in countries' rates of progress. Aiyar *et al.* (2013) focus on the probability of a growth slowdown measured in terms of a large, sustained deviation from the predicted growth path. Eichengreen *et al.* (2013) develop a similar concept but define it differently. It is measured as an episode whereby a fast-growing country with a seven-year average growth of at least 3.5 per cent grows at just 2 per cent in the subsequent seven years. In these definitions, countries may be 'trapped' in a slowdown for some time but then escape and resume growth. Indeed, South Korea in the early 1970s and Malaysia in the early 1980s experienced marked slowdowns according to these two studies.

Another approach to the trap is to consider it as being stuck in a level of GDP per capita (which is set somewhat arbitrarily). Felipe (2012) defines the trap by assessing the historical experience of countries graduating from lower to upper middle-income status and subsequently to high-income status. A country is stuck in a trap if it stays in lower middle-income status longer than its historical experience. By this definition, the East Asian countries that were successful in escaping lower middle-income status in 1950 and moving to upper middle-income include China, Malaysia, South Korea, Taiwan (China) and Thailand (Felipe, 2012). The countries that reached upper middle-income status after 1950 and graduated to high income are the Tigers, which include Hong Kong (China), Japan, Singapore, South Korea, and Taiwan (China) (Felipe, 2012). The East Asian countries that were considered to be in a trap in 2010 were the Philippines (stuck at lower middle-income status) and Malaysia (stuck at upper middle-income status).[2]

For the purposes of this chapter, we compare the human capital development in East Asia's economic Tigers with that in those countries that have yet to achieve high-income status. The former include Japan, South Korea, Taiwan (China), Hong

Kong (China) and Singapore. Some parts of China, such as Shanghai and other eastern cities, have broken out, but by and large the others have not. The middle-income economies of Indonesia, Malaysia, Thailand, the Philippines and Vietnam are still vulnerable to being trapped. This chapter also draws on observations from India, which, while not part of East Asia, has broken through to middle-income country status with its quite robust economic growth in nearly two decades.

How can human capital help countries avoid being 'trapped'?

The literature points to two distinct but related dimensions of what it means to avoid the trap. One is to avoid a slowdown after growth episodes – that is, being able to sustain growth, as stressed by Aiyar *et al.* (2013) and Eichengreen *et al.* (2013). Another dimension is to reach the GDP per capita of the next 'accepted' economic category and maintain that position by competing with higher-income economies and moving up the value chain in production.[3] The implications for human capital are profound for both dimensions.

The accounting of economic growth is deceptively simple. Growth per person comes from four sources: more capital per unit of labour, more labour relative to the number of people, more productive labour and technical progress. That said, how to stimulate each, and in what combination, is difficult and complex. The Growth Commission (2008) found no single tried-and-tested formula for sustaining economic growth. But in all of these efforts, investment in human capital through education is a necessary (though by no means sufficient) condition for economic growth. It is beyond the scope of this chapter to review the extensive literature on education and growth (for a comprehensive treatment, see Barro and Lee, 2015).[4] We provide a brief recap here.

Early models of economic growth presented a growth-accounting framework, as mentioned earlier. For 83 economies, Barro and Lee (2015) estimate that almost one-quarter of growth between 1960 and 2010 can be attributed to human capital. Later 'endogenous' growth theories postulated that human capital had additional economic benefits through externalities such as spillovers of knowledge across workers or technological accumulation and adaptation. Cross-country regressions show that, beyond a certain threshold, educational attainment contributes positively to economic growth (Barro and Lee, 2015). Some of the nuances have changed. Research in the 1990s showed that the economic performance of the East Asian Tigers pointed to primary education as 'by far the largest single contributor to the high performing Asian economies' predicted growth rates' (World Bank, 1993: 52). Recent studies (for example, Barro and Lee, 2015) show that secondary and tertiary education contribute more to growth, which is not surprising given the universal gains in primary education achievement.

There is much less research on the role of education in avoiding the more recent notion of 'growth traps'. Aiyar *et al.* (2013) do not directly analyze the contribution of human capital per se, but their paper discusses how higher dependency ratios – the proportion of non-working age to working-age population that is so crucial to the demographic dividend mentioned earlier – increase the probability of a growth slowdown in subsequent periods.

Eichengreen *et al.* (2013) investigate this issue more directly. Their paper finds that while average years of schooling alone have no impact, the number of secondary and tertiary education graduates lowers the likelihood of a slowdown. More advanced education seems to be valuable by moving production into more technologically advanced goods and services. Moreover, they find that when holding constant the number of secondary and higher education graduates, average years of education become significant – that is, for countries that have achieved less in higher education levels, more education can accelerate growth – but this effect diminishes when they move upmarket and are challenged from below.

These results support the importance of the other aspect of avoiding the trap: moving up the value chain to raise productivity. Moving upmarket means having more higher value-added industries and sectors and, within any sector, raising productivity through new technologies. As noted in a recent Organization for Economic Cooperation and Development (OECD) document, the countries that have avoided the trap succeeded in 'export-led growth by targeting strategic industries that facilitated gradual diversification and upgrading into new products that required similar skills and inputs' (Jankowska *et al.*, 2012). The main drivers are modernized manufacturing and services sectors.

Another pathway through which human capital helps countries avoid traps is reducing inequality. There is an increasing body of evidence that shows that higher inequality is not conducive to growth. For example, economists at the International Monetary Fund find that inequality affects the duration of growth: a one Gini-point increase is associated with a decrease in a growth spell of 7 per cent (Ostry *et al.*, 2014: 23). Some investments in human capital may be more inequality reducing than others. Subsidizing human capital investments for the poor (such as basic education) will reduce inequality compared with costly universal (untargeted) subsidies to higher education.

How might human capital trap countries?

As noted earlier, the demographic dividend is not automatic. To realize the gains from a lower dependency ratio (specifically, a prolonged period when there are more people of working age than people of non-working age) as the East Asian Tigers have done, countries aspiring to high-income status have to invest in developing human capital and deploying it productively in their labour force. Moreover, this demographic dividend is not available indefinitely. Inevitably, the bulge in the working-age population, which is youthful in the early stages of the demographic transition, will decrease as workers age and eventually retire. To understand this trap, one needs to consider what happens during demographic transitions.

In the initial stages of development, a country experiences high rates of population growth because it benefits from health improvements that reduce mortality rates while fertility remains high. This leads to a population age pyramid, with large numbers of very young children and fewer numbers at older age cohorts. This was the situation in Taiwan, China and the other Tigers in the 1950s, and is the situation in the high-fertility countries in Africa today.

A demographic transition occurs when fertility declines so that there are relatively fewer young children while more people enter the working-age cohort. The population structure is no longer a pyramid because a bulge occurs in the middle age groups. During this period, which could last for several generations, the number of people who are not of working age declines – either because they are too young or because they are too old – relative to the number of those of working age (the dependency ratio). A lower dependency ratio leads to a demographic window of opportunity for an economic dividend – one the Tigers reaped earlier and that emerging Asian economies are reaping. It is estimated that about 0.8 to 1 per cent of growth in South East Asia is due to demographic change (Bloom and Williamson, 1998). Bloom and Williamson's study also pointed to a second demographic dividend, since a large working-age cohort typically saves more.

The demographic window of opportunity eventually closes when the bulge of workers age. Japan is confronting an inverted population pyramid, and its dependency ratio is rising again due to an aging population. This is a challenge, but having achieved high-income status some time ago, it has the resources to sustain its level of income and even to grow. Countries that grow old before they get rich will find it more difficult to sustain growth – hence the trap. Countries such as Argentina and those in Eastern Europe and Central Asia face this challenge. The emerging countries of Asia are not yet in this situation, but the reckoning will inevitably come.

The nature of human capital and what it means for avoiding the trap: building skills

How precisely does human capital help middle-income countries avoid slowdowns and compete with richer economies? To answer this question it is important to examine how East Asian economies that have successfully reached high-income status have formed different types of skills through the right investments in human capital. Their experiences can offer lessons for those middle-income countries that have aspirations to join them at the next levels. The literature has discussed three types of skills: cognitive, non-cognitive and creative. We discuss these in turn in the next sections.

Developing cognitive skills

Cognitive skills encompass a broad array of skills that go beyond the affective or motor domains but which influence a person's value in the workplace. They include basic numeracy and literacy but also subject matter knowledge in specialized fields. These are the skills that are mostly taught in education systems throughout the world, although these skills can also be self-taught or learned through more informal means.[5]

What kind of skills does it take to avoid a trap?

As mentioned in the previous section, avoiding the trap means that countries should move from competing on the low-skill margin to competing on the high-skill margin. This then leads to the question, what is the nature of that high-skill margin? Hanushek *et al.* (2013: 15) analyzed Programme for the International Assessment of Adult Competencies data for 22 countries to estimate individual earnings functions and found that education quality, as measured by cognitive skills, increases individual earnings:

> Across the 22 countries, a one-standard deviation increase in numeracy skills is associated with an average 18 percent wage increase among prime age workers. Moreover, because of measurement errors in skills, these estimates should be thought of as lower bounds on the return to skill.
>
> But this overall measure of returns to skill also masks considerable cross-country heterogeneity: Returns are below 15 percent in eight countries, including all four participating Nordic countries, and above 21 percent in six countries, with the largest return being 28 percent in the United States. Estimated returns tend to be largest for numeracy and literacy skills and smaller for problem solving skills, although the relative importance of different skill dimensions varies across countries. Estimates prove highly robust to different earnings measures, additional controls, and various subgroups.

In an earlier study using standardized test scores from the Programme for International Student Assessment (PISA) and Trends in Mathematics and Science Study (TIMSS), Hanushek and Woessmann (2008: 7) found that 'test scores that are larger by one standard deviation (measured at the student level across all OECD countries in PISA) are associated with an average annual growth rate in GDP per capita that is 2 percentage points higher over the whole 40-year period'. Moreover, this effect of educational quality is larger for higher-income relative to lower-income countries.

There is recognition that the changing needs of the labour market and the greater role of technology are putting more pressure on education systems. When long periods are needed to fill vacancies, one reason is that the skills and competencies of workers do not match the technical requirements of the unfilled jobs. It takes about six weeks to fill professional vacancies in Malaysia and Thailand, and more than four weeks in China and Mongolia (World Bank 2012). According to employer surveys, in East Asia, 'more than 30 percent of firms cite skills as at least a moderate obstacle to growth. This increases to 40 percent for low-income countries' (World Bank, 2012: 5). Moreover, those firms that are technologically intensive and export oriented are more likely to report skills as a constraint. In China, graduates are ending up in professions unrelated to their major (31 per cent of university and 38 per cent of vocational college graduates), partly because there are not sufficient job openings related to their major and partly because graduates do not meet the skills requirement for jobs related to their majors (Molnar *et al.*, 2015).

What is the track record?

There is no question that the East Asian Tigers achieved impressive increases in school enrolments. In 1950, about one-half of the population in these countries had no education; by 2010, this fraction had shrunk to less than one-tenth. In 1950, one-tenth had secondary education; by 2010 this had increased to nearly one-half. Focusing on the past 20 years, the average years of schooling of the population aged 15 and over increased by about two years – faster than the increase in Latin America or Eastern Europe (Barro and Lee, 2010). There is also a marked difference in post-primary educational attainment between the Tigers and the rest of the region, with Japan's and South Korea's net enrolment rates in secondary education being nearly universal (Table 8.1). The average years of schooling attained by the age cohort 25–9 in each country most captures the impact of these high enrolments and continuation rates. Young adults in South Korea, Japan and Singapore have continued to increase their educational attainment in the past decade and they are among the most highly educated job entrants in the world.[6]

The Tigers' record on education quality has been equally impressive. Based on international tests such as PISA and TIMSS, students in these countries, on average, outperform students in other countries, including those in the OECD. Singapore, Hong Kong (China), South Korea, Japan, Taiwan (China) and two Chinese cities (Shanghai and Macau) ranked in the top 10 in the 2012 PISA tests (OECD, 2012) in mathematics (Table 8.2).[7] Shanghai, Singapore, Hong Kong, Japan and South Korea also ranked as the top five in reading comprehension. Note that five Tigers also topped the 2011 TIMSS tests for eighth graders (IEA, 2011).

The emerging Asian economies – the region's Tiger Cubs – have greatly expanded their school enrolments, too, not only at the primary level but also at the secondary and tertiary levels. The net enrolment rates for Malaysia, for example, rose from 84 per cent in 1970 to 97 per cent in 2005 at the primary level, with nearly all children who enter primary school reaching the last year of the cycle, and from 33 per cent to 67 per cent at the secondary level during the same period. Tertiary-level enrolments have also expanded in these countries – for example, Malaysia's gross enrolment rate is now 36 per cent and Thailand's is 51 per cent. As a result of these increases in enrolment, these countries have achieved a steady rise between 1950 and 2010 in the average years of schooling of their population aged 15 and above (Figure 8.1).

Despite these gains, there are several reasons to be concerned. Less than one-fifth of enrollees complete their first degree in these countries, except in Thailand where the completion rate is 30 per cent; in comparison, the completion rate is 40 per cent in Japan and 49 per cent in South Korea. Progress in the past decade has been slow in the Philippines, where the net enrolment rate at the primary and

Table 8.1 Selected education indicators, East Asian countries, 1999–2012

Country	Persistence to last primary grade (%)			Net secondary enrolment rate (%)			Gross tertiary enrolment rate (%)			Average years of schooling, 25–9 years old		
	Mean 1999–2001	Mean 2004–6	Mean 2 2009–12	Mean 1999–2001	Mean 2004–6	Mean 2 2009–12	Mean 1999–2001	Mean 2004–6	Mean 2 2009–12	2000	2005	2010
Japan	100.0	99.9	99.9	99.6	98.8	98.9	48.4	55.2	59.3	13.1	13.4	13.4
Korea, Rep.	98.8	98.2	99.2	95.6	95.3	95.8	78.6	93.7	100.4	13.6	14.2	14.7
Singapore	n.a.	n.a.	n.a.	n.a.	n.a.	n.a.	n.a.	n.a.	n.a.	12.5	12.6	14.4
China	n.a.	n.a.	n.a.	n.a.	n.a.	n.a.	8.1	18.3	24.0	8.4	8.8	8.9
Hong Kong SAR, China	n.a.	99.3	99.2	69.4	72.4	79.1	n.a.	32.1	58.1	12.9	14.1	14.0
Macau SAR, China	n.a.	n.a.	98.3	68.4	83.9	77.9	33.3	65.0	62.7	8.6	9.6	10.3
Taiwan, China	n.a.	n.a.	n.a.	n.a.	n.a.	n.a.	n.a.	n.a.	n.a.	12.2	13.1	13.3
India	n.a.	n.a.	n.a.	n.a.	n.a.	n.a.	7.7	9.3	16.3	6.0	7.0	7.8
Indonesia	85.9	83.4	89.6	50.2	56.7	71.4	14.8	17.5	26.8	5.2	7.7	9.2
Malaysia	n.a.	93.6	99.2	65.9	69.3	66.0	24.5	28.8	36.3	10.7	11.6	12.4
Philippines	75.3	71.7	n.a.	50.3	59.2	61.4	29.6	27.9	28.2	8.8	9.0	9.4
Thailand	87.6	n.a.	n.a.	n.a.	67.1	79.1	35.8	43.4	50.7	8.1	10.1	10.5
Vietnam	85.5	92.1	95.6	n.a.	n.a.	n.a.	9.7	16.2	22.8	6.3	7.9	8.4

Sources: UNESCO data at World Bank, EdStats (http://datatopics.worldbank.org/education/wDataQuery/QProjections.aspx), February 2014; Barro-Lee (2010).

Table 8.2 Average test scores as a percentage of South Korea's average test scores, specific years (per cent)

Country	Reading, PISA					Math, PISA					Science, PISA					Math, Grade 8, TIMSS			
	2000	2003	2006	2009	2012	2000	2003	2006	2009	2012	2000	2003	2006	2009	2012	1999	2003	2007	2011
Japan	99.4	93.3	89.6	96.5	100.4	101.8	98.5	95.6	96.9	96.8	99.6	101.9	101.7	100.2	101.7	98.5	96.7	95.4	93.0
South Korea	100.0	100.0	100.0	100.0	100.0	100.0	100.0	100.0	100.0	100.0	100.0	100.0	100.0	100.0	100.0	100.0	100.0	100.0	100.0
Singapore	n.a.	n.a.	n.a.	97.6	101.1	n.a.	n.a.	n.a.	102.9	103.4	n.a.	n.a.	n.a.	100.7	102.4	102.9	102.8	99.2	99.7
Hong Kong	100.0	95.5	96.4	98.9	101.7	102.4	101.5	100.0	101.6	101.3	98.0	100.2	103.8	102.0	103.2	99.1	99.5	95.9	95.6
Macau	n.a.	93.3	88.5	90.4	95.0	n.a.	97.2	96.0	96.2	94.8	n.a.	97.6	97.9	95.0	96.8	n.a.	n.a.	n.a.	n.a.
Shanghai	n.a.	n.a.	n.a.	103.2	106.3	n.a.	n.a.	n.a.	109.9	110.6	n.a.	n.a.	n.a.	106.9	107.8	n.a.	n.a.	n.a.	n.a.
Indonesia	70.7	71.5	70.7	74.6	73.9	67.1	66.4	71.5	67.9	67.7	71.2	73.4	75.3	71.2	71.0	68.6	69.7	66.5	63.0
Malaysia	n.a.	n.a.	n.a.	76.8	74.3	n.a.	n.a.	n.a.	74.0	76.0	n.a.	n.a.	n.a.	78.4	78.1	88.4	86.3	79.3	71.8
Philippines	n.a.	n.a.	n.a.	n.a.	n.a.	n.a.	n.a.	n.a.	n.a.	n.a.	n.a.	n.a.	n.a.	n.a.	n.a.	58.7	64.1	n.a.	n.a.
Thailand	82.1	78.7	75.0	78.1	82.3	79.0	76.9	76.2	76.7	77.1	79.0	79.7	80.7	79.0	82.5	79.6	n.a.	73.9	69.7
Vietnam	n.a.	n.a.	n.a.	n.a.	95.0	n.a.	n.a.	n.a.	n.a.	92.2	n.a.	n.a.	n.a.	n.a.	98.1	n.a.	n.a.	n.a.	n.a.

Note: PISA is Programme for International Student Assessment; TIMSS is Trends in International Mathematics and Science Study.

Source: World Bank EdStats online database (http://datatopics.worldbank.org/education/wDataQuery/QLearning.aspx).

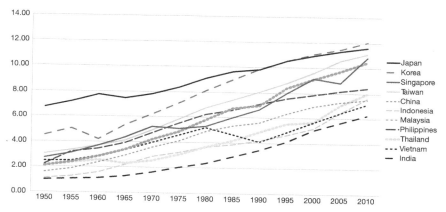

Figure 8.1 Average years of schooling in East Asia, population aged 15+ years, 1950–2010

secondary levels in 2000 has fallen behind those of its neighbours, and the tertiary enrolment rate has stagnated in the past decade (Table 8.1). India lags even further behind, with just 16.3 per cent gross enrolment rate at the tertiary level and strikingly large differences across states – for example, it is 16.8 per cent in Uttar Pradesh and 38 per cent in Tamil Nadu. Inequality across states, and across demographic groups and castes, is a major challenge in India.

The performance of the Tiger Cubs on the quality of education, as measured by performance on international tests, falls far below that of the Asian Tigers. The test scores of 15-year-old Thai, Malaysian and Indonesian students are between 68 and 77 per cent of the average PISA math scores of South Korean students and between 74 and 82 per cent of the average reading comprehension scores of South Korean students (Table 8.2).[8] But average test scores reveal only one aspect of the academic disparity between these two groups of countries; there are also wide disparities in the distribution of competencies. In Indonesia, three-quarters of students have test scores that correspond to the two lowest levels of competency in math; in Malaysia and Thailand, one-half of the test scores are at these levels (Figure 8.2). By comparison, the corresponding proportion for the Asian Tigers is about one-tenth (Japan) or smaller (South Korea, Singapore). These results imply that the basic abilities of young people who enter the labour force in these two groups of countries are also hugely different.

The low level of cognitive skills in the Tiger Cubs, despite increases in average years of schooling, may be one reason why wage gaps (or wage premiums) persist between those with and without secondary or tertiary education across a number of countries. In 2007–8, the wage premium for workers with upper secondary education and employed in primary (natural resources and agriculture) and secondary (manufacturing) industries ranged from 0.2 to 0.4 in diverse countries such as Cambodia, China, the Philippines and Vietnam. In services, the premium exceeded 0.5 in all four countries – double what it was a decade before (World Bank, 2012). Another possible explanation is that technologies have been shifting

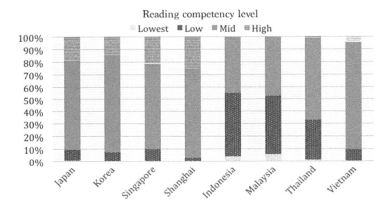

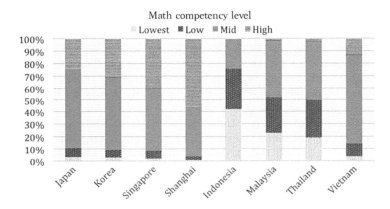

Figure 8.2 Percentage distribution of competency levels based on PISA test scores, 2012

Notes: (1) The "lowest" competency scale pertains to the percentage of 15-year-old students scoring below the lowest proficiency level on the PISA reading scale. Students at this level (less or equal to 262 points) usually do not succeed at the most basic reading tasks that PISA measures. The "low" competency level is the sum of two PISA levels (level 1A and 1B). This includes the percentage who score higher than 262 but lower than or equal to 407. Tasks at Level 1A require the reader to locate one or more independent pieces of explicitly stated information; tasks at level 1B require the reader to locate a single piece of explicitly stated information in a prominent position in a short, syntactically simple text with a familiar context and text type, such as a narrative or a simple list. The "high" competency level pertains to the percentage who score higher than 626 on the PISA reading scale. They are able at least to retrieve information requiring the reader to locate and organize several pieces of deeply embedded information, inferring which information in the text is relevant. (2) The "lowest" competency level pertains to the percentage of 15-year-old students below the lowest proficiency level (scoring 358 or below) on the PISA mathematics scale; students at this level may be able to perform very direct and straightforward mathematical tasks. The "low" competency level pertains to the percentage who score higher than 358 but lower than or equal to 420 points on the PISA mathematics scale; at this level, students can answer questions involving familiar contexts where all relevant information is present and the questions are clearly defined. The "high" competency level pertains to the percentage who score higher than 607, and corresponds to PISA levels 5 and 6. At this level, students can develop and work with models for complex situations, identifying constraints and specifying assumptions.

in favour of higher skills, essentially increasing the demand for and relative productivity of higher-skilled workers.

India was missing from the 2012 PISA round. Two of its states participated in the 2009 round, with the intention of expanding participation to other states in 2012, but the two states together ranked at 72nd of 73 systems, and India opted out of the 2012 round. However, a long series of national standardized tests in the early grades portrays the state of education quality in the country. The 2014 annual report by Pratham (2015),[9] which is based on a survey of children in rural areas, finds that one-half of Class 8 students cannot read a Class 2-level text, although there have been gains since 2012. Maths also continues to be a serious concern, with only one-quarter of Class 3 children able to perform two-digit subtractions, and only about one-quarter of Class 5 children able to do division. Kingdon (2007: 3) makes the comparison with countries in East Asia – in particular, China – in quite stark terms: 'India is more than 30 years behind China in terms of the proportion of the population with completed secondary and post-secondary schooling.'

The hopeful news with respect to learning outcomes is the performance of Vietnamese students, who achieved 92 and 95 per cent of the average maths and reading comprehension scores, respectively, of South Korean students – outperforming even the average OECD student. Vietnam's performance indicates that it is possible for a low-income, emerging-economy country to push and support its education system towards academic excellence.

Developing non-cognitive skills and personality

What will it take to escape the trap?

Due to technological and market changes, the skills demanded by employers have shifted in developed countries, including in the Tiger economies – from skills for manual, routine work to skills for manual, non-routine tasks and even more analytical, non-routine work.[10] These shifts intensify the demands on education systems. Increases in average years of schooling are no longer enough. They must be accompanied by higher cognitive and technical skills, as noted above. In addition, students are increasingly expected to demonstrate capacities for critical thinking, problem-solving and communication.

Previous studies have concluded that innate cognitive ability (usually measured by IQ), family economic status and demographics are the principal determinants of a student's academic success (for example, Glewwe, 2002). There is also a growing body of evidence from multiple disciplines (psychology, behavioural economics and neuroscience) that aspects of a student's personality predict academic performance. Indeed, these associations are long lasting, affecting adult productivity and labour market success. In brief, the evidence indicates that '[t]he hallmark of successful individuals is that they love learning, they seek challenges, they value effort, and they persist in the face of obstacles' (Dweck, 2000).

With respect to academic performance, some evidence in fact indicates that personality may be more important than intelligence. Grit – defined as the tendency to be organized, responsible and hard-working, and focused on pursuing long-term goals with sustained zeal – has been shown to be a robust predictor of achievement in academic, vocational and avocational domains (Duckworth *et al.*, 2012; von Culin *et al.*, 2014). In the United States, for example, increasing non-cognitive ability has a greater effect on lowering attrition from high school and increasing transition to college than increasing cognitive ability (Heckman *et al.*, 2006). Not surprisingly, the impact of personality traits seems even larger as a student reaches higher education levels (Deke and Haimson, 2006).

In the workplace, these positive personality traits distinguish productive workers from others. Self-esteem, generalized self-efficacy, locus of control and emotional stability are among the best predictors of job performance and job satisfaction (Judge and Bono, 2001; Roberts *et al.*, 2007). Bowles *et al.* (2001) conclude that, although introducing a measure of cognitive performance into an earnings equation reduces the coefficient of years of education by an average of 18 per cent, much of this labour market return actually reflects factors that cognitive tests do not capture. In the United States, 'employers of new college graduates report that communications skills, motivation/initiative, teamwork skills, and leadership skills are all more highly valued than academic achievement/GPA' (Kuhn and Weinberger, 2005: 1). Among German workers, an internal locus of control – attributing success or failure to one's own effort rather than to external circumstances – predicts substantially higher earnings (Heineck and Anger, 2010). Motivated and dependable workers who possess control over their lives tend to challenge themselves and so are able to have a job that requires more education than they have acquired.

What is the track record?

Because there are no commonly accepted standard measures of non-cognitive and behavioural skills, it is difficult to get the same kind of evidence in this area that we have for cognitive skills. Nonetheless, data from employer surveys are instructive. In middle-income East Asian countries, employers expect workers to possess technical and cognitive skills such as information technology skills. But, as shown in Table 8.3, non-cognitive skills such as communication, problem-solving, leadership and the ability to learn continuously also rank very high on employers' 'wish lists'.

Fostering creativity

One element of individual skill that deserves special mention, because it contributes to productivity both at the individual and the economy-wide levels, is creativity (King and Rogers, 2014).

What is creativity and why is it needed to escape the trap?

Creativity has many definitions, but the core idea is that it is the ability to generate novel ideas or products that are of value. The future challenge of moving upmarket

Table 8.3 Critical skills for professionals in East Asia

	Vietnam	Indonesia	Malaysia	Philippines	Thailand	Mongolia	Average
Technical	7	5	7	7	5	5	6.0
Communication	6	7	5	5	4	4	5.2
English language	5	3	4	4	7	7	5.0
Problem solving		5	4	6	4	3	4.4
Leadership		4	4	6	4	4	4.4
Information technology		4	6	3	6	6	5.0
Creativity		6	5	4	4	4	4.6
Work attitude	7	6	4	4	3	3	4.5

Source: World Bank (2012).

for emerging economies is daunting given the rapid technological evolution happening in the global economy. The popular press has written about a 'third industrial revolution' in manufacturing sectors. The first such revolution was spawned by the mechanization of Britain's textile industry in the late eighteenth century, which led to the modern factory replacing the handicrafts of hundreds of individual weavers. The second was propelled by the technical change brought about by new forms of energy such as steam, electricity and petrol, and by the practices of mass production brought about by the moving assembly line. The third promises to be no less disruptive as manufacturing becomes more dependent on digital technology through the convergence of computer technology, robotics, informatics and new processes such as three-dimensional printing (*The Economist*, 2012).

Stimulating creativity is not only about sparking a person's imagination. Research has identified common traits in personality, lifestyle and environment in creative people. Most creative people show intense interest in their field even at an early age, and most have benefited from a highly supportive mentor in their area of interest. One characteristic of creative people is said to be the skill for 'divergent production': the ability to generate a diverse but appropriate response to a given situation. Researchers also point to sustained cognitive processes of problem-solving and building expertise in a specific field, requiring a huge number of hours.[11]

What is the track record?

The assessment of creative problem-solving in PISA 2012 concludes that East Asian 15-year-old students – in Singapore, South Korea, Japan, Chinese Taipei, Hong Kong (China), Macau (China) and Shanghai – outperform students in other countries (OECD, 2013b), so perhaps the East Asian education system, which has emphasized basic skills, has not necessarily stymied creativity. The first OECD survey of skills of adults further shows that adults who engage more often in literacy- and numeracy-related activities and use information and communication technologies more, both at and outside work, have greater proficiency in literacy, numeracy and problem-solving skills, controlling for educational attainment (OECD, 2013a). In this survey, Japan tops the performance of 22 participating countries. While South Korea performs just below the average, its young adults (aged 15–34) are among the top performers – revealing a large generation gap in the country that reflects its recent, rapid educational progress.

Patenting activities are, at best, rough indicators of creativity because many other creative endeavours – in the arts, for example – are generally not patentable. Using this indicator, however, industry in the Tiger economies is clearly able to find creative workers (Veugelers, 2013). Japan is the most important patenting country in the region, and China clearly has the ambition 'to become a world leading innovator, creating and capturing high-tech value added, particularly in targeted areas' (Veugelers, 2013: 11). Despite South Korea's smaller population, it has a similar number of patents to China. The patenting activities in these three countries have outpaced their research and development (R & D) spending, such that their share of world patents is now almost twice as high as their share of global R & D expenditure.[12]

But can creativity be taught and, if so, how? The evidence on the characteristics of creative people suggests that an education system that promotes both cognitive and personality skills should also be able to promote creativity. However, some have argued that traditional schools are stifling, not stimulating, creativity by promoting uniformity and standardization (Robinson, 2006). Indeed, a common view of education systems in East Asia, especially in the Tiger economies, is that they inhibit creativity (Niu and Sternberg, 2003) because of an excessive focus on rote memorization and test-taking, and an excessive respect for hierarchy.

What works to improve cognitive and non-cognitive skills in East Asia?

Directions for policy change

What should countries do to develop cognitive and non-cognitive skills? It is beyond the scope of this chapter to make specific policy recommendations (those need to be tailored to each country context), but the general priorities for policy are reasonably clear: countries must address both the supply of and the demand for human capital.

On the supply side, a paper prepared for PAFTAD 35 (Jimenez *et al.*, 2013) suggests the following policy directions for Malaysia and Thailand: ensure that public funds are spent so as to optimize social returns; reform various aspects of the education system at all levels; and invest in early child development (ECD).

In their initial phases of development, the successful Tiger economies devoted scarce public resources to expand primary and lower secondary education, which at the time yielded the highest social returns. These investments laid a solid and broad foundation for growth – a generally literate and numerate workforce. South Korea demonstrates the benefits of having an education system that is able to respond to and support its different stages of economic development. In the 1960s, to meet increasing demand for junior secondary education, South Korea's government removed entrance examinations to that level and provided short-term teacher training in order to grow its teacher force quickly. In the 1970s and 1980s, its priority shifted to senior secondary education, two-year colleges and open universities. The government transformed private schools into 'privately managed public schools' and provided subsidies to private providers, effectively expanding school supply at the secondary level and raising the enrolment rate from 70 to nearly 100 per cent between 1970 and 2002 (Lee, 2013).

While the emerging economies should improve the reach and quality of basic education, they cannot afford to neglect ECD or the post–basic education levels. As discussed below, there is a growing body of evidence of the long-run benefits of ECD. Attention to tertiary education does not necessarily mean providing subsidies for universal access, but rather addressing capital market failures through targeted means-tested stipends and loan programmes that enable low-income students to have the same opportunities as better-off students. Also, it means having a diversified system that includes general, technical and vocational secondary schools, community colleges, polytechnics, teaching universities, research-focused universities and shorter training programmes. And students should be supported with the right amount of information about the labour market and their own skills to be able to choose among these options. This requires oversight and the right amount of regulation, which are often lacking for non-university tertiary education and for technical vocational education and training institutions.

No one solution or intervention will fix most problems in an education system; mid-course corrections or refinements to a reform are going to be the norm, and frequent and rigorous assessments of education outcomes can help improve the reform as well as build political support for its continuation or improvement. According to Murnane and Ganimian (2014: 13):

> Interventions . . . will not enable countries to develop high-performing education systems such as those in South Korea and Singapore. The remarkable progress of these educational systems results from system-wide efforts over several decades. These efforts included defining learning standards in core subjects for every grade level, developing curricula well-aligned with the learning standards, producing assessments that measured student mastery of the standards, and developing teacher training programs that attracted talented students and prepared them to teach the demanding curriculum effectively. Designing and managing such systemic change successfully requires a remarkably high level of governmental capacity.

Moreover, education reforms need to go beyond investing in school inputs. They involve improving the interrelationships among the key parts of the system and addressing misalignments in its governance framework, management and financing mechanisms, and performance incentives. Countries in East Asia have tried programmes that aim to bring about broad institutional reforms, including decentralizing responsibility and devolving decision-making authority to schools

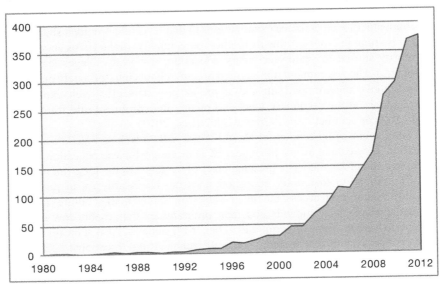

Figures 8.3 Impact evaluations published, by year, 1981–2012

and their communities, as in China and Indonesia. East Asian countries have also shown openness to the role of the private sector in education, by mobilizing, or at least allowing, the private sector to help finance, operate and manage education services. An important policy decision that the countries have faced is how much and for whom governments should subsidize or contract non-state organizations to provide education. Another is how best to ensure good quality and relevance of the services, as well as secure access for disadvantaged students.

Charting the way forward through better evidence: an unfinished agenda

What is the evidence that programmes and policies that act on these general recommendations, if implemented, would be effective in raising educational outcomes? This is a crucial question to ask, especially if there is no one formula that applies to all contexts. Impact evaluation methods that have been used primarily in science and medical research are now being used to inform innovations in education policy, much of them related to expanding enrolment and promoting cognitive skills.[13] Such evaluations are proving useful for assessing alternative programme designs and implementation approaches, as well as for holding programme implementers accountable.

Unfortunately, the evaluation evidence base on education policies and programmes is thin in East Asian countries, and certainly not proportional to the income levels and numbers of children and youth in the region. According to a recent study of all impact evaluations published from 1980 to 2014 (Cameron *et al.*, 2016: Figure 3), there are 649 education-related evaluations in developing countries. Of these, 121 (or about six a year) are on countries in East Asia, with almost half of them on China.[14] Since context matters, countries should build up their own capabilities to conduct such assessments if they are to be useful. India, in contrast to the East Asian economies, has been the subject of a growing body of evaluation research in education, although more research is needed that focuses on building cognitive, non-cognitive and vocational skills.

This evidence gap needs to be filled because knowledge about what works and what does not can help these countries address their skills deficits more effectively and efficiently. We provide a few examples of how rigorous evidence can be used to ensure that policies and programmes are the right ones for the context and time in East Asia.

Early child development

As noted earlier, there is ample evidence from several developed countries and now from a few developing countries that ECD is one of the most effective investments in human capital. In the Philippines, longitudinal data on children from birth through to the end of the primary cycle suggest that malnutrition up to the second year of life has long-term consequences for cognitive development and later educational outcomes (Glewwe *et al.*, 2001). The study suggests returns to investments in ECD in the order of 3:1 – results that are comparable with those found in the United States and elsewhere.

However, design and implementation matter: the right policy may fail when implementation is deficient. Consider the mixed results in Cambodia. In one policy experiment, the government implemented three kinds of interventions to stimulate ECD: formal ECD classrooms; a community-based ECD programme; and a home-based ECD programme. It then supported a rigorous impact evaluation that relied on the random assignment of these interventions across areas, with the expected outcome being measured with standardized tests of problem-solving skills.[15] The result? No significant short-term effects for any of the modalities tested – a disappointing outcome that was attributed to poor implementation and low uptake due to deficiency in promoting the programme.

But another early education programme in Cambodia appears to have been not only more comprehensive in its approach but also better aligned with the existing Grade 1 curriculum. The School Readiness Program includes a number of components: the development of special curricular documentation, 14 days of training to orient teachers to the programme, a regular monitoring regimen, physical upgrading of classrooms and student assessment for monitoring and reporting purposes. The programme evaluation found that children in the treatment group significantly outperformed children in the control group in the language test (Nonoyama-Tarumi and Bredenberg, 2009). This intervention may be one way to compensate for the unavailability of good-quality preschools or ECD centres before children enter primary school.

Improving school quality

Much of the attention to skill building ultimately focuses on reforms to how well schools function. What inputs matter for improving school quality? There are many recent empirical evaluations and studies that help answer this question, though not many involving East Asia, and they have spurred a number of reviews. The clearest findings from one such review by Glewwe *et al.* (2014: 47) are that the following appear conducive to student learning: (a) 'having a fully functioning school – one with better-quality roofs, walls, or floors, with desks, tables, and chairs, and with a school library'; (b) 'having teachers with greater knowledge of the subjects they teach, having a longer school day, and providing tutoring'; (c) teachers' knowledge of the subjects they teach; and (d) higher teacher salaries (although contract teachers who earn less have a positive effect on student performance compared with regular teachers, perhaps as a result of stronger incentives to perform better). Other reviews of evaluations arrive at slightly different conclusions but they tend to agree on the initiatives to improve teachers' ability and effort.[16]

How school inputs are used in the classroom can make all the difference in their impact on learning. For example, many education systems are enthusiastic about the potential benefits of using computers for teaching and learning – and there is good reason for such enthusiasm. In Beijing, the evaluation of a 'one laptop per child' programme in schools found that, after six months of intervention, the programme produced large improvements in learning, with gains in student computer skills and maths scores of 0.33 and 0.17 standard deviations, respectively. The programme also increased students' time using educational software and decreased their time watching television (Mo *et al.*, 2013).

However, computers in classrooms have not always proven to be effective learning tools. In India, an evaluation concludes that when students use computers instead of interacting with teachers during classroom hours, computers have a significant negative effect on test outcomes (0.57 of a standard deviation); but when students use computers after school as a complement to their classroom experience, they show some improvement (0.28 standard deviation) (Linden, 2008).

Another example of this point is about the effective use of textbooks and learning materials. A short-term (31-day) reading marathon programme in the Philippines provided age-appropriate reading materials, trained teachers in their use, supported teachers' initial efforts for about a month and encouraged students to read more on their own at home. The programme evaluation found that students' reading skills improved by 0.13 standard deviations (Abeberese *et al.*, 2014). This positive effect lasted for three months after the programme ended but it had diminished to 0.06 standard deviations by then. The results suggest that teachers do need more training in the use of learning materials and also that a longer-running programme may have yielded a more lasting effect on reading habits and skills.

Addressing health to improve skills

Sometimes the returns to relatively simple interventions, some of which go outside the school system, such as child health, also pay off handsomely. One such intervention is to ensure that children are well nourished. Iron deficiency, or anaemia, leads to lethargy, fatigue, poor attention and prolonged physical impairment. China's Centers for Disease Control found that up to 40 per cent of first-year students in junior high schools suffer from anaemia. In Shaanxi Province, a randomized control trial gave fourth-grade students a daily dose of iron supplements to reduce anaemia; the programme significantly raised the standardized test scores in maths of the students who received the multivitamins (Luo *et al.*, 2009).

More trials are needed to investigate whether other micronutrients affect various cognitive domains – such as short-term memory, visual perception, retrieval ability, sustained attention and cognitive processing speed – in different ways. The results of these interventions can vary depending on which outcome is measured. A meta-analysis (NEMO Study Group, 2007) of hundreds of evaluations of micronutrient supplementation programmes finds the possibility of only a small positive effect on fluid intelligence (or reasoning ability), a positive effect on academic performance in only a handful of trials, and no effect on crystallized intelligence (or acquired knowledge).

Another relatively simple health-related intervention with dramatic effects on motor and cognitive outcomes has been to correct for poor vision – a problem that affects millions of children in East Asia. The leading cause of visual impairment among children is refractive error. A recent study in rural western China raised consciousness among parents and teachers and provided free glasses to randomly selected students. The evaluation found that a short-sighted child performs twice as well in standardized tests if provided with corrective glasses (Ma *et al.*, 2014).

Vocational and technical education

Since the focus of this chapter is skills for a growing economy, vocational and technical education (VTE) deserves special mention. Indeed, it may be important to rebalance an education system that is heavily focused on academic programmes to one that also offers attractive VTE and training at the secondary level. This seems like a sensible approach and one that South Korea, given its perhaps overly high tertiary enrolment rate, has been attempting to do by expanding its 'Meister high school' programme (Lee, 2013). But what is the evidence that a more vibrant VTE programme would build more relevant skills? The relatively scant empirical research on this issue for East Asia signals that caution is needed.

One study in China found that using vocational schooling as a substitute for academic schooling may fail to build the types of skills needed in a competitive economy. A survey of 10,000 students attending academic and vocational high schools in Shaanxi and Zhejiang provinces found that those attending vocational schools did not do well, not only in terms of general skills but also in terms of specific job-related skills (Loyalka, *et al.*, 2013). Analyses of longitudinal data from household surveys in Indonesia examine the labour force participation rates and wages of individuals who chose different education tracks (Chen, 2009; Newhouse and Suryadarma, 2011). The studies did not find better labour market outcomes for those who chose a vocational track over the academic track.

These results do not necessarily imply that VTE – through formal schooling or short training programmes – is not an effective means to build skills. Rather, such programmes may fail to deliver outcomes if they are under-resourced and under-supervised, if their teachers are ill prepared for teaching VTE skills, and if their curricula are not sufficiently informed by the needs of employers. In other regions, such as Latin America, new programmes that bring in private sector perspectives systematically show some promise.

Gaps in evidence

The topic of teachers deserves special attention because the relationship between teachers and students in the classroom lies at the core of the learning process. Various countries have experimented with ways to raise the motivation and performance of teachers through financial incentives, accountability pressure and professional rewards. In terms of financial incentives, Singapore pays teachers for undertaking 100 hours of professional development each year. In terms of professional rewards, China and South Korea encourage teachers who teach the same subject to share information about their experience and solve problems together (Lee, 2013; Wang, 2012). These are promising initiatives that need to be examined so that lessons can be shared with other countries.

In contrast to East Asian countries, in India, there are a larger number of evaluations of teacher-related interventions. For example, one experiment in rural primary schools in Andhra Pradesh provided modest financial rewards to teachers and succeeded in raising student outcomes by 0.27 and 0.17 standard deviations in maths and language, respectively (Muralidharan and Sundararaman, 2011). How well similar rewards would work in different settings in East Asia remains to be seen.

There are no rigorous impact evaluations yet of how to enhance non-cognitive outcomes and creativity in the East Asian context. Past evaluations have focused on assessing interventions to raise enrolment or cognitive skills. Beyond basic education, there is much more to learn from current and future initiatives related to VTE, informal skills training and higher education. Important innovations in these largely uncharted areas in the region warrant the type of research that is now being used to understand successful programmes in basic education.

Concluding remarks

In this chapter we focused on the importance of developing cognitive, non-cognitive and creative skills as part of a country's growth strategy. The rise of the East Asian Tigers points to high-quality skills as a necessary, albeit insufficient, condition for escaping the 'middle-income trap' and spurring further growth. As the demand for skills in the workplace continues to shift towards more advanced tasks, and as jobs increasingly involve analyzing and communicating information, those individuals (and their countries) with low cognitive and non-cognitive skills are also increasingly likely to be left behind in the global economy.

A small, though key, part of this human capital and growth agenda should be to measure the progress in developing skills. Internationally comparable standardized tests such as TIMSS and PISA have been instrumental in raising consciousness about the disparities and changes in skills levels worldwide. The high performance of the East Asian Tigers has made them the standard against which many countries, including those in the OECD, measure their educational performance. Though imperfect measures of the full set of skills in demand now, student assessments galvanize public opinion and set benchmarks for performance that can be tracked. Not all the countries in the region, however, belong to the consortium of countries that applies these tests (Table 8.2). Among the middle-income countries, China (as a whole), India and the Philippines did not participate in the recent assessment rounds; Vietnam joined PISA in 2012 (and did remarkably well). Low-income countries such as Laos and Cambodia would reap benefits from participating now, as they reform their education systems. And countries in the Pacific such as Papua New Guinea and Fiji should consider measuring themselves against international benchmarks.

As part of building the evidence base for better policies and investments, we have argued also for more analyses of which specific investments build skills and under what conditions. There are now scientifically valid methods that are being used in the social sciences to measure such impacts. And because context matters for effective design and implementation, there is ample need for more evaluations in the emerging East Asian economies.

Notes

1   Indeed it was the theme of a recent PAFTAD Conference. See Dobson (2013).
2   The varying definitions of what is a middle-income trap have led to different judgements as to who is in it and who is not. Using a definition closer to that of Aiyar *et al.* (2013), Watson (2014: 14) claims that Thailand is in the trap, Vietnam is a candidate for it, the Philippines is 'shaky but improving' and Indonesia is reasonably solid. Much of the discussion is about the institutional framework in these countries.
3   For example, in Malaysia from 1987 to 2007, output per worker in the sector rose almost fourfold. In the services sector, productivity doubled. In contrast, agricultural productivity rose less than 20 per cent in the same period (Flaaen *et al.*, 2013). Can these gains be sustained? Analysts claim that this will happen only if countries such as Malaysia are able to stimulate their exports of modern services in telecommunications, computer and information services as well as financial services, which at the moment are still outstripped by traditional services in travel, construction and personnel areas.
4   We are grateful to Jong-Wha Lee, a discussant of this chapter, for bringing this work to our attention.
5   South Korea stands out in this respect because of its high rates of private tutoring (Dang and Rogers, 2008). South Korean parents spend considerable resources on private tutoring to boost their children's academic performance, and there is evidence that these investments are positively associated with maths and English test scores (Park *et al.*, 2011).
6   In South Korea and Singapore, the enrolment rate at the tertiary level is so high that some analysts, writers in the popular press and policymakers have expressed concern about 'over-education' (for example, Chen, 2015).

7 Although technically not a Tiger economy because it is a city within a country, Shanghai (China) also kept pace with the other Asian countries.

8 Using the 2011 TIMSS data, the average maths scores in Indonesia, Malaysia and Thailand relative to South Korea's scores range from 63 per cent in Indonesia to 72 per cent in Malaysia. The Philippines does not participate in PISA and last participated in TIMSS in 2003; in 2003, its average maths score was 64 per cent of South Korea's average score that year.

9 Pratham is an Indian non-governmental organization that facilitates and publishes the Annual Status of Education Report (ASER), which is based on an annual rural household survey, to assess children's basic learning levels in reading and arithmetic. One government school in each sampled village is also visited. The survey is carried out by a local organization or institution in each district. ASER 2014 is the tenth such report.

10 We wrote about this in Jimenez and King (2013).

11 Research has shown a negligible relationship between creativity and IQ scores, indicating that even students with low IQ scores can be creative. There are different ways of testing for creativity, and a meta-analysis of hundreds of studies shows that 'when creativity tests are administered in a game-like context, the creativity test scores have smaller relationships with IQ test scores than when creativity tests are administered in a test-like context' (Kim, 2005: 65). The analysis also finds that IQ scores are more closely associated with creativity scores for younger groups than for older groups.

12 Note also the success of East Asian emigrants in dynamically innovative areas such as Silicon Valley, suggesting that these countries' education systems have stimulated creative thinking (Wadhwa *et al.*, 2012).

13 For more information on impact evaluations, see the 3ie website: www.3ieimpact.org.

14 Much of the Chinese work is done through a partnership between Stanford University and Chinese researchers in an initiative called the Rural Education Action Project (REAP). See Boswell *et al.* (2011) for a description. The website is http://reap.fsi.stanford.edu/research.

15 Some 1,500 children were tested between 2009 and 2011 (Bouguen *et al.*, 2013).

16 See Conn (2014); Glewwe *et al.* (2014); Kremer *et al.* (2013); Krishnaratne *et al.* (2013); McEwan (2014); and Murnane and Ganimian (2014).

References

Abeberese, AB, Kumler, TJ and Linden, LL 2014. Improving reading skills by encouraging children to read in school: A randomized evaluation of the Sa Aklat Sisikat reading program in the Philippines. *Journal of Human Resources*, 49(3), 611–33.

Aiyar, MS, Duval, MRA, Puy, MD, Wu, MY and Zhang, ML 2013. *Growth slowdowns and the middle-income trap*. IMF Working Paper No. 13–71. Washington, DC: International Monetary Fund.

Barro, RJ and Lee, J-W 2010. *Barro–Lee: Educational Attainment Dataset*. Available online at: www.barrolee.com.

Barro, RJ and Lee, J-W 2015. *Education Matters: Global Schooling Gains from the 19th to the 21st Century*. Oxford: Oxford University Press.

Bloom, D and Williamson, JG 1998. Demographic transition and economic growth in East Asia. *World Bank Economic Review*, 12(3), 419–55.

Bloom, D, Canning, D and Malaney, P 2000. Demographic change and economic growth in East Asia. *Population and Development Review*, 26, 257–90.

Boswell, M, Rozelle, S, Zhang, L, Liu, C, Luo, R and Shi, Y 2011. Conducting influential impact evaluations in China: The experience of the Rural Education Action Project. *Journal of Development Effectiveness*, 3(3), 420–30.

Bouguen, A, Filmer, D, Macours, K and Naudeau, S 2013. *Impact evaluation of three types of early child development interventions in Cambodia.* World Bank Policy Research Working Paper No. 6540. Washington, DC: The World Bank.

Bowles, S, Gintis, H and Osborne, M 2001. The determinants of earnings: A behavioral approach. *Journal of Economic Literature,* 39(4), 1, 137–76.

Cameron, D, Mishra, A and Brown, A 2015. The growth of impact evaluation for international development: How much have we learned. *Journal of Development Effectiveness* 8(1), 1–21.

Chen, D 2009. *Vocational schooling, labor market outcomes, and college entry.* Policy Research Working Paper Series. Washington, DC: The World Bank.

Chen, S 2015. Singapore wants kids to skip college: Good luck with that. *Bloomberg News,* 3 May. Available online at: www.bloomberg.com/news/articles/2015–05–03/singapore-wants-kids-to-skip-college-good-luck-with-that.

Conn, K 2014. Identifying effective education interventions in sub-Saharan Africa: A meta-analysis of rigorous impact evaluations. Unpublished ms. Columbia University, New York.

Dang, HA and Rogers, FH 2008. The growing phenomenon of private tutoring: Does it deepen human capital, increase inequality, or waste resources? *World Bank Research Observer,* 23(2), 161–200.

Deke, J and Haimson, J 2006. *Valuing Student Competencies: Which Ones Predict Postsecondary Educational Attainment and Earnings, and for Whom?* Princeton, NJ: Mathematica Policy Research Inc.

Dobson, W (ed.) 2013. *Human Capital Formation and Economic Growth in Asia and the Pacific.* London: Routledge.

Duckworth, AL, Weir, D, Tsukayama, E and Kwok, D 2012. Who does well in life? Conscientious adults excel in both objective and subjective success. *Frontiers in Psychology,* 3, 356–65.

Dweck, CS 2000. *Self-Theories: Their Role in Motivation, Personality, and Development.* New York: Psychology Press.

The Economist 2012. Manufacturing: The third industrial revolution. *The Economist,* 21 April.

Eichengreen, B, Park, D and Shin, K 2013. *Growth slowdowns redux: New evidence on the middle-income trap.* NBER Working Paper No. 18673. Cambridge, MA: National Bureau of Economic Research.

Felipe, J 2012. *Tracking the middle-income trap: What is it, who is in it and why? Part I.* Economics Working Paper Series No. 306. Manila: Asian Development Bank.

Flaaen, A, Ghani, E and Mishra, S 2013. *How to avoid middle income traps: Evidence from Malaysia.* Policy Research Working Paper. Washington, DC: The World Bank. Available online at: http://elibrary.worldbank.org/doi/abs/10.1596/1813–9450–6427.

Glewwe, P 2002. Schools and skills in developing countries: Education policies and socioeconomic outcomes. *Journal of Economic Literature,* 40(2), 436–82.

Glewwe, P, Hanushek, EA, Humpage, S and Ravina, R 2014. School resources and educational outcomes in developing countries: A review of the literature from 1990 to 2010. In P Glewwe (ed.), *Education Policy in Developing Countries.* Chicago: University of Chicago Press, 13–64.

Glewwe, P, Jacoby, H and King, EM 2001. Early childhood nutrition and academic achievement: A longitudinal analysis. *Journal of Public Economics,* 81(3), 345–68.

Growth Commission 2008. *The Growth Report: Strategies for Sustained Growth and Inclusive Development.* Washington, DC: The World Bank.

Hanushek, EA and Woessmann, L 2008. The role of cognitive skills in economic development. *Journal of Economic Literature*, 46(3): 607–68.

Hanushek, EA, Schwerdt, G, Wiederhold, S and Woessmann, L 2013. *Returns to skills around the world: Evidence from PIAAC*. OECD Education Working Paper No. 101. Paris: OECD Publishing. Available online at: http://dx.doi.org/10.1787/5k3tsjqmvtq2-en.

Heckman, JJ, Stixrud, J and Urzua, S 2006. The effects of cognitive and noncognitive abilities on labor market outcomes and social behavior. *Journal of Labor Economics*, 24(3), 411–82.

Heineck, G and Anger, S 2010. The returns to cognitive abilities and personality traits in Germany. *Labour Economics*, 17(3), 535–46.

International Association for the Evaluation of Educational Achievement (IEA) 2011. *Trends in International Mathematics and Science Study (TIMMS)*. Amsterdam: IEA. Available online at: www.iea.nl/timss_2011.html.

Jankowska, A, Nagengast, A and Perea, JR 2012. *The middle-income trap: Comparing Asian and Latin American experiences*. OECD Development Centre Policy Insights No. 96. Paris: OECD Publishing.

Jimenez, E and King, EM 2013. The skills of 'Tigers'. In W Dobson (ed.), *Human Capital Formation and Economic Growth in Asia and the Pacific*. London: Routledge, 19–36.

Jimenez, E, Nguyen, VT and Patrinos, HA 2013. Human capital development and economic growth in Malaysia and Thailand: Stuck in the middle? In W Dobson (ed.), *Human Capital Formation and Economic Growth in Asia and the Pacific*. London: Routledge, 141–62.

Judge, TA and Bono, JE 2001. Relationship of core self-evaluations traits – self-esteem, generalized self-efficacy, locus of control, and emotional stability – with job satisfaction and job performance: A meta-analysis. *Journal of Applied Psychology*, 86(1), 80–92.

Kharas, H and Kohli, H 2011. What is the middle income trap, why do countries fall into it, and how can it be avoided? *Global Journal of Emerging Market Economies*, 3(3), 281–9.

Kim, KH 2005. Can only intelligent people be creative? A meta-analysis. *Journal of Secondary Gifted Education*, 16(2–3), 57–66.

King, EM and Rogers, FH 2014. Intelligence, personality, and creativity: Unleashing the power of intelligence and personality traits to build a creative and innovative economy. Conference Edition. Seoul symposium on 'Achieving HOPE: Happiness of People through Education. Innovation in Korean Education for a Creative Economy', November 2014.

Kingdon, GG 2007. The progress of school education in India. *Oxford Review of Economic Policy*, 23(2), 168–95.

Kremer, M, Brannen, C and Glennerster, R 2013. The challenge of education and learning in the developing world. *Science*, 340(6,130), 297–300.

Krishnaratne, S, White, H and Carpenter, E 2013. *Quality education for all children? What works in education in developing countries?* International Initiative for Impact Evaluation (3ie) Working Paper No. 20. New Delhi.

Kuhn, P and Weinberger, C 2005. Leadership skills and wages. *Journal of Labor Economics*, 23(3), 395–436.

Lee, JH 2013. *Positive Changes: The Education, Science & Technology Policies of Korea*. Updated edn. Seoul: Korea Economic Daily & Business Publications, Inc.

Linden, L 2008. Complement or substitute? The effect of technology on student achievement in India. JPAL Working Paper. Cambridge, MA: MIT. Available online at: www.poverty actionlab.org/evaluation/complement-or-substitute-effect-technology-student-achievement-india.

Loyalka, P, Huang, X, Zhang, L, Wei, J, Yi, H, Song, Y, Ren, B, Shi, Y, Chu, J, Maani, M and Rozelle, S 2013. *The Impact of Vocational Schooling in Deveoping Countries: Evidence from China*. Stanford, CA: Stanford Rural Education Action Program (REAP). Available online at: http://reap.fsi.stanford.edu/sites/default/files/Impact_of_Vocational_Schooling.pdf.

Lucas, RE 1993. Making a miracle. *Econometrica*, 61(2), 251–72.

Luo, R, Shi, Y, Zhang, L, Liu, C, Rozelle, S and Sharbono, B 2009. Malnutrition in China's rural boarding schools: The case of primary schools in Shaanxi Province. *Asia Pacific Journal of Education* 29(4), 481–501.

Ma, X, Zhou, Z, Yi, H, Pang, X, Shi, Y, Chen, Q, Meltzer, ME, le Cessie, S, He, M, Rozelle, S, Liu, Y and Congdon, N 2014. Effect of providing free glasses on children's educational outcomes in China: Cluster randomized controlled trial. *BMJ* 349:g5740. Available online at: www.bmj.com/content/bmj/349/bmj.g5740.full.pdf.

McEwan, PJ 2014. Improving learning in primary schools of developing countries: A meta-analysis of randomized experiments. *Review of Educational Research*, 20(10), 1–42.

Mo, D, Swinnen, J, Zhang, L, Yi, H, Qu, Q, Boswell, M and Rozelle, S 2013. Can one-to-one computing narrow the digital divide and the educational gap in China? The case of Beijing migrant schools. *World Development*, 46, 14–29.

Molnar, M, Wang, B and Gao, R 2015. *Assessing China's skills gap and inequalities in education*. OECD Economics Department Working Paper No. 1220. Paris: OECD Publishing. Available online at: http://dx.doi.org/10.1787/5js1j1805czs-en.

Muralidharan, K and Sundararaman, V 2011. Teacher performance pay: Experimental evidence from India. *Journal of Political Economy*, 119(1), 39–77.

Murnane, RJ and Ganimian, AJ 2014. *Improving educational outcomes in developing countries: Lessons from rigorous evaluations*. NBER Working Paper No. 20284. Cambridge, MA: National Bureau of Economic Research.

NEMO Study Group 2007. Effect of a 12-mo micronutrient intervention on learning and memory in well-nourished and marginally nourished school-aged children: 2 parallel, randomized, placebo-controlled studies in Australia and Indonesia. *American Journal of Clinical Nutrition*, 86(4), 1082–93.

Newhouse, D and Suryadarma, D 2011. The value of vocational education: High school type and labor market outcomes in Indonesia. *World Bank Economic Review*, 25(2), 296–322.

Niu, W and Sternberg, RJ 2003. Societal and school influences on student creativity: The case of China. *Psychology in the Schools*, 40(1), 103–14.

Nonoyama-Tarumi, Y and Bredenberg, K 2009. Impact of school readiness program interventions on children's learning in Cambodia. *International Journal of Educational Development*, 29(1), 39–45.

Organization for Economic Cooperation and Development (OECD) 2013a. *OECD Skills Outlook 2013: First Results from the Survey of Adult Skills*. Paris: OECD Publishing.

Organization for Economic Cooperation and Development (OECD) 2013b. *PISA 2012 Results in Focus: What 15-Year-Olds Know and What They Can Do With What They Know*. Paris: OECD Publishing.

Ostry, JD, Berg, A and Tsangarides, CG 2014. *Redistribution, inequality, and growth*. IMF Staff Discussion Note SDN14/02, April. Washington, DC: International Monetary Fund.

Park, H, Byun, S-Y and Kim, K-K 2011. Parental involvement and students' cognitive outcomes in Korea focusing on private tutoring. *Sociology of Education*, 84(1), 3–22.

Pratham 2015. *2014 Annual Status of Education Report*. New Delhi: Pratham.

Roberts, BW, Harms, PD, Caspi, A and Moffitt, TE 2007. Can we predict the counter productive employee? Evidence from a child-to-adult prospective study. Evidence from a 23-year longitudinal study. *Journal of Applied Psychology*, 92(1), 427–36.

Robinson, K 2006. Changing education from the ground up. TED Talks.

Veugelers, R 2013. *The world innovation landscape: Asia rising?* Bruegel Policy Contribution No. 2013/02, February. Brussels: Bruegel.

von Culin, K, Tsukuyama, E and Duckworth, A 2014. Unpacking grit: Motivational correlates of perseverance and passion for long-term goals. *Journal of Positive Psychology*, 9(4), 306–12.

Wadhwa, V, Saxenian, AL and Siciliano, FD 2012. *America's New Immigrant Entrepreneurs: Then and Now*. Kansas City, MO: Ewing Marion Kauffman Foundation.

Wang, Y 2012. *Education in a Changing World: Flexibility, Skills, and Employability*. Washington, DC: The World Bank.

Watson, WT 2014. *Beating the Middle Income Trap in Southeast Asia*. Special Report No. 156, 27 August. Washington, DC: The Heritage Foundation.

World Bank 1993. *The East Asian Miracle. Policy Research Report*. Washington, DC: Oxford University Press.

World Bank 2012. *Putting Higher Education to Work: Skills and Research for Growth in East Asia*. Washington, DC: The World Bank.

9 Escaping the middle-income trap

Trade, investment and innovation

Shiro Armstrong and Tom Westland

Introduction

The Asia-Pacific region, especially East Asia, is home to a number of economies that have managed to graduate from middle-income status into the high-income group of economies. Starting with Japan's rapid rise from the ashes of World War II, South Korea, Taiwan and Singapore all successfully caught up to the technological frontier, and their peoples enjoy high incomes. Only 13 of 101 countries globally have been able to move from middle-income to high-income status since 1960 and catch up to the technological frontier.

China and other countries in South East Asia have succeeded in emulating the rapid catch-up growth of Japan and the newly industrialized economies (NIEs), but have yet to make the transition to high income. Some middle-income countries, such as Thailand and Malaysia, appear to be stuck in the middle-income range – using the World Bank Atlas method of categorizing economies, this means that they are countries with per capita gross national incomes of between US$1,045 and US$12,746 – and are having difficulty in reaching the technological frontier. Others such as China are experiencing a slowdown in growth as they rapidly approach higher middle-income levels, and a major policy preoccupation is with maintaining growth momentum and avoiding getting stuck in a middle-income trap.

The 'middle-income trap' is still rather nebulously defined in the literature. There is no strong agreement on the definition of the trap, its causes or its potential remedies. Some authors consider that the trap is absolute – that is, a phenomenon encountered by countries at a particular stage of their economic development (Felipe *et al.*, 2012). This might suggest structural pitfalls that are common to economies at different stages of development. Another interpretation suggests the middle-income trap should be conceived in relative terms – that is, essentially, it describes a failure of some countries to converge to the income levels of the high-income countries, even though they may experience continual growth (Robertson and Ye, 2013). Others – without necessarily using the phrase 'middle-income trap' – examine 'growth slowdowns', as in Eichengreen *et al.* (2013), Aiyar *et al.* (2013) and Pritchett and Summers (2014), in order to understand why rapidly growing economies may slow and not achieve potential.

Depending on which definition of the trap is used, some possible causes are relatively straightforward. Conceived as a relative slowdown, the trap may be explained via simple convergence mechanisms like that suggested by the Solow model, whereby the accumulation of factors that exhibit diminishing marginal returns permits fast catch-up growth when an economy is a long way from the frontier, but leads to relatively slow economic growth closer to it. In this case, productivity growth becomes more important, suggesting that countries may need to invest in human capital or research and development in order to continue converging to the frontier. Other possible causes of the trap include a loss of competitiveness in export industries as countries reach the Lewis turning point and real wages begin to rise, without the countervailing increases in technology and human capital that would facilitate a move into high value-added industries (Cai, 2012; Kharas and Kohli, 2011).

The East Asian growth model, which allowed some Asian economies to avoid or escape the middle-income trap, has been studied extensively owing to the region's record of remarkable development in a short time. The policies that led to the very fast growth first of Japan early in the post-war period, then of the NIEs of Taiwan, South Korea (hereinafter Korea), Hong Kong and Singapore in the 1970s and 1980s, have been of immense interest in understanding not only the factors that facilitated or encouraged rapid growth, but also how these countries reached high-income levels and the global technology frontier. Figure 9.1 shows that the Asian economic experience has been extraordinarily diverse in the past 60 years: some countries have risen from very low levels of per capita income to converge closely to US per capita gross domestic product (GDP); others, on the other hand, have stagnated at low or middle levels of income.

The Asian growth story is strongly linked to openness in international trade. All the major economies that have transitioned from low through middle to high income in Asia were natural resource-deficient economies that were dependent on efficient specialization in the international economy through exporting labour-intensive, then capital-intensive and technology-intensive products to make this transition. This story has been analyzed and elaborated on famously in this conference series (Garnaut, 1979). Policymakers in Asia and elsewhere recognize the importance of openness to trade and investment for economic development. They accept that both rapid catch-up growth for low-income countries and growth in reaching the technology frontier for middle-income countries have required openness to trade and investment. The production networks and deep integration that now typify Asian economic interdependence are a result of openness to trade and investment.

This chapter considers the middle-income trap as a relative trap – that is, as a failure of convergence to the frontier. We therefore look at economic growth in countries that are at 'middle distance' from the technological frontier, as defined by US GDP per worker. As Kharas and Gill argue in their contribution to this volume, there has been a gap in economic theory when it comes to growth in middle-income countries. We therefore take our inspiration from Schumpeterian growth theory and, in particular, from the model of Acemoglu *et al.* (2006). Their

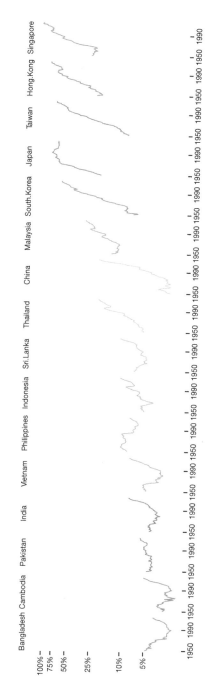

Figure 9.1 Ratio of real GDP per capita (PPP) in Asian countries to US, 1950–2013

Note: Per capita GDP is calculated on a purchasing power parity (PPP) basis.

Source: Authors' calculations; Maddison database (www.ggdc.net/maddison/maddison-project/home.htm).

model distinguishes between a 'catch-up' and an 'innovative' phase of growth. In this context, the 'trap' is considered as a difficulty in transitioning from the one into the other.

In particular, this chapter considers the middle-income 'trap' as a product of the interaction between institutional and policy settings and the developmental level. In particular, it looks at the importance of trade and foreign direct investment (FDI) for catch-up growth and inquires into the nature of its importance for innovative growth. Openness to trade and investment appears a necessary but not sufficient condition for both phases of growth. But the kind of openness that facilitates fast growth in the catch-up and innovative growth phases is likely to be quite different. The traditional kind of openness – lower tariffs and openness to foreign capital – facilitates catch-up growth as well as innovative growth. But as countries reach a certain stage of development, it can be hypothesized, a deeper kind of openness is required: one that facilitates the entry and exit of firms, and thus the 'creative destruction' of Schumpeterian growth.

There are several well-known mechanisms that explain why openness is necessary for growth. To have access to frontier technology, for example, it is necessary to be open to trade in capital goods or in goods that embody the technology that is to be adopted. Just as importantly, international trade leads to fiercer competition for markets in the home country, which encourages domestic firms to raise their productivity. Openness also encourages economic specialization in areas of comparative advantage, leading to higher allocative efficiency. Openness to international investment also promotes growth by facilitating the transfer of technology, increasing competition and encouraging efficiency gains.

The impact of this process of opening, however, may not be the same at all stages of development. Consider the case of tariffs. The deadweight loss of a tax is proportional to the square of the tax rate, so reductions in relatively low tariffs, although still positive for growth and efficiency, will not have the same impact as reductions in very high tariffs. But countries with relatively low tariffs often have other barriers to economic competition that, for example, impede firm entry and exit or regulate financial markets in ways that may starve innovative, productivity-enhancing firms of the capital they require to expand.

The importance of trade and investment can therefore be considered in the context of different growth stages: catch-up growth at the beginning of the economic development and industrialization process, growth closer to the global technology frontier, and the transition between the two. This chapter is concerned with the experience of Asian economies in these two stages of development or growth, and those that may get stuck in between the two.

Importance of trade and investment for growth

That trade and investment are important for economic growth and development is widely accepted; they are a necessary but not sufficient condition for growth (IMF, 2014). Opening up to trade allows specialization in production, realization of comparative advantage, and therefore a more efficient allocation of resources. East Asian economies are exemplars of the success of commitment to open trade and investment regimes for integration into the global economy, rapid development and lifting incomes.

Openness to trade and investment would seem to be necessary for growth at all stages of economic development. Rapid catch-up growth for developing countries would not be possible without trade and investment. Even when growth slows as countries lose the advantage of backwardness and the ability to leapfrog early stages of development, the transition to more value-added growth continues to require adoption of technologies from abroad. And growth closer to the technology frontier would require maintaining that openness.

We illustrate this stylistically in Table 9.1, which uses the Konjunkturforschungsstelle (KOF) *de jure* measure of economic globalization that ranges from zero to 100. The *de jure* measure includes hidden import barriers, the mean tariff rate, taxes on international trade as a percentage of current revenue and capital account restrictions. The table presents average annual per capita growth rates in Asia for economies with KOF economic globalization scores of less than (greater than) 75. For countries with labour productivity between one-quarter and one-half of US labour productivity, having very high openness is associated with a small additional positive impact on average growth rates. Countries between one-half and three-quarters as productive as the United States have a larger pay-off to openness; however, the countries that see the largest impact of this deep 'openness' are those that are close to the US technological frontier. In Figure 9.2, we show values for this KOF *de jure* index for selected Asian countries. Key episodes from recent economic history in Asia, such as India's dramatic liberalization, starting in 1990, can clearly be seen.

Upgrading technology and catching up to, or remaining at, the global technology frontier require trade and FDI. FDI brings not only foreign capital, but also technology, knowledge, know-how and best-practice management; and is crucial to technological progress (Almeida and Fernandes, 2008). Trade embodies technology with significant spillovers to the importing country. The global technology frontier is expanding with innovation wherever that may occur and requires openness for adoption and adaptation.

As middle-income countries are defined by their distance from the global technology frontier, the ability to upgrade, catch up and innovate is important to them closing that distance. To reach that technology frontier, countries need to be open to ideas and have institutions that allow for more complex interactions across the

Table 9.1 The impact of 'deep' openness on average annual per capita GDP growth rates in Asia, 1970–2010 (per cent)

	GDP per worker relative to the US			
	0–25	*25–50*	*50–75*	*75–100*
Openness < 75	3.056	6.04	2.27	2.14
Openness > 75	n.a.	6.212	3.421	4.575

Sources: GDP per worker from Penn World Tables v.8; openness from KOF Index of Globalization, Economic Globalization (Restrictions Sub-index).

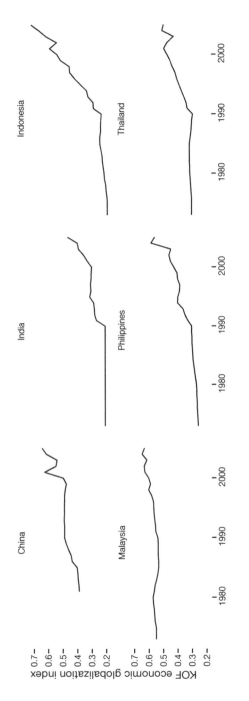

Figure 9.2 Economic openness in selected Asian countries, 1970–2005

Source: KOF Index of Globalization, ETH Zurich (http://globalization.kof.ethz.ch/).

economy. That would seem to include good governance characterized by decentral-ized decision-making and confidence in a well-functioning and flexible market system.

Figure 9.3 shows the correlation between openness and annual growth rates for economies between 1975 and 2009 by income group. There is a positive relationship between an economy's growth rate and its level of openness across time and across income groups.

Low-income countries that have below $1,045 gross national income (GNI) as defined by the World Bank at any particular point show a strong relationship between growth and opening up from autarky. It would appear high middle-income (with a GNI between $4,125 and $12,746) and high-income countries (above $12,746) require higher degrees of openness to grow significantly. Lower middle-income countries (with a GNI between $1,045 and $4,125) exhibit a relationship between growth and openness that is unexpected, with high rates of growth at both higher levels and relatively lower levels of openness, but not between.

Much of the literature – and Figure 9.3 illustrates this through simple correlation – is clear on the necessity of openness for growth. What is less clear in the literature is the empirical evidence of exact causal links, the magnitude of the effect of trade on growth and the channels by which trade and investment can accelerate growth.

The empirical evidence in traditional trade models, and some more recent literature, has generally found modest gains from trade (see, for example, Arkolakis *et al.*, 2012). Those models typically measure gains from changes in aggregate trade following liberalization and aggregate elasticities. These models do not account for heterogeneous firms and therefore resource allocation within industries

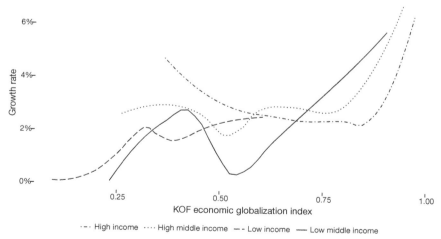

Figure 9.3 Historical relationship between growth rates and openness at different stages of development, 1970–2005

Note: The fits are non-parametric (loess) regressions for each income category. Each country-year is one observation.

Source: Penn World Tables; KOF Index of Globalization.

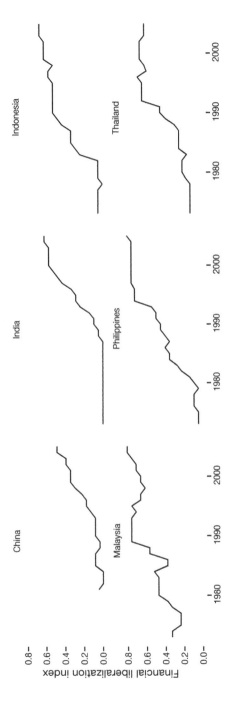

Figure 9.4 Financial liberalization in selected Asian countries

Source: Aiyar et al. (2013).

towards more productive firms. Ricardian trade models and others based on restrictive assumptions around homogeneous firms, such as that of Arkolakis *et al.* (2012), capture the gains of trade from moving from autarky, signs of which can be seen for low-income countries in Figure 9.1.

In reconciling the difference in observed welfare gains and productivity growth from trade liberalization and the trade models, a new class of models has been developed in the past decade that demonstrates that gains from trade occur from increased varieties for consumers (Broda and Weinstein, 2006), allocative efficiency gains and trade-induced productivity gains (Melitz, 2003). The gains from trade are, in this class of model, largely driven by the increased competition from foreign firms and new entrants domestically, and the ability of productive incumbent firms to expand and also inefficient firms to exit the market and free up resources (Melitz and Redding, 2013).

Increased competition – from both international and domestic entrants – and access to a larger market internationally are important for reducing mark-ups for firms, realizing economies of scale and achieving higher aggregate productivity for firms and industries (Melitz and Ottaviano, 2008; Melitz and Redding, 2013). An important condition for realizing these gains is free entry and exit of firms. The extent of barriers to entry for firms is an important indicator of well-functioning institutions (Acemoglu *et al.*, 2006; Djankov *et al.*, 2002), and high barriers to entry for new firms mean that innovation is impeded and incumbent firms are protected and do not have the incentive to innovate (Aghion *et al.*, 2005). Barriers to exit, or poor bankruptcy laws, mean that inefficient firms cannot easily exit the market and hold up valuable resources that could be put to better use (Lee *et al.*, 2011). Economies with high barriers to entry and exit are often characterized by inefficient firms with lost innovation potential and may need subsidies to survive.

The gains from trade are magnified when innovation and deeper specialization occur in production chains. Melitz and Redding (2013) show that domestic productivity growth due to specialization in the production networks that characterize trade and investment in global commerce today is in addition to any dynamic gains from trade and technology spillovers. These effects can be expected to be particularly prominent in Asia, where production networks are more extensive than anywhere else in the world (Baldwin and Lopez-Gonzalez, 2014). Those gains from trade and FDI due to technology diffusion and spillovers are often identified as necessary for escaping the middle-income trap (Lee and Narjoko, 2015). The model of Melitz and Redding (2013) shows that fragmentation of production across borders, which induces reorganization of production, is a significant source of endogenous change in domestic productivity.

The experience of Asian and other economies shows that catch-up growth requires openness to goods trade and liberalized FDI across key industrial sectors. An export-oriented growth strategy, which many in Asia have followed, requires policies and institutions that allow adoption of technology and favourable conditions for exporting to the global market.

The policy strategies and institutions that encourage export-oriented growth may not be suitable for more innovative growth, which requires higher productivity services input, efficiency in production and more flexibility in resource allocation, as well as a wider array of arm's-length market interactions. That would seem to require a different kind of openness to goods and services trade, openness to international and domestic competition, and more foreign participation and linkages across more of the economy.

Catch-up growth and growth at the technology frontier

Institutions and policies suited to growth and development differ at different stages of development. There is a large body of literature that shows institutions different from those that are considered best practice may serve developing countries sufficiently well. These second-best institutions are important in the context of developing countries that have specific market and government failures that cannot be remedied in the short run (Rodrik, 2008).

The experience of many Asian countries demonstrates that second-best institutions and policies have been a feature during rapid catch-up growth. Rents and barriers to entry may be an element in developing countries that stimulate entrepreneurship, investment and exports (Klinger and Lederman, 2006; Rodrik, 2008). Such second-best institutions are often then seen as a drag on growth once those economies develop to the point where the underlying market and government failures can be remedied. Rajan and Zingales (2000) suggest that the very institutions and practices that were responsible for Asia's growth success played a role in the Asian Financial Crisis because the countries failed to change their growth models or reform their institutions as they narrowed the distance to the technology frontier. The institutions that played an important role in Japan's rapid growth – such as labour practices, a repressed capital market that directed the allocation of capital to preferred sectors and industrial organization arrangements – are now seen as a drag on growth since the economy reached the technology frontier and growth has slowed (Ozawa, 2005).

It is therefore important to recognize the different policy regimes and institutional settings that might be suited to different stages of growth in any analysis of the importance of trade and investment for moving from one stage of growth to another.

Acemoglu *et al.* (2006) develop a model to show that catch-up growth or, as they characterize it, growth that depends on *adoption* of technologies from the global technological frontier, will be fostered by a different set of policies and institutional arrangements than is required for an economy closer to the frontier that requires innovation. The key difference between firms in catch-up economies and those in countries that are closer to or at the technology frontier, according to Acemoglu *et al.* (2006), is whether or not firms are protected from competition.

Investment and capital formation are important for an economy in the catch-up phase of growth, when it is adopting technology instead of innovating (Acemoglu *et al.*, 2006). Investment in this phase of development is commonly encouraged by non-competitive arrangements, including protection from competition, state intervention and long-term relationships between firms and banks (Gerschenkron,

1962). Without that protection, firms and managers may not have the incentive to invest, but that protection becomes a hindrance to productivity-raising investment as an economy moves closer to the frontier.

Beyond catch-up growth through capital accumulation and the utilization of cheap labour, firms need to innovate and not just adopt or imitate technology to reach the global technology frontier. That requires the selection of more efficient, productive and innovative managers, more highly skilled labour and more flexible firms. As a country approaches the global technology frontier in the Acemoglu *et al.* (2006) model, in order to move to innovation-based growth, these protections need to be removed to allow natural (better) selection of firms and managers. A country will become stuck in a non-convergence trap – trapped in the investment-based strategy and failing to transition to the innovation-based strategy – if it maintains these non-competitive arrangements. With more competition, international and domestic firms are less likely to retain unsuccessful workers, and the opportunity costs of subsidies to unsuccessful firms that fail to innovate become more costly.

Acemoglu *et al.* (2006) do not refer to the middle-income trap. Their model is concerned solely with domestic competition and does not include an external sector, but the model provides a useful framework for thinking about these two different growth strategies. In the Acemoglu *et al.* (2006) framework, the difference between catch-up growth and growth closer to the frontier is simplified to the difference between high barriers to entry and low barriers to entry. Their empirical results suggest that barriers to entry are more harmful to growth as a country moves closer to the frontier.

Firm entry and exit is one of the main drivers of the gains from trade in the new trade theory models with heterogeneous firms, as explained above (Levchenko and Zhang 2014; Melitz, 2003; Melitz and Redding, 2013). Efficiency and productivity gains from low barriers to firm entry and exit cannot be realized for economies in the catch-up phase of growth given the underdeveloped markets in developing countries. Other conditions that are required for innovative growth, such as high levels of human capital, would also seem to be necessary to ensure flexibility and gains from low barriers to entry. The allocative efficiency gains and the trade-induced productivity gains from trade liberalization may be even more important when an economy is closer to the technology frontier. Protection of incumbents and barriers to firm entry mean that the industry does not realize the potential allocative efficiency gains and productivity gains through natural selection.

Market intervention in Asia and transition to innovation

Governments in Japan, Korea, Taiwan and China countered market failure in factor markets with interventions to facilitate the establishment and growth of industrial sectors that were consistent with their comparative advantage (Amsden, 1989; Kwon, 1994; Wade, 1990). Export-promoting growth strategies were pursued through different interventions across these economies. Such second-best or third-best policies were embraced for political stability and to allow a gradual approach to marketization given the many vested interests and the circumstances of those countries (Perkins, 1994). Another reason North East Asian economic policies achieved a high degree of success was that the interventionism typically worked by influencing rather than replacing private market decisions (Kuznets, 1988).

Market distortions in East Asia during the rapid catch-up growth periods have been mainly focused on government intervention in trying to fix or overcome underdeveloped markets (for earlier work, see Corden, 1974; Myint, 1973). As Perkins (1994) and Saxonhouse (1983) argue, in Japan and East Asia, industrial policy and government intervention were often aimed at assisting particular industries in overcoming the underdevelopment or suppression of factor markets. That was often done instead of addressing the more difficult underlying problem of an underdeveloped market – seen prominently in financial but also other markets.

There is another stream in this literature, which shows trade liberalization requires well-functioning credit markets for convergence (Peters and Schnitzer, 2012). Well-functioning capital markets are important to realizing the gains from trade that come from a reallocation of resources within and between industries, because the efficiency and productivity gains come from existing productive firms – which are able to innovate and compete by expanding production – and from new entrants – who are able to raise capital to enter the industry. Suppressed capital markets do not intermediate savings to productive investments via market forces and do not encourage inefficient firms to exit the market and the reallocation of those resources to efficient incumbents or potential new entrants.

Developing East Asian economies were no different from other developing countries in having shallow, underdeveloped capital markets. Firms had a difficult time raising capital in such circumstances, and many investment and growth opportunities went unrealized. But North East Asian economies in particular overcame some of these constraints via the nature of the capital market distortions that were put in place, whether from direct intervention in the capital market or by financial market repression, coupled with industrial policies that generally gave priority to exporters and saw rapid exports and high investment rates, which contributed greatly to rapid GDP growth.

During rapid catch-up growth in Japan, government intervention and government lending through strategic industrial policy overcame some of the drawbacks of a suppressed capital market (Patrick, 1972). Saxonhouse (1983: 271) argues that 'Japanese industrial policy has been a substitute, and not an unfair complement, for the market allocation of capital'.

The distortions in Chinese factor markets that repressed labour, capital, land and resource costs acted as subsidies to producers and were important in increasing investment (Huang, 2010). The factor market repression, combined with liberalization of product markets and goods trade, helped China achieve competitiveness in international markets. As the Chinese economy moves closer to the global technology frontier and innovation-based growth becomes more important, it will need to reform those underlying market failures in its factor markets (Huang, 2010).

These second-best institutions are not congenial to factor-augmenting, or innovative, growth. Countries can get stuck in a non-convergence trap if an economy does not switch out of its investment-based policies (Acemoglu *et al.*, 2006).

Capital market development, openness and creative destruction

In order to examine the hypothesis that a different and deeper kind of openness is necessary for countries to move from catch-up to innovative growth, this chapter adapts the empirical strategy in Acemoglu *et al.* (2006). In particular, we use two composite indices of openness: the *de jure* measures of economic globalization in the KOF globalization index, and a financial repression index.

The Acemoglu *et al.* (2006) empirical results suffer from a number of short-comings. The results also have inconsistent specifications between regressions, and the description of variables is inconsistent within the text. Their empirical exercise is used to motivate their paper rather than demonstrate empirical evidence for the theoretical model they develop. Most notably, their measure of high and low barriers – taken from Djankov *et al.* (2002) and measuring the number of procedures required to open a business – is time invariant. While it is conceivable that, if the process of reform proceeds in a linear fashion, countries that were 'high barrier' countries in 2002 were also 'high barrier' countries in 1965, when the Acemoglu *et al.* (2006) panel began, it is unlikely that all countries with low barriers today also had low barriers in 1965.

In contrast, we use two variables that vary across time as well as across countries. This makes our results easier to interpret. We use a measure of capital market repression instead of a measure of high or low barriers to entry to proxy for the different institutional and policy settings in the catch-up and innovative growth phases. As explained above, financial or capital market repression is characteristic of developing countries with high growth. And the lack of a well-functioning capital market acts as a barrier to entry for new firms and for expansion of all efficient or productive incumbents.

In order to investigate the notion that openness and financial market repression may have differing impacts at different levels of development, we investigate the relationship between three-yearly average growth rates and measures of openness and financial market repression in a diverse panel of 69 countries from 1973 to 2005. The model is estimated for a large set of countries to provide context for Asia's experience, which is the focus of this study.

As our measure of openness, we use the *de jure* economic globalization measure that forms part of the KOF globalization index, which measures legal restrictions on trade and investment. Financial market repression is measured by the financial metric found – with a more detailed explanation of its construction – in Abiad *et al.* (2010). It incorporates coded measures of reserve requirements, credit direction, subsidized credit, interest rate liberalization and financial sector entry and exit. Real GDP, population and employment figures are taken from the latest version of the Penn World Tables. Summary statistics for all variables are presented in Appendix 9.1.

We then construct two dummy variables, FAR and MIDDLE, as measures of a country's distance from the technological frontier. A country is 'far' from the frontier if its labour productivity at time *t* is less than 30 per cent of US labour productivity at time *t*. A country is in the 'middle' of the technological spectrum if its labour productivity at time *t* is between 30 per cent and 60 per cent of US labour productivity at time *t*. Using dummies in this way allows us to capture non-linearities in the interaction between our variables of interest and the distance from the technological frontier. For example, a given increase in magnitude of financial openness may have a higher (or lower) impact on countries in the middle of the productivity range than it does on those closer to (or further away from) the technological frontier. This may be difficult to capture with a simple linear interaction term. Our basic equation therefore takes the following form (Equation 9.1).

$$\text{growth} = \beta_0 + \beta_1\text{dejure} + \beta_2\text{finance} + \beta_3\text{far} + \beta_4\text{MIDDLE} +$$
$$\beta_5\text{FAR·dejure} + \beta_6\text{MIDDLE·dejure} + \beta_7\text{FAR·finance} +$$
$$\beta_8\text{MIDDLE·finance} + \text{crisis} + u \qquad \text{Equation 9.1}$$

We estimate this equation with time and country fixed effects, so, for example, the coefficient on the openness variable may be interpreted as the extent to which increasing or decreasing openness will cause a deviation from the country's average growth rate, also taking into account the average growth rate among all countries for that year.

As in Acemoglu *et al.* (2006), we then include a human capital control in regression (2). In regression (3), we replace our measure of financial liberalization with the residuals from a regression of financial liberalization on real GDP per capita. This gives us a measure of the extent to which an economy has a liberalized financial sector for its level of development.

In all three specifications, openness has a positive impact on growth for high-income countries; however, there is no statistically significant effect for middle-income and far-income countries. There is some evidence of convergence, with countries far from the frontier and at mid-distance from it growing faster. As expected, systemic banking crises have a negative impact on growth in all specifications. Financial reform has an insignificant impact on growth for countries close to the frontier (that is, when the 'far' and 'middle' dummies are zero); its impact is, however, positive and significant for countries at far and middle distance from the frontier. In the first and third specifications, the point estimate of the effect of financial reform is larger for mid-distance than for far-from-frontier countries; the difference is, however, statistically insignificant. Increases in human capital have a significantly negative impact for countries very far from the frontier, perhaps because of the opportunity cost of education. In the third specification, the magnitude of relative financial liberalization is larger than the absolute financial liberalization estimates in the first two regressions. This may suggest that financial liberalization relative to a country's stage of development is important, along the lines suggested by Dollar in his contribution to this volume.

Conclusion

This chapter has demonstrated that openness to trade and investment is a necessary but not sufficient condition for escaping the middle-income trap and reaching the technological frontier. In order to graduate from being a middle-income country to a high-income country that is close to the global technology frontier, there are a number of conditions that would seem necessary, including a highly educated workforce, institutions that encourage innovation and efficiency, and confidence in a well-functioning market system. Rapid catch-up growth also requires openness to trade and investment in order to acquire technology, know-how and the global markets for reallocating resources domestically to more productive uses and realization of comparative advantage. But to shift from catch-up growth to innovative growth at the frontier requires a deepening of liberalization and openness across the economy, including, importantly, openness to domestic as well as international competition.

To reach the global technology frontier, and to remain there, it is necessary to have low barriers to new firms entering the market, and human capital and good institutions (including well-functioning markets), as well as openness to trade and investment. Not only openness and exposure to competition, but also openness to ideas and change are necessary for productivity growth and better resource allocation. High barriers to competition domestically – represented in this chapter by the level of capital market suppression – become more costly the closer a country gets to the technology frontier, and financial market development and liberalization, as well as other regulatory reforms to reduce barriers to entry, would appear to be important for escaping the middle-income trap.

One interesting question is what leads to or obstructs this deeper openness. As an economy grows in its catch-up phase, it will likely generate larger and larger economic rents, making reform increasingly difficult if firms and individuals who benefit from the rents exert political pressure. Governments can also derive significant implicit revenue from financially repressive or anticompetitive policies (Aloy *et al.*, 2014; Giovannini and de Melo, 1991; Reinhart and Sbrancia, 2011). However, the amount of implicit revenue/debt relief that is obtainable by financial repression is limited by opening up to foreign trade and capital (Jinjarak, 2013).

A democratic polity may be more or less conducive to reforms than other styles of government. Quinn (2000), for example, finds that financial reforms are more likely to occur under democratic rule. Giuliano *et al.* (2013) find that democratic systems, broadly, are more likely to engage in reforms, including in the financial sector, the capital account, product markets, agricultural markets, trade and the current account. A model of the political economy of the middle-income trap that endogenizes changes in domestic regulation could therefore shed further light on why some countries remain 'trapped' at middle-income status and others do not.

Appendix 9.1 Summary statistics

Statistic	N	Mean	St. Dev.	Min	Max
year	740	1,989.099	9.481	1,974	2,004
pop	740	55.478	162.630	1.349	1,277.826
rgdpe	740	324,522.400	625,809.800	3,454.154	6,251,935.000
emp	738	23.818	80.000	0.408	748.048
hc	707	2.245	0.564	1.095	3.448
lp	738	23,346.950	20,499.210	626.504	82,243.450
rgdpc	740	9,681.731	9,641.766	308.662	41,385.140
frontier	740	67,571.820	11,033.860	54,869.580	88,039.630
frontier_ratio	738	0.345	0.288	0.009	0.946
growth	740	0.019	0.040	−0.154	0.180
ifs	740	384.091	227.341	112	939
directedcredit	740	1.511	1.157	0.000	3.000
creditceilings	399	0.602	0.474	0.000	1.000
creditcontrols	740	1.543	1.130	0.000	3.000
intratecontrols	740	1.755	1.292	0.000	3.000
entrybarriers	740	1.677	1.183	0.000	3.000
bankingsuperv	740	0.719	0.921	0.000	3.000
privatization	740	1.250	1.146	0.000	3.000
intlcapital	740	1.650	1.085	0.000	3.000
securitymarkets	740	1.464	1.111	0.000	3.000
finreform	740	10.056	6.381	0.000	21.000
finreform_n	740	0.479	0.304	0.000	1.000
large_reversal	739	0.006	0.055	0.000	1.000
reversal	739	0.043	0.120	0.000	0.667
reform	739	0.230	0.272	0.000	1.000
large_reform	739	0.048	0.135	0.000	1.000
status_quo	739	0.673	0.319	0.000	1.000
Advanced	740	0.312	0.464	0	1
Emerging_Asia	740	0.161	0.368	0	1
Latin_America	740	0.238	0.426	0	1
SSA	740	0.193	0.395	0	1
Transition	740	0.007	0.082	0	1
MENA	740	0.089	0.285	0	1
open	730	0.005	0.002	0.001	0.010
facto	730	0.478	0.205	0.038	0.983
jure	730	0.514	0.249	0.059	0.960
far	738	0.557	0.497	0	1
middle	738	0.178	0.382	0	1
uhat	740	−0.000	0.234	−0.572	0.566

References

Abiad, AG, Detragiache, E and Tressel, T 2010. A new database of financial reforms. *IMF Staff Papers*, 57(2), 281–302.

Acemoglu, D, Aghion, P and Zilibotti, F 2006. Distance to frontier, selection, and economic growth. *Journal of the European Economic Association*, 4(1), 37–74.

Aghion, P, Bloom, N, Blundell, R, Griffith, R and Howitt, P 2005. Competition and innovation: An inverted-U relationship. *Quarterly Journal of Economics*, 120(2), 701–28.

Aiyar, S, Duval, R, Puy, D, Wu, Y and Zhang, L 2013. *Growth slowdowns and the middle-income trap.* IMF Working Paper No. 13/71. Washington, DC: International Monetary Fund.

Almeida, R and Fernandes, AM 2008. Openness and technological innovations in developing countries: Evidence from firm-level surveys. *Journal of Development Studies*, 44(5), 701–27.

Aloy, M, Dufrénot, G and Péguin-Feissolle, A 2014. Is financial repression a solution to reduce fiscal vulnerability? *Applied Economics*, 46(6), 629–37.

Amsden, AH 1989. *Asia's Next Giant: South Korea and Late Industrialization.* Oxford: Oxford University Press.

Arkolakis, C, Costinot, A and Rodriguez-Clare, A 2012. New trade models, same old gains? *American Economic Review*, 102(1), 94–130.

Baldwin, R and Lopez-Gonzalez, J 2014. Supply-chain trade: A portrait of global patterns and several testable hypotheses. *The World Economy.* doi:10.1111/twec.12189.

Broda, C and Weinstein, DE 2004. Variety growth and world welfare. *American Economic Review*, 94(2), 139–44.

Cai, F 2012. Is there a 'middle-income trap'? Theories, experiences and relevance to China. *China & World Economy*, 20(1), 49–61.

Corden, M 1974. *Trade Policy and Economic Welfare.* Oxford: Clarendon Press.

Djankov, S, La Porta, R, Lopez-de-Silanes, F and Shleifer, A 2002. The regulation of entry. *Quarterly Journal of Economics*, 117(1), 1–37.

Eichengreen, B, Park, D and Shin, K 2013. *Growth slowdowns redux: New evidence on the middle-income trap.* Working Paper No. 18673. Cambridge, MA: National Bureau of Economic Research.

Felipe, J, Abdon, A and Kumar, U 2012. *Tracking the middle-income trap: What is it, who is in it, and why?* Working Paper No. 715. New York: Levy Economics Institute of Bard College.

Garnaut, R (ed.) 1979. *ASEAN in the Changing Pacific and World Economy.* Canberra: The Australian National University Press.

Gerschenkron, A 1962. *Economic Backwardness in Historical Perspective.* Cambridge, MA: Belknap Press of Harvard University Press.

Giovannini, A and de Melo, M 1991. *Government revenue from financial repression.* Working Paper No. 3604. Cambridge, MA: National Bureau of Economic Research.

Giuliano, P, Mishra, P and Spilimbergo, A 2013. Democracy and reforms: Evidence from a new dataset. *American Economic Journal: Macroeconomics*, 5(4), 179–204.

Huang, Y 2010. Dissecting the China puzzle: Asymmetric liberalization and cost distortion. *Asian Economic Policy Review*, 5(2), 281–95.

International Monetary Fund (IMF) 2014.

Jinjarak, Y 2013. Economic integration and government revenue from financial repression. *Economic Systems*, 37(2), 271–83.

Kharas, H and Kohli, H 2011. What is the middle income trap, why do countries fall into it, and how can it be avoided? *Global Journal of Emerging Market Economies*, 3(3), 281–9.

Klinger, B and Lederman, D 2006. *Diversification, innovation, and imitation inside the global technological frontier.* World Bank Policy Research Working Paper No. 3872. Washington, DC: The World Bank.

Kuznets, PW 1988. An East Asian model of economic development: Japan, Taiwan, and South Korea. *Economic Development and Cultural Change*, 36(3 Sup.): S11–S43.

Kwon, J 1994. The East Asian challenge to neoclassical orthodoxy. *World Development*, 22(1994), 636–44.

Lee, C and Narjoko, D 2015. Escaping the middle-income trap in Southeast Asia: Micro evidence on innovation, productivity, and globalization. *Asian Economic Policy Review*, 10(1), 124–47.

Lee, SH, Yamakawa, Y, Peng, MW and Barney, JB 2011. How do bankruptcy laws affect entrepreneurship development around the world? *Journal of Business Venturing*, 26(5), 505–20.

Levchenko, AA and Zhang, J 2014. Ricardian productivity differences and the gains from trade. *European Economic Review*, 65(C), 45–65.

Maddison, A 2003. *The World Economy: Historical Statistics*. Paris: OECD Publishing.

Melitz, MJ 2003. The impact of trade on intra-industry reallocations and aggregate industry productivity. *Econometrica*, 71(6), 1695–725.

Melitz, MJ and Ottaviano, GI 2008. Market size, trade, and productivity. *The Review of Economic Studies*, 75(1), 295–316.

Melitz, MJ and Redding, SJ. 2013. *Firm heterogeneity and aggregate welfare*. CEPR Discussion Papers 9405. London: Centre for Economic Policy Research.

Myint, H 1973. *The Economics of the Developing Countries*. London: Hutchinson University Library.

Ozawa, T 2005. *Institutions, Industrial Upgrading, and Economic Performance in Japan: The 'Flying Geese' Paradigm of Catch-up Growth*. Northampton, MA: Edwin Elgar.

Patrick, H 1972. *Finance, Capital Markets and Economic Growth in Japan*. New York: New York University Press.

Perkins, D 1994. Completing China's move to the market. *The Journal of Economic Perspectives*, 8(2), 23–46.

Peters, F and Schnitzer, M 2012. *Trade liberalization and credit constraints: Why opening up may fail to promote convergence*. CEPR Discussion Papers 8942. London: Centre for Economic Policy Research.

Pritchett, L and Summers, LH 2014. *Asiaphoria meets regression to the mean*. Working Paper No. 20573. Cambridge, MA: National Bureau of Economic Research.

Quinn, DP 2000. *Democracy and International Financial Liberalization*. Washington, DC: McDonough School of Business, Georgetown University.

Rajan, RG and Zingales, L 2000. *The great reversals: The politics of financial development in the 20th century*. OECD Economics Department Working Paper No. 265. Paris: OECD Publishing.

Reinhart, CM and Sbrancia, MB 2011. *The liquidation of government debt*. Working Paper No. 16893. Cambridge, MA: National Bureau of Economic Research.

Robertson, P and Ye, L 2013. *On the existence of a middle-income trap*. Economics Discussion Paper 13.12. Perth: University of Western Australia.

Rodrik, D 2008. *Second-best institutions*. Working Paper No. 14050. Cambridge, MA: National Bureau of Economic Research.

Saxonhouse, GR 1983. What is all this about 'industrial targeting' in Japan? *The World Economy*, 6(3), 253–74.

Wade, R 1990. *Governing the Market: Economic Theory and the Role of Government in East Asian Industrialization*. Princeton, NJ: Princeton University Press.

Index

For Product Safety Concerns and Information please contact our EU
representative GPSR@taylorandfrancis.com Taylor & Francis Verlag GmbH,
Kaufingerstraße 24, 80331 München, Germany

Printed and bound by CPI Group (UK) Ltd, Croydon, CR0 4YY
08/05/2025
01864534-0002